GIVING FOR SOCIAL CHANGE

FOUNDATIONS, PUBLIC POLICY, AND THE AMERICAN POLITICAL AGENDA

Althea K. Nagai, Robert Lerner,
and Stanley Rothman

PRAEGER

Westport, Connecticut
London

Library of Congress Cataloging-in-Publication Data

Nagai, Althea K., 1954–
    Giving for social change : foundations, public policy, and the
American political agenda / Althea K. Nagai, Robert Lerner, and
Stanley Rothman.
        p.   cm.
    Includes bibliographical references and index.
    ISBN 0–275–94697–5 (alk. paper)
    1. Endowments—Political aspects—United States.   2. Charities—
Political aspects—United States.   3. Elite (Social sciences)—
United States.   4. United States—Social policy.   I. Lerner,
Robert, 1953– .   II. Rothman, Stanley, 1927– .   III. Title.
HV91.N23   1994
361.7′632′0973—dc20   93–25060

British Library Cataloguing in Publication Data is available.

Library of Congress Catalog Card Number: 93–25060
ISBN: 0–275–94697–5

First published in 1994

Praeger Publishers, 88 Post Road West, Westport, CT 06881
An imprint of Greenwood Publishing Group, Inc.

Printed in the United States of America

The paper used in this book complies with the
Permanent Paper Standard issued by the National
Information Standards Organization (Z39.48–1984).

10 9 8 7 6 5 4 3 2 1

To our parents, Kaoru and Yaeko Nagai, and Frances and Monroe Lerner.

To my fathers Jack Rothman and Samuel Schwartz. They were good men who did their best for those they loved. Both died before their time.

CONTENTS

TABLES AND FIGURES

TABLES

FIGURES

PREFACE

We undertook this study of philanthropic foundations as part of a larger project on social and political elites in the United States. This book is the integration of a wealth of unexplored material on the foundation elite, a unique survey of the ideology of foundation leaders, and a content analysis of public policy grants.

Our book revolves around foundation leaders as a strategic elite—that is, elite members of a strategic sector in U.S. society, not as an extension of upper-class domination. Our sociodemographic data clearly show that foundation leaders are far from being the repository of the white, Anglo-Saxon, Protestant establishment that scholars often picture them to be. Only one in three of the foundation elite is a WASP. The foundation leaders are richer than other elite groups, but many achieved leadership starting from relatively modest backgrounds. Also, their backgrounds are considerably less affluent than those of leaders of the most liberal elite groups in the United States: public interest group leaders.

In this book, we demonstrate that foundation leaders are the most politically polarized of U.S. elite groups. We also examine the philanthropic ethos of the foundation elite. Some aspects of this ethos are not related to political ideology, but, as we shall see, other aspects are clearly ideologically driven. Many foundation leaders are strongly committed to providing a safety net against unfettered *laissez-faire* capitalism. At the same time, foundation leaders think philanthropy should support projects ignored by the welfare state.

Foundation leaders, regardless of ideology, also partake in the American tradition of voluntarism and progressivism. They believe that foundations, by supporting a variety of alternative approaches to social change, contribute to pluralism.

In actual public policy grant-making, however, our data show that their theoretical commitment to philanthropic pluralism does not extend to the ideological sphere. Foundation pluralism is in fact much more limited. Most foundation spending for public policy projects tilts toward the left.

Many people and institutions helped us with this research. The following foundations made this project possible: the J. M. Foundation, the John M. Olin Foundation, the Smith Richardson Foundation, The Donner Foundation, the Earhart Foundation, and the Sarah Scaife Foundation. Smith College provided institutional support, and the Survey Research Institute of the University of California at Berkeley conducted the survey. Willa Johnson and her staff at the Capital Research Center were extremely helpful in answering our many questions about U.S. philanthropy.

Many Smith students helped us with the collection, cleaning, and statistical analysis of our data. We wish to thank Janice Mason, who contributed considerable time and skill in the preparation of the manuscript. Althea Nagai would also like to acknowledge those at her undergraduate school who doubted her capacity to make it through graduate school.

The study is sponsored by the Center for the Study of Social and Political Change at Smith College, directed by Stanley Rothman.

The codebooks, questionnaires, and tapes for the analysis of disbursal of funds for grants and the survey of the philanthropic elite have been placed on file at the Roper Public Opinion Center at the University of Connecticut. They will be released for use by other scholars as of September 1995.

GIVING FOR SOCIAL CHANGE

CHAPTER 1

INTRODUCTION

This book shows how philanthropic foundations ideologically and substantively help shape the American political agenda. Elites in certain strategic sectors such as business, the federal judiciary, education, and the public interest movement bring about societal change from the top down. The philanthropic foundation elite guides one of these strategic, change-producing sectors.

We find that a critical mass of social-change foundations attempts to push the national agenda in a liberal direction, despite the prominence of a few conservative foundations. This book demonstrates the extent of this tilt, with a survey of the ideological views of the foundation elite and an examination of foundations' public policy grants.

Our large, multifaceted study adds to the literature on foundations and public policy, an important but neglected area. Academics, on the whole, pay scant attention to social-change foundations. The general neglect occurs because the two disciplines most concerned with national public policy—economics and political science—focus on markets and government, respectively, while the philanthropic foundation is neither. It is a privately held, not-for-profit, grant-making organization. Since it is not for profit, it is generally ignored by economists; since it is neither a governmental body nor an important interest group, the political science field overlooks it as well.

Yet some foundations actively take upon themselves the role of funding pilot programs for future government intervention. In this regard, funding policy-relevant projects helps set the national agenda. Since little is known about U.S. foundations and the nonprofit sector as a whole, we hope this book will play a part in integrating foundations into the study of public policy.

WHAT IS PHILANTHROPY AND WHAT IS A FOUNDATION?

The Nonprofit Sector

To quote Dwight Macdonald, a philanthropic foundation is "a large body of money completely surrounded by people who want some" (1989, p. 3). More precisely, the philanthropic foundation falls under the category of nonprofit organizations, which are basically defined by the Internal Revenue Service. While logically one might think that "nonprofit" organizations are those not allowed to make a profit, technically this is not the case. Nonprofit organizations are ones that cannot distribute their profits to their owners or other private persons. As such, they receive special tax treatment.

The Philanthropic Foundation: A Definition

The philanthropic foundation is one kind of nonprofit organization. It is a private organization with a large endowment and achieves its goals by making grants. The grants must go to an individual or other private organizations that serve some public purpose. These include organizations in such areas as health care, social services, culture, education, and religion.[1] Foundations and recipient organizations are all tax exempt.

The confusion as to what foundations do and what they ought to do rests in part with a misinterpretation of the terms *charity* and *philanthropy*. Americans sometimes use the words *charity* and *philanthropy* interchangeably, but they are not the same thing. Charity means helping the poor. Foundations do not directly help the poor because they do not disburse dollars to the needy but go through an intermediary nonprofit organization to accomplish this end. Moreover, many foundations award grants to groups that have little to do with aiding the poor.[2]

Sociologist Christopher Jencks in "Who Gives to What?" refers to all contributions to a tax-deductible organization as philanthropy, not charity, insofar as most contributions do not go to the penniless. Charity, Jencks argues (1987, p. 322),

conjures up images of the rich helping the poor: medieval lords endowing almshouses, John D. Rockefeller giving away dimes, or the average citizen tossing money in the Salvation Army kettle at Christmas. Very few [contributions] are "charitable" in this sense. . . . [T]he prospective beneficiaries are seldom indigent and are often quite affluent.

He notes that most of Americans' "charitable contributions" go to churches, hospitals, and institutions of higher education, none of which are poor. Jencks is correct to point out such a distinction but neglects the reasoning behind such giving. As we will discuss in our history of philanthropic foundations, much American giving since Puritan times has centered on building institutions. Such institutions are designed to give individuals the opportunity to rise to the top, regardless of their position at birth. To provide for an equality of opportunity, Americans before the welfare state hated to rely on the federal government. Instead, they preferred, and still prefer, to a lesser extent, to rely on local voluntary associations.

Should we, given Jenck's definition, call all givers "philanthropists"? The question is rhetorical, and, in any case, Jencks would argue that we are not all conventional philanthropists. The function of philanthropy, Jencks argues, is twofold. The first function applies to the "nonrich" who make contributions to personal voluntary associations such as their church or local Red Cross. Jencks calls this "paying your dues." Jencks argues that most of our giving serves primarily to reinforce group membership. Jencks maintains that informal standards evolve regarding the "right amounts." These standards balance a notion that the richer should give more with a notion that group members are relatively equal. The result, Jencks argues, is that nonprofit contributions rise with income, but not proportionately. In fact, Jencks believes that most of us seek to give "the minimum respectable gift" (1987, p. 324).

The second type of giving is what Jencks and most of us think of as philanthropy, which he defines as the giving away of "surplus income." Moreover, it goes beyond the need to maintain local group cohesion. As philosopher William K. Frankena (1987) points out, to be a philanthropist involves more money and greater systematic effort than the typical donation. At the same time, Frankena notes, it does not necessarily come from a feeling of benevolence. Waldemar Nielsen's (1972) history of the large foundations provides empirical evidence for this claim. Many original donors set up foundations for less than noble purposes, the most obvious being tax and family considerations. Nielsen (1985, pp. 16–17) observes that roughly half of America's thirty-six largest foundations emerged from a serious commitment to doing "good works." "[I]n half the cases or more the donors endowed their foundations simply because they were running out of time, were drowning in money, and were unable to think of anything better to do with it." In some of the most notorious cases, the term *philanthropy* clearly departs from its original Greek roots in which *philanthropia* means "love of mankind."

A philanthropist frequently turns his or her "surplus income" into an endowment for a philanthropic foundation. In turn, the philanthropic foundation becomes the organization that gives away the philanthropist's wealth or, more frequently, the interest earned from the endowment. In *Philanthropic Foundations* (1956), Frank Emerson Andrews, former president of the Foundation Center, provides a widely used definition of the philanthropic foundation, which we use in this book. A foundation is "a nongovernmental, nonprofit organization having a principal fund of its own, managed by its own trustees or directors, and established to maintain or aid social, educational, charitable, religious or other activities serving the common welfare" (Andrews, 1956, p. 11).

Andrews emphasizes that the endowment distinguishes an organization as a foundation. This is an important point because many organizations call themselves "foundations" without necessarily being such. "[T]he prestigeful name foundation has been adopted by many organizations . . . [which] have no proper right to its use. These include agencies which solicit contributions instead of disbursing from an established fund, and some which are trade associations, pressure groups, or outright rackets" (p. 12).

With the advent of the philanthropic foundation, numerous persons such as trustees and foundation staff are designated by the donor to come between the donor and the donor's wealth. The philanthropist proper thus has to be distinguished from "the philanthropoid." The philanthropoid, to quote Macdonald (1989, p. 96) again, is the "middleman between the philanthropist and the philanthropee." Frederick P. Keppel first coined the term, and it has become a standard label applied to those whose profession is "the giving away of other people's money" (Macdonald, 1989, p. 96). For the older foundations, where there are few or no ties to the original philanthropist, the philanthropoids become critical to running the foundation and sometimes charting its course.

Like the media, the foundation world is a relatively new strategic sector in American society. Foundations are new in the sense that they are the products of mass industrial society and were created by the wealth of great industrialists. Like other organizational outcomes of mass industrial society, foundations manifest a tendency toward a specialization of function and a division of labor. Although not as extensively bureaucratic as the largest of modern corporations or the federal government, the largest foundations have a professional and clerical staff, officers, and a president who serve at the pleasure of boards of trustees. The foundation managers run the day-to-day operations, while the board meets periodically to set general policy and goals.

In short, the officers and trustees of the United States' largest foundations are a new strategic elite in this country. In discussing their role in social change, and because the large foundations play a significant role in setting the policy agenda for this country, this book places them in an explicitly political context and presents them as the product of larger shifts in American culture and society. Because they are a new strategic elite, we also compare, where possible, the foundation elite with other U.S. elites such as business, the military, the media, and social movement leaders.

Foundations, however, play a significant social role only in the United States. They are not found in large numbers in other industrialized countries. This means that foundations are also a product of U.S. culture, not merely U.S. industrialization. The philanthropic foundation is set up because Americans prefer to rely on these nonprofit associations to distribute and use "surplus" wealth for the sake of the public good.

Equating foundations and other nonprofit activity with the public good, however, has become problematic with the rise of the welfare state. How people of the United States define "the public good" and how they think it should be achieved profoundly shape the course of foundation giving. When the "public good'' is synonymous with the activities of the welfare state, foundations become extensions of government. When conservatives and liberals define ''the public good'' in radically different terms, foundation giving becomes politicized giving. This book traces these cultural changes up to the present. We show that these changes have generally been in a liberal direction and that a significant segment of the foundation elite see themselves as part of the cutting edge of social change.

Despite the recognized prominence of foundations since the 1950s, partisan political attacks on large foundations (which we discuss in chapter two), and the role of foundations in public policy in using ''private wealth for public purposes,'' scholars have done little quantitative analysis of foundations. Our book remedies this lack. It is the first quantitative study of foundations based on a survey of the opinions of the foundation elite and a systematic content analysis of public policy grants. The book also places this important U.S. institution in the context of larger sociopolitical changes and other scholarly work on ideology and American elites. Finally, it integrates our empirical findings with both the scholarly and popular literature on foundations, as well as the more general social science paradigms that currently frame the debate about these organizations.

This book consists of 3 conceptual parts: a brief history of philanthropy in the United States, an analysis of a survey of the foundation elite, and an analysis of public policy giving. The survey of the foundation elite provides detailed information on political and social attitudes, demographic attributes, their views of how foundations should operate, and what they should spend money on. The second body of data is an examination of more than 4,000 public policy grants distributed by 225 of the largest foundations in the United States.

The following chapter traces the historical development of the foundation and its relationship to the establishment of the helping professions and the rise of the welfare state, focusing on the current understanding of philanthropy and social change. The chapter traces modern philanthropy, which started after the Civil War, when the previous belief in individual actions like the Good Samaritan gave way to a belief in science, rationalism, and utilitarianism. This encouraged the rich to move from the role of civic stewardship to the more distant position of money giver in the emerging large-scale industrial society. While the ''Gilded Age'' is thought of as the height of Social Darwinistic *laissez-faire* capitalism, it is also the era in which groups such as the Charity Organization Societies (COS) movement attempted to put charity and philanthropy on a scientific yet voluntary basis.

The clearest articulation of the organizational mission of the modern foundation, however, is found in the Progressive Era. The Progressives favored scientific, planned approaches, not only to charity but to solving social problems in general. This coincides with the rise of expertise, the establishment of the research university, and the growth of the professions. Foundations were created with the hope of contributing to general social betterment rather than as palliative individual acts of charity.

We then look at foundations after the New Deal, which broke the monopoly of private benevolence and created the framework of the modern welfare state. We examine the role of the state in shaping philanthropy from the New Deal up through the 1960s and 1970s, and focus on the interplay between liberal innovation in the foundation world and the conservative response. By the midsixties, many liberal members of the foundation elite viewed the primary role of private philanthropy as creating pilot programs for government to take over, essentially acting as a handmaiden to the expanding welfare state.

The last section of chapter two traces the activities of the foundations in the 1970s and 1980s, and the conservative response. The response has been twofold. Conservatives encourage philanthropy as a substitute for government funding. Second, conservatives fund research and activities supportive of conservative causes, in such fields as economics, public law, human rights, and foreign policy.

Chapters three and four set our general debate. Chapter three addresses the charge that the foundation elite is an extension of the American upper class. We argue instead that the foundation elite is a strategic elite. We define these terms and analyze the socially diverse backgrounds of members of this elite. Many, in fact, do not come from highly educated, wealthy, white-collar families. Chapter four presents alternative views to the ruling class model of foundation leaders. Some elites maintain that the foundation world is a manifestation of U.S. pluralism. Others, generally conservative intellectuals, see the foundation as one repository of a political subculture essentially hostile to American values. Simply stated, one model claims that foundations seek to maintain the status quo; another model claims that foundations, like other U.S. institutions, are actually pluralistic in orientation; and yet a third claims that the large foundations work hand-in-glove with other new groups to bring about massive social change in a radical direction. Each of these paradigms—the ruling elite model, the pluralist model, and the model of the adversary culture—is based on key propositions that we systematically elucidate, partly by working through their theoretical assumptions and partly by developing testable empirical propositions that we subsequently apply to our data.

The ruling class versus pluralism versus adversary culture orientations are examined extensively in chapters five and six. We show that the foundation elite is neither wholly a power elite nor totally representative of the adversary culture. Chapter five looks at the political attitudes of the foundation elite. It is the most polarized, but also one of the most ideologically sophisticated, of all U.S. elite groups. Some can be considered part of "the establishment," but others partake of a liberal-left culture. We compare the foundation elite with the business elite and more liberal elites (journalists, public interest leaders, television and movie makers) along six dimensions of ideology, including the dimensions we call collectivist liberalism, alienation, expressive individualism, foreign policy, crime, and affirmative action.

Chapter six shows that the foundation elite is more ideologically sophisticated than most other elite groups. Their political beliefs affect their evaluation of contemporary leaders and celebrities, their views of the news, and their thoughts on broad-based goals for American society.

Chapter seven examines how political ideology among foundation leaders affects the organizational ethos of foundations. We show that three different dimensions constitute the foundation ethos: support for a nonprofit sector; support for "societally conscientious" investments; and issues regarding who controls the money. We find that some dimensions of the philanthropic ethos stem from political attitudes, and we show that political liberalism guides the desire for organizational innovation within a foundation and a preference for "social-change" spending (e.g., projects in support of the peace movement, gay-lesbian rights, and affirmative action for women and minorities). Liberal members of the foundation elite also claim to be more influenced by foundation staff. Political conservatives and moderates have more traditional views regarding foundations (such as favoring volunteer work and following the original intent of the donor) and prefer to spend funds on noncontroversial projects (such as medicine, science, and social welfare projects).

In chapter eight, we examine the impact of politicized foundations—that is, foundation support of public policy recipients. Most public policy grants have a definite ideological tilt. Roughly 2,000 grants in our sample support liberal causes, while only slightly more than 600 go to conservative groups. Translated into total dollar amounts, liberal projects receive four times as much as do conservative projects or groups. This, paradoxically, also results in a conservative grantee receiving more dollars on average than a liberal, since there are relatively few conservative recipients and many liberal ones.

Finally, chapter nine reviews our findings and recapitulates our overall argument. This gives us the material to reexamine the claim of foundation professionals that "philanthropic pluralism" is the proper orientation for large foundations. We compare philanthropic pluralism to political and other forms of pluralism, and discuss the ways in which pluralism, professionalization, accountability, and the original philanthropic enterprise are in inherent tension. We argue that a critical segment of the foundation elite are proponents of a new polarized pluralism that contributes to the fragmentation of U.S. political culture and that places many members of the foundation elite far to the left of the American public.

The book thus integrates the professional literature on philanthropic foundations with a larger debate about the structure of power in U.S. society. We support our arguments with a substantial body of quantitative data. Based on our theory regarding the professionalization of foundations in the context of sociopolitical change, we show how modern liberalism has become—and remains—the "common sense" framework of thought and action among many elites in the United States, including the foundation elite.

NOTES

1. Organizations that receive tax-deductible contributions make up the overwhelming majority of the nonprofit sector. Besides philanthropic foundations and nonprofit, tax-exempt recipient groups, there are private, nonprofit commercial enterprises (e.g., mem-

bership cooperatives) and social groups (e.g., hunting clubs), where the organizations exist solely to benefit their members. Noncharitable nonprofit organizations also include social clubs, labor unions, chambers of commerce, and various ''private interest'' lobby groups. Gifts to these groups are not tax deductible.

2. The confusing definitional relationship between not-for-profit, tax-exempt giving and charity (which we think should be limited to helping the poor) is also in part due to U.S. ''tax'' language, which refers to contributions to any tax-exempt nonprofit as ''charitable''' contributions.

CHAPTER 2

PHILANTHROPY AND SOCIAL CHANGE:
A HISTORICAL OVERVIEW

Populism has always rendered Americans suspicious of large fortunes, including those that created the large independent foundations in the early twentieth century. But the foundations created from these fortunes have played a far greater role in shaping public life in the United States than that of any other country. Their very existence has reflected the inherent and continuing tension between two deeply felt American principles: voluntarism and equality. At the same time, Americans' profound suspicion of government action to meet public needs has sustained the large foundations and other nonprofit organizations.

In this chapter, we trace the rise of the large U.S. foundation in the context of how the United States dealt with its less fortunate people. In *The Protestant Ethic and the Spirit of Capitalism* (1930 trans.), Max Weber focuses on how religious belief encouraged the proper attitude toward work that inevitably led to the development of capitalism. Americans developed a parallel structure to modern capitalism to deal with the less fortunate. From prerevolutionary times, Americans depended on individuals and voluntary associations to help those that could not help themselves. This was the beginning of the American nonprofit sector—neither business nor government.

Large-scale disruptions in the form of wars, migrations, industrialization, depressions, and the welfare state forced changes upon how the country took care of its less fortunate. How the United States responded to these disruptions, such as with the rise of the welfare state and in the 1960s with greater conflict among significant elite groups, profoundly altered the structure and norms of the nonprofit sector. We analyze these changes, starting with the American Puritan community and its dependence on voluntary action, in the next section.

THE AMERICAN PURITAN TRADITION AND THE CHARITABLE IMPULSE

The philanthropic foundation has deep roots in the American Puritan tradition. As Tocqueville writes in *Democracy in America*, "Puritanism was not just a religious doctrine; in many respects it shared the most absolute democratic and republican theories" (Tocqueville, 1969 trans. and ed., p. 36). Tocqueville makes Puritanism the point of departure for studying democracy in the United States, and we do the same in our history of U.S. philanthropy.

The Puritans made achievement in everyday life central to the American creed, whereby rational, practical effort became the sign of religious salvation. Americans in turn transformed their Calvinist faith into a political faith of liberal individualism, which became the civil religion of the new republic (Bellah, 1970). In the Puritan view, liberty by nature was a uniquely moral liberty. Thought to be embodied in the "personal covenant between God and man," liberty was constrained by a strict moral code. True liberty meant restraining impulse and subordinating the sexual and aggressive passions. A demand for hard work set stringent limits upon the expression of liberty.

Puritanism also fostered upon its members a notion of a special kind of community. A specific ethical and spiritual creed, based on equality rather than divisions based on heredity and birth, held the community together. Puritan founder Jonathan Winthrop describes his "city on a hill" in these words: "We must delight in each other, make others conditions our own, rejoice together, mourn together, labor and suffer together, always having before our eyes our community as members of the same body" (quoted in Bellah, et al. 1985, p. 85).

Within this new American community, people pursued wealth within the framework of communal assumptions of Christian stewardship. The Puritan faith did not deplore wealth but decidedly frowned upon accumulation for its own sake. William Perkins, the premier theologian of Puritan thought in the 1600s, writes, "Men are honored for their riches. . . . I meane not riches simple but the use of riches; namely as they are made instruments to uphold and maintain virtue" (Baltzell, 1979, p. 77). Seeking wealth to the exclusion of community spirit was sinful; miserliness was both wrong and self-defeating.

The spirit of Christian stewardship to the community carried well into the nineteenth century. By the early 1800s, leading citizens were becoming trustees of permanent charities, while teachers, ministers, and the press heralded them as model moral stewards. The model citizen was a conscientious churchman who gave extensively to schools, churches, and public works projects. More important, each Christian steward personally attended to the poor and regularly made rounds to their homes.

Benjamin Franklin was the most famous of these Christian stewards. Heavily influenced by the Christian idea of civic stewardship and Cotton Mather's essays of 1710, Franklin put into practice many of his self-help ideas to organize and fund voluntary associations in Philadelphia. He promoted libraries, the College

of Philadelphia, and the Pennsylvania Hospital. He accomplished his philanthropic endeavors in a most calculating and efficient manner. He developed
extensive lists of prospective donors; he relied on personal visits to solicit contributions; and he used the public press to promote ongoing contributions. (For
an extensive list of Franklin's many contributions to the public wealth, see the
chart in Baltzell, 1979, pp. 152–53.)

The wealthy citizens of New York also developed a network of civic stewards,
although John Pintard complained that New York lacked a true aristocracy of
wealth to "attend to the multiplied demands on humanity and benevolence. . . .
Here, these duties fall oppressively heavy on the few public spirited citizens,
whose necessities compel them . . . to toil for their support" (Heale, 1968,
p. 164). Despite his complaints, Pintard was the model humanitarian New
Yorker. He actively supported New York's Society for the Prevention of Pauperism, the Historical Society, the American Bible Society, the Free School
Society, and the American Academy of Fine Arts.

The practice spread to the Midwest. A young, displaced New Englander by
the name of Philo Carpenter became a noted Christian steward of Chicago. The
son of a distinguished family from the East, Carpenter settled in Chicago at the
age of twenty-eight to become a successful pharmacist. He then established the
city's first Sunday school, the Chicago First Presbyterian Church, and the Chicago Temperance Society. He opened his home to the underground railroad,
made weekly visits to the poor, and personally ministered to countless victims
during Chicago's devastating cholera epidemics. Carpenter donated large sums
to his favorite institutions: $50,000 to the First Congregational Church of Chi-
cago; $110,000 to the Chicago Theological Seminary; and lesser amounts to
Oberlin College, Berea College, the Chicago Missionary Society, and the Chicago Historical Society (McCarthy, 1982, p. 57).

This is not to say that the Christian stewards of the past were of better character
than leaders of today. Many affluent individuals were merely acting according
to expectations imposed on them by the larger society, which glorified the
personal traits of the Christian gentleman. Antelbellum treaties and church sermons called for the rich to honor their civic and spiritual obligations through
personal ministry. Obituaries, sermons, and news stories scrutinized the achievements and faults of the rich upon their death. When one very wealthy Chicagoan
died before the Civil War, he left what seemed to be almost nothing to charity.
The newspaper attacks were so severe that friends had to step forward to clear
his name (McCarthy, 1982, p. 60).

Americans, in short, expected their moneyed elite to live modestly and not
overtly display their wealth. The wealthy should use their leisure time to benefit
the community instead of solely pursuing pleasure. Visible devotion to family,
community, charity, and cultural patronage were thought to curb the acquisitive
spirit while justifying the process of accumulation itself.

The aims of noted Christian stewards such as Franklin, however, were of two
distinct types: one was merely to make men moral; and the other was to make

less wealthy men better. The first aim of Christian stewardship in the United States involved attempts to morally reform the degenerate, poor, neglected, and deviant. Making men moral, they believed, would solve their problems. The Society for the Prevention of Pauperism declared that almost all poverty and wretchedness "proceeds directly or indirectly from the want of correct moral principle" (Heale, 1968, p. 166). Because paupers, drunks, gamblers, and criminals were immoral individuals, the proper inculcation of religion and virtue would reduce poverty, drunkenness, crime, general debauchery, and other social ills.

The examples of Franklin, Pintard, and Carpenter make clear, however, that private wealth for public purposes involved more than morally reforming the poor. It also involved building institutions that would enable the less fortunate to lift themselves from poverty through learning and culture, as well as through moral reform. It included support for institutions such as local churches, schools, universities, theological seminaries and public libraries, and societies for the fine arts, for those who could not provide for such on their own.

The impact of Puritan ideas on wealth, giving, and philanthropy is undeniable. Historian Peter Dobkin Hall and sociologist E. Digby Baltzell independently develop the contrast between general charity and Puritan philanthropy. In his monumental study of Quaker Philadelphia and Puritan Boston, Baltzell distinguishes between the spontaneous charity characteristic of the Catholic and aristocratic ethic, on the one hand, and the institution building that characterized the American Puritans, on the other (1979, see, for example, pp. 77–78, 94). According to Baltzell, the uniquely Puritan form of giving is philanthropy, "an infinitely Puritan and rational response to social conditions that . . . were dysfunctional to the best use of talent in promoting an efficient division of labor" (1979, p. 78). The purpose of Puritan-derived philanthropy is a hard, unsentimental, rationalistic view of societal improvement.

In contrast, giving based on a Catholic or aristocratic ethos (to which Baltzell likens the Quaker response to the problem of poverty) takes the characteristic form of charity. It is a "spontaneous, stop-gap, and Christian response to the poor" (p. 77); underlying the Catholic and aristocratic ethos is the understanding that the poor shall always be with us. It accepts the idea that persons are the product of their estates, where one would be born, live out one's life, and die.

Hall (1987) attributes the national spread of philanthropy and of nonprofit organizations to the Puritan culture of philanthropy. Hall also believes that Puritan philanthropy promotes institution building. These nonprofit institutions and voluntary associations across the country all seemed to have their roots in New England. "Such an association was almost invariably the work of a migrant New Englander with evangelical connections" (Hall, 1987, p. 7). Hall points out that the migrating New Englanders and their descendants produced a public but nongovernmental "culture of organization." Like Baltzell, Hall draws a picture of emerging philanthropy, not ameliorative charity.

Philanthropy in pre–Civil War times already centered on giving for public purposes. The focus on institution building would become even more prominent with the rise of the great industrialists after the Civil War. Eventually, American philanthropy would turn into a calculating, nonspontaneous, and long-term support of the nonprofit sector.

HELPING THE POOR IN THE "GILDED" AGE

After the Civil War, faith in science, rationalism, and utilitarianism eroded the religious underpinnings of the American community. In everyday life, Americans attempted to cope with modern science by separating ways of understanding the world into two categories. They distinguished between the world we could know through empirical evidence and the unknowable world of faith. In the end, however, a triumph of science in the mundane world could not help but reduce the salience of the sacred. (For extensive analysis of the consequences of this erosion, see Rothman, Lichter, and Lichter, forthcoming.)

The cultural shift from religion to science in modern industrial society accompanies significant structural changes—of increasing specialization and differentiation of occupations. In tandem with the gradual erosion of religion in everyday life, the Christian Steward more or less disappeared as the model of doing good for the cultural elite by the end of the nineteenth century. The belief in science, progress, and technology increased the demand for "professionals," "efficiency," and "expertise" as Americans tried to cope with new urban problems brought about by the industrialization of the United States.

The rise of professional specialization and differentiation meant a reduced value placed on volunteers. The idealization of the expert, especially in such fields as medicine and social work, pushed aside the ideal of relying on wealthy, nonspecialized amateurs to deal with new urban problems.

Further specialization thus occurred when society redefined the notion of providing for the public good from voluntarism and civic stewardship to the more distant position of general money-giving. The rich would come to fulfill their societal obligations by giving money away—a far cry from Winthrop's community that labored together and suffered together.

Many industrialists went one step further. Retaining Puritanism's rationalistic outlook, they set about to restructure institutions of charity to look like modern corporations. The postwar era saw many popular business techniques applied to organizing charity so that needs of the poor could be efficiently addressed and quickly handled (McCarthy, 1982, p. 62). In the quest for improving the administration of charity, the demand was for a hard-nosed approach—increasing centralization, maintaining better staff control, and increasing efficiency.

All these changes did not mean that spontaneous giving, voluntary efforts, and general good works vanished. Rather, new organizational forms emerged alongside old practices for helping the poor, but adapted the earlier benevolent impulses to a new era.

The Charity Organization Societies (COS) movement is one example. S. Humphreys Gurteen, an English Episcopal clergyman, pioneered them in 1877. The American Charity Organization Societies copied the London Society for Organizing Charitable Relief and Repressing Mendicancy (Lubove, 1965, p. 2). The societies spread rapidly from their original founding in Buffalo, New York. City leaders established societies in New Haven and Philadelphia in 1878, and in Brooklyn, Cincinnati, and Boston (Leiby, 1978, p. 114) the following year. Josephine Shaw Lowell and others founded the New York Society in 1882. A decade later there were ninety-two societies, serving a population of more than 11 million (Lubove, 1965, p. 2).[1]

The COS movement updated Christian charity to deal with a major problem of industrializing the United States—the depression of 1873, which produced large-scale national unemployment. The increasing urbanization of America diminished the effectiveness of the face-to-face, one-on-one interaction between rich and poor, characteristic of the Christian gentleman approach. The COS movement attempted to fill the gap.

The COS movement was distinctive, insofar as the *laissez-faire* views of the day defined the movement's approach, and was based on the notion that, in general, personal character defects led to poverty. Movement leaders strongly believed that "the dependent poor needed not alms but a friend" (Kramer, 1981, p. 63). These societies sought to eliminate the system of "outdoor relief," which provided monetary aid to those living outside of state-run institutions. Supporting those not in institutions, leaders believed, was simply subsidizing vice and indolence.[2]

Instead of indiscriminate charity, the movement attempted to coordinate the charitable agencies in the community so that they would be working together. More important, the leaders of the COS devised a strategy for categorizing those without work during this depression into the deserving and undeserving poor.

COS work programs "let the labor axiom be the test" of whether "the able-bodied applicant [would be] as willing to do as much work as his condition [allowed]" (quoted in Olasky, 1990). Leaders categorized those able and willing to work, along with children and disabled handicapped, as part of the deserving poor; they would be helped. Those who would not "do as much work as [their] condition allow[ed]" were considered the undeserving poor and would be excoriated.

The COS helped industrious persons find direct employment and gave deserving clients loans without interest (Olasky, 1990). Advocates of the COS approach, which they referred to as "scientific charity" or "scientific philanthropy," often compared it favorably to the impulsive, casual handout given to a beggar and to the indiscriminate dole of the soup kitchen. Handouts failed to alleviate the conditions of the poor, while soup kitchens contributed to the demoralization of the person receiving benefits. The COS cure required individualized treatment for each case, recognizing both the material and "the subjective aspect" of welfare dependency (Leiby, 1978, p. 114).

The COS approach, however, was not the most popular. Recipients were told they personally had to do something about their problems that beset them from without. Donors were told that their money giving and voluntarism were half-hearted and self-defeating. Frank Dekker Watson, a supporter of the COS approach and professor of sociology at Haverford College, writes, however, that while the stable organization provided for by the COS societies may not be the spontaneous charity that "Lords and Ladies Bountiful" would desire, charity balls could not take the place of social work (1922, p. 496).

The "radicals" (Watson's term), though, proved to be the more formidable critic of the COS movement and were ultimately responsible for burying it in obscurity, especially in academic circles. The radical opponents to the COS argued that private charity, including the COS approach, would injure the poor's self-respect. Much of the radical criticism became embodied in efforts to deal with the 1932 depression. We deal with public welfare later on in this chapter but want to note here that the radical critics countered the ideology of the COS movement with the argument that public assistance can and should be granted as a matter of right, not based on personal character evaluations. The critics contended that charity work, including what the COS did, is at best a palliative and not a real cure for poverty. The underlying, real cause of urban poverty was *laissez-faire* capitalism.

Despite the radical critics of the COS, the movement did have an effect. Even today, Americans still tend to believe that those in need should receive government welfare only when the market, family, and other nonprofit organizations fail to function. Ironically, Lubove (1965) notes that the COS's emphasis on character rehabilitation and professional supervision of the poor client discredited public assistance. "Charity organization leaders convinced themselves and countless Americans that public relief was incompatible with efficient, scientific philanthropy because it ultimately pauperized the character of its recipients. Unaccompanied by satisfactory investigation and rehabilitation procedures, public relief disrupted the social and economic order by reducing all incentive to work" (Lubove, 1965, p. 52).[3]

THE PROGRESSIVE ERA AND RISE OF PROFESSIONALS IN THE PHILANTHROPIC WORLD

The Progressive Era marked yet another change in the relationship between wealth and philanthropy. By the end of the nineteenth century, American institutions were evolving in new directions. The country had rapidly industrialized; a new, powerful, capitalist, urban society had emerged; public education, high culture, and mass communication networks were swiftly expanding. Government at all levels turned to experts for practical help in dealing with complex social problems. On the state level, Wisconsin Governor Robert M. La Follette relied upon the university "brain trust" for expert advice. On the national level, Theodore Roosevelt and Woodrow Wilson did the same.

As it did with these other institutions, Progressivism dominated the organization of charity and philanthropy in the United States in the early twentieth century. The new enlightened view was that the social environment shaped people's attitudes and conduct, of both rich and poor, and that the environment was ultimately the cause of deviance and poverty. To truly help the deviant, the poor, and the unfortunate, one had to reform institutions. This required criticizing the "leisure" class and overthrowing their previously established moral claims to personal wealth (Bell, 1976; Lasch, 1977; Janowitz, 1978).

Writers now encouraged the wealthy to honor responsibilities, but the urgings were tinged with implied threats. The middle class professionals of the Progressive Era encouraged wealthy individuals to try to understand the poor and accommodate their needs rather than paternalistically make their decisions for them (McCarthy, 1982, p. 101). The corollary was that if the rich failed to provide needed assistance, the poor would revolt and take what was rightfully theirs in the first place.

Even the leaders of the COS movement were not immune to these shifts in opinion. Many came to reject any connection between poverty and moral character. By 1907, the Buffalo COS broke from prior practice and began providing simple relief. The editor of *Charities*, the official publication of the New York Charity Organization Society, approvingly pointed to the fact that the poor were no longer regarded as the moral inferiors of the rich. Leaders of the movement also explicitly repudiated the belief in a connection between poverty and virtue (Trattner, 1979, p. 88).

The settlement house movement, though, emerged as the main competitor of the COS movement. Popularly associated with Jane Addams and Lillian Wald (see, for example, Trattner, 1979, pp. 134–59), the settlement house idea, like the COS, was imported from England. Its inspirational model, Toynbee Hall, however, was founded by Christian socialists, such as Fredric Maurice and Charles Kingsley, and other critics of capitalism, such as John Ruskin. Advocates of the settlement houses were critical of the Spencerian individualism that motivated the COS efforts. Jane Addams summed up the motivations of the founders as promotion of "actual social democracy." Settlement leaders encouraged participants in the movement to better understand the poor by living in their neighborhoods.

Settlement houses exhibited features similar to the COS movement, particularly in their use of volunteers and in their interest in people's spiritual as well as material conditions (Trattner, 1979, p. 137). Their differences, however, reflected changes in cultural conceptions of poverty and reform, from the earlier era of self-reliance, rugged individualism, and *laissez-faire* to the Progressive Era. Settlement house workers sought to promote social and economic reform as a primary means of improving the condition of the poor. Unlike the COS movement, they made no distinction among the indigent, between the "deserving'' and the ''undeserving'' poor. They preferred to stress the social and material conditions that kept them poor. Settlement house leaders lived in the indigent neighborhoods in an attempt to avoid what they felt was the paternalism of the COS movement. They sought more ''democratic'' and egalitarian relationships between themselves and the poor.

The settlements had no clearly defined goals other than the general one of group improvement. They advocated specific programs such as kindergartens, schools, nurseries, and day-care centers and the use of extensive facilities for neighborhood groups. Interested in practice rather than theory, the three Rs of the movement were Residence, Research, and Reform. Settlement house leaders aligned themselves with the working rather than the employing classes, and they gave many young people a sense of mission in life (not unlike the Peace Corps was for a later generation of idealistic youth).

The primary focus of the settlement house movement was not individual character reform but promoting social change in the industrial order. Movement leaders believed that reform in the interest of ''social justice'' was more important than changes in personal morality. Their reform efforts took two forms—preventive legislation and social insurance (Trattner, 1979, p. 150). Preventive legislation included ''fair'' standards of wages, hours, and housing; the prohibition of child labor; the regulation of dangerous trades; the establishment of public health programs; and the development of more practical education. Social insurance reforms included compulsory social insurance against unemployment, old age, sickness, disability, and the death of the family bread winner.

The settlement house leaders did not achieve their social justice objectives in the short run, but they eventually provided the basic program of the modern welfare state. In fighting for their programs, the settlement house leaders proved to be brilliant publicists on behalf of the poor. Judith Ann Trolander (1987) notes that one study of fourteen well-known settlement leaders showed that they produced at least forty-five books (p. 16).[4]

Increasingly, Progressives saw philanthropists as self-serving people who donated money as a convenient mechanism to achieve respectability and fame. The motives of the well-to-do were suspect, their wealth decried; businessmen became ''robber barons,'' and their wives ''society queens.'' There was a growing sense that beneficiaries had a right to the benefactor's donation. Money was to be rendered without the expectation of gratitude, and many middle class professionals who dealt with urban problems came to view the ''charitable donation'' as an entitlement (McCarthy, 1982, p. 166).

THE EMERGENCE OF THE FOUNDATION

Wealthy Americans, in response to such criticisms, established a number of different institutions to carry on philanthropic work to deal with the root causes of the United States' problems. Many of these men donated large fortunes based on the concept of ''surplus wealth.'' At the age of thirty-three, a good thirty years before he set upon his career as a philanthropist, Andrew Carnegie laid out the philanthropist's thesis in his "Gospel of Wealth," which would legitimize the nontaxed, general purpose foundation in American life. Carnegie's thesis combines the communitarianism of an earlier era (binding the rich and the poor) with a confidence in his own individual superiority over others. "The problem of our age is the proper administration of wealth, that the ties of brotherhood may still bind together the rich and poor in harmonious relationship" (Carnegie, 1983, p. 97). Concentrated wealth in the hands of a few, however, does not negate wealth's true aim, which is the pursuit of the common good. "We start, then, with a condition of affairs under which the best interests of the race are promoted, but which inevitably gives wealth to the few" (p. 100).

Carnegie's view of the lifestyle of the rich embodies a strong belief in community and hierarchy. In Carnegie's eyes, wealth is not ultimately private. It should not be spent solely for the sake of those who have it. The life of the wealthy should be:

to set an example of modest, unostentatious living, shunning display or extravagance; to provide moderately for the legitimate wants of those dependent upon him; and after doing so, to consider all surplus revenues which come to him simply as trust funds, which he is called upon to administer, and strictly bound as a matter of duty to administer in the manner which, in his judgment, is best calculated to produce the most beneficial results for the community—the man of wealth thus becoming the mere trustee and agent for his poorer brethren, bringing to their service his superior wisdom, experience, and ability to administer, doing for them better than they would or could do for themselves. (p. 104)

In 1911, Andrew Carnegie created the first broad-purpose foundation, the Carnegie Corporation, to implement his philosophy of general philanthropy. Other millionaires, such as John D. Rockefeller, followed his example, and within twenty years such foundations as Russell Sage, Rosenwald, Duke, Guggenheim, Kellogg, Mellon, and Phelps-Stokes came into existence. Like Carnegie, they were all broad-based institutions founded on great fortunes.

Like other elites of the nineteenth and early twentieth centuries, these particular individuals admired science and technology. They were also spirited men of action, guided by the practical experience they obtained from running large-scale corporate enterprises. Julius Rosenwald, founder of the Julius Rosenwald Fund established in 1917, captures the sentiment behind what the philanthropic foundation would do:

I do not like the "sob stuff" philanthropy. What I want to do is to try to cure the things that seem to be wrong. I do not underestimate the value of helping the underdog. That, however, is not my chief concern, but rather the operation of cause and effect. I try to do the things that will aid groups and masses rather than individuals. (quoted in Boorstin, 1983, p. 136)[5]

Rosenwald and his like-minded philanthropists clearly rejected the COS notion of "relief through individual effort." The hope of these donors was that a board of trustees would be responsive to their original vision and devote themselves to improving human welfare through the broadest possible interplay between scientific knowledge and an efficient, flexible organization. In tandem with the large, general-purpose foundation, the great donors also created the research university (as exemplified by Johns Hopkins and the University of Chicago), the independent research institute (such as the Carnegie Institution and Rockefeller University), the single-purpose reform trust (such as the Carnegie Foundation for the advancement of teaching); and the newly developed profession of social work (Karl and Katz, 1981, pp. 245–46). These institutions would then mount a sustained attack on the real causes of problems in the industrial United States.

Historians Barry Karl and Stanley Katz consider the general-purpose foundation "a noble and heroic endeavor" (1981, p. 246) and the most innovative organizations developed by the great industrialists to promote the general welfare. The invention of the foundation did not pass without criticism, however. The donors' relatively extensive wealth caused Congress, through the Populist-based Walsh Commission in 1915, to attack the foundation as a bastion of corporate capitalism and as subversive to American democracy. Congress aimed its attack primarily at John D. Rockefeller (JDR) II and the Rockefeller Foundation. Rockefeller had many enemies, including Teddy Roosevelt, and Populists at that time reviled the philanthropists' donations as "the kiss of Judas and the Trojan Horse" (Whitaker, 1974, p. 102).

The Walsh Commission denounced the Rockefeller Foundation for funding a study of labor unions and strikes by Mackenzie King (future Canadian prime minister), shortly after the violent Ludlow Massacre. When asked about this foundation-sponsored study, JDR II replied, "Our office staff is a sort of family affair. . . . We have not drawn sharp lines between business and philanthropic interests" (Whitaker, 1974, p. 102).

The commission recommended the following legislation: that foundations no longer be perpetual; that they be limited in size; that they not accumulate income; and that trustees would also come from the federal government. (In his original proposal to Congress for the purpose of chartering a general-purpose foundation, Rockefeller made a similar proposal.) Congress took no action, but the Rockefeller Foundation did stop the labor study and for some time thereafter concentrated primarily on funding noncontroversial medical research. Despite the Walsh Commission, foundations quickly won acceptance. According to Karl and Katz, "by 1929, the foundation had come to appear traditional, inevitable, and acceptable" (1981, p. 253).

Despite the prominence of the famous large foundations in the 1920s, the presidencies of Harding, Coolidge, and Hoover ironically mark this period before the New Deal as one of political conservatism. But this was also the period when college administrators, academics, foundation managers, and civil servants started a growing managerial network among foundations, recipient organizations, and government, culminating in President Hoover's government-foundation collaboration, *Report on Recent Social Trends* (Hofstadter, 1948).

The rise of the professions and the professionalization of the nonprofit sector had a profound impact on foundations. The growth of foundation wealth and activity during and after World War I and the death or retirement of original donors further deepened reliance on the foundation manager. Eventually, the composition and philosophy of the boards of trustees at many foundations paralleled the professionalization of voluntarism. Untrained Good Samaritans no longer involved themselves in the day-to-day decisions of foundation work but left the task to professionals. The separation of ownership from control paralleled that of the corporate world. In order for philanthropists to decide how best to distribute their excess wealth, they were expected to work together on important problems with those who had professional expertise.

In 1930, Frederick Keppel, of the Carnegie Corporation, captured the general orientation of the philanthropic foundation and its professionalization, mostly in terms of its close relationship with the research university:

It is only natural that the relations between the [foundations and universities] have always been close. The foundations have learned by experience that one of the most satisfactory ways of disposing of their burdens of responsibility is to lay them upon the universities as operating agencies. The experience of the university, on the other hand, is constantly bringing to light opportunities for the foundation in the form of enterprises which no institution could carry through unaided, but from which all institutions and all communities might profit. (Keppel, 1930, p. 11)

In the pre–New Deal era, foundations contributed mightily to the elimination of "pellagra, hookworm, typhoid, yellow fever, and numerous other physical ailments which throughout history damaged and shortened life" (Karl and Katz, 1981, p. 252). In addition, foundations contributed to the development of survey research and the founding of the Social Science Research Council, the National Bureau of Economic Research, the first think-tank (the Brookings Institute), and the first library school at the University of Chicago (Karl and Katz, 1981, pp. 266–67). In fact, in the early years the major contributions by foundation grants to furthering the public good are so vast that Warren Weaver requires several hundred pages and many coauthors to describe them (Weaver, 1967, pp. 223–448).

Those in recipient institutions also felt the rapid encroachment of professionalism. Fund raising by the University of Chicago is a good example (McCarthy, 1982, pp. 160–61). In the 1890s, before the professionalization of giving, two Baptist clergymen, Frederick Taylor Gates and Thomas Wakefield Goodspeed, were in charge of raising enough money to match John D. Rockefeller's grant to the university. They barely met their goal. In the 1920s, the university had another fund-raising drive, during which the responsibility fell upon a professional fund raiser, the Jones Corporation, headed by John Price Jones. The professionals carefully selected target groups, and efficiently solicited gifts. Professional fund raising, like the professionalization of other activities, removed the wealthy even further from control over their donations.

Professional fund raisers couched their efforts in scientific terms, referring to "the psychology" of the donor, "compiling data," "analyzing," and "manipulating donor needs." The managerial task of philanthropy now focused on what William Rainey Harper called "the amassing of large sums at a distance" (quoted in McCarthy, 1982, p. 164).

Free from central government control, professionals worked with volunteers in the public arena. This mix gave a distinctive and uniquely American shape to the collection of organizations now referred to as the independent sector or the third sector. These organizations include both donor groups (foundations) and recipients (hospitals, universities, charity groups) (Cornuelle, 1965; Nielsen, 1979).

Until the New Deal, this nonprofit sector had a specific activist design, while the federal government's role in promoting the general welfare was very limited. Much of the responsibility fell on the private, nonprofit domain to further the public good (Nielsen, 1979, p. 183).

The government's role was indirect, mostly through providing legal privileges and tax exemptions. Government would not trespass on the freedom of educational, scientific, medical, cultural, and religious institutions to perform their missions (Nielsen, 1979). In return, nonprofits would refrain from direct lobbying activities and commercial activities.

THE NEW DEAL AND CHANGING THE THREE SECTORS' BALANCE

The Great Depression was the major turning point for foundations, nonprofit recipients, and the federal government. The habit of sending problems to Washington grew with the inability of private charity to meet the needs of the time. Robert H. Bremner (1980) details the extensive efforts of President Herbert Hoover during the Depression to stimulate private, state, and local nonprofit activity. His activities were consistent with his philosophy, which was the traditional view of limiting federal government while encouraging nonprofit activity to meet public needs. The American Red Cross even spurned a proposed congressional grant of $25 million and undertook a relief effort with $5 million from its general campaign and an additional $15 million from a special campaign (Bremner, 1988, p. 138).

In 1931, Hoover planned and carried out a major national campaign, the Organization for Unemployment Relief, which raised over $100 million from both local and private sources of charity. As the crisis deepened, Hoover, with congressional authorization of the Reconstruction Finance Corporation, gradually shifted toward the kind of central government involvement characteristic of the New Deal, but without Roosevelt's optimistic enthusiasm for collective action and resulting political success.

The literature on the government's response to the Great Depression is so vast that even to summarize it would take more space than we have available (see, for example, Sitkoff, 1985, for bibliographies; McCraw, 1985, on New Deal economic policy; and Bremner, 1988, on social welfare policies). Hoover's policies, with their stress on "morale" and morality, contrasted radically with Roosevelt's optimism. The latter would not make the political mistakes of his predecessors but based his New Deal policies on the "common man" and "the forgotten man" (a phrase ironically coined by William Graham Sumner, the sociologist and a principal advocate of rugged individualism). Roosevelt and the New Deal quite successfully remolded U.S. politics.

Roosevelt's search for a solution to the unexpectedly severe crisis led to an unprecedented mobilization of experts from the nonprofit sector for governing. Some were law school professors; others were in economics and the newer social sciences of sociology, psychology, and political science; and most were oriented toward social planning. Believing that social problems were the outcome of faulty institutions rather than the result of individual failures, these academic experts strongly contended that the government should seek widescale institutional reforms to solve social problems. The continued seriousness of the nation's problems led to the proliferation of New Deal agencies and expanded the size of the federal bureaucracy.

Several features of the New Deal should be noted as relevant for foundations. First, the credibility of traditional *laissez-faire* individualism vanished along with the political fortunes of Herbert Hoover, its most articulate defender (see, for example, Hofstadter, 1948). Second, while FDR certainly did not introduce socialism to the United States, his innovative, often radical, experimentation with national government programs for dealing with what were previously private, state, and local matters dramatically altered earlier practices. As T. V. Smith pointed out, in his essay "The New Deal as a Cultural Phenomenon," Roosevelt "was enormously successful in *politicizing* the whole of American life" (quoted in Lawson, 1985, p. 156). Roosevelt's national planning blurred the lines between the three sectors of business, government, and nonprofit organizations.

Federal government activity did not have the short-run effects that many conservatives feared or some radicals hoped. It nevertheless set an important precedent for the later Great Society programs and contributed mightily to the redefinition of *liberalism* to include a generous measure of government intervention in domestic affairs and a permanent ambition for "completing" the programs initiated by the New Deal. Roosevelt himself said in his speech accepting the Democratic nomination, "Let it be the task of our Party to break foolish traditions" (quoted by Smith, 1949, p. 212).

Private giving during the New Deal faced new problems, the biggest one being the inability of the nonprofit sector to handle the Depression without active government help. The Depression itself, notes Bremner, put a great strain on the resources of many nonprofit institutions and the commitment of many of the large foundations. Nonetheless, several large foundations came into being after the Great Depression, including the Andrew Mellon Charitable and Educational

Trust (1930), the Kellogg Foundation (1930), and the Sloan Foundation (1934), while many like the Rockefeller Foundation continued their good works.

The real impact of the New Deal on U.S. political life, however, went way beyond government's eclipsing of the nonprofit sector in providing for the public good. The New Deal led to a new conventional wisdom that redefined the meaning of American liberalism. This new conventional wisdom favored greater federal government responsibility for welfare, education, scientific research, higher education, and culture (i.e. art) and for greater governmental influence over the policies and performances of private, nongovernmental institutions (Nielsen, 1979). The dominance of this view, especially in intellectual circles, became so strong that the literary critic Lionel Trilling in 1950 writes, "In the United States liberalism is not only the dominant but even the sole intellectual tradition. For it is the plain fact that nowadays there are no conservative or reactionary ideas in general circulation" (quoted in Nash, 1976, p. 58).[6]

While there has been extensive literature on the growth of the welfare state, the nonprofit sector and its relationship with the welfare state has been largely ignored by the scholarly literature until recently (e.g., Cornuelle, 1965; Nielsen, 1979; Powell, 1987), although there are exceptions. Waldemar A. Nielsen (1979), for example, offers three converging lines of intellectual support for government expansion. First is the argument of the realist, that the problems faced by the nation are too large to be handled by private nonprofits alone. The second line of support is managerial, that planning and coordination of large-scale enterprises are most efficiently done by the central government. Nielsen himself describes private welfare institutions as sentimental relics.[7] The third line of argument for government activism over nonprofit activity is ideological. It rests on the notion that benefits for the unfortunate are due them by right and not charity. "It is the dignified, participatory, equitable and democratic way" (Nielsen, 1979, p. 22). Nielsen notes that in Europe, attitudes toward private philanthropy are less favorable than here (p. 234). While there are large numbers of "left-over" charities, most, he claims, are relics of the past and exist in name only. Some of the European left charge philanthropy with delaying the expansion of government-controlled benefits; others decry its elitism.

While support for the welfare state among most intellectuals and academics in the United States is overwhelming, Americans generally support it rather reluctantly (Wilensky, 1975). Americans place far greater weight than do the peoples of other nations on the values of individualism, private property, the free market, and minimum government (e.g., Lipset, 1963). More recently, Nathan Glazer (1986) makes the same point, as do Robert Y. Shapiro and John T. Young (1989), with a large amount of comparative public opinion data.

The post–New Deal definition of *liberalism*, which made the welfare state the primary provider of the public good, profoundly transformed the mission of the philanthropic foundation. In effect, the entire nonprofit sector experienced a massive crisis of confidence after the New Deal (and World War II). What was the mission of the whole nonprofit sector, if government was going to do it all and do it better? The next section discusses the long-range impact of the New Deal era and how it ultimately redefined government-nonprofit relations. Offsetting this crisis was the sudden surge of optimism and massive activism on the part of the Ford Foundation, to which we now turn.

POSTWAR FOUNDATIONS

Despite government expansion, foundations flourished after World War II (Walton and Andrews, 1960, pp. x–xi). In 1915, the Russell Sage Foundation listed 27 foundations in their directory. In 1930, 185 foundations were reported, and by 1946 the number had increased to 505. The 1948 edition of *American Foundations and Their Fields* contained data on 899 foundations, while the 1955 edition reported on 4,164 foundations.

By the mid–1980s, the *Foundation Directory* listed more than 25,000 foundations (Foundation Center, 1987). These foundations all had assets of over $1 million and/or gave away at least $100,000 annually. Roughly 3 out of 4 of these appeared after 1950; fewer than 1 in 10 existed before World War II.

In the 1950s, the Ford Foundation emerged as the giant among philanthropic foundations and was also the target of numerous political attacks. Several congressional probes, for the most part led by anticommunist Populists, targeted foundations.

While the Walsh Commission of 1915 sought to curtail the power of robber-baron capitalism, subsequent congressional attacks were quite different. The Cold War and the deaths of Roosevelt and Wilkie created new ground for congressional attacks on foundations and "liberal internationalism," in the form of two ideological sentiments. One was a foreign policy outlook against international communism. The other was a domestic view hostile to the welfare state and in favor of restoring "rugged individualism." These ideological currents fueled much of the congressional investigations in the 1950s.

The Cox Committee

In 1952, Congress set up the Select Committee to Investigate Tax-Exempt Foundations and Comparable Organizations—the Cox Committee—chaired by Georgia Congressman Edward Eugene Cox. The committee was authorized to hold hearings on whether foundations and other nonprofits were using funds to support anti-American subversive activists or "for purposes not in the interest or tradition of the United States" (Whitaker, 1974, p. 106).

Supporters of Joseph McCarthy pushed for the committee's establishment. After all, Alger Hiss was former president of the Carnegie Endowment for International Peace. The political coalition also included supporters of Republican Robert Taft, such as Cox and Robert McCormick. The coalition attacked the Eastern, liberal, internationalist wing of the Republican Party. The internationalist faction of the Republicans included such notables as President Eisenhower, the Rockefeller brothers, and Paul Hoffman, president of the Ford foundation.

Bipartisan committee members and staff (with exception of Cox), however, conducted the hearings with little animosity toward foundations. Most testimony before the committee supported private foundations, pointing out that the alternative to private philanthropy would be large government (Weaver, 1967; Whitaker, 1974; Hall, 1987). The final committee report criticized some grants but found little subversive activity. The report did encourage greater disclosure of fiscal data, including lists of donors and recipients. Nevertheless, the committee also recommended the reexamination of tax laws to further encourage foundations (Weaver, 1967, pp. 172–74; Whitaker, 1974, pp. 106–7).

Congressman B. Carroll Reece (R.-Tennessee), former chairman of the Republican National Committee and member of the Cox Committee, was far from satisfied. He demanded further study, noting the short period of time (six months) given the committee to compile its report. In response, Congress authorized the formation of the Reece Committee, headed by Congressman Reece, to conduct further hearings.

The Reece Committee

The Reece Committee pursued the same agenda as the Cox Committee but resulted in a majority and a minority report. Rather than praising the role of private philanthropy in the United States, the Reece Committee's majority warned foundations to be ''chary of promoting ideas, concepts and opinion-forming material which runs contrary to what the public currently wishes, approves, and likes'' (Whitaker, 1974, p. 109). Many in and out of politics criticized the majority report. The minority report, authored by Democrat Wayne Hays, accused the committee and staff of a witch-hunt. ''This was not an investigation in which the purpose was to gather facts, to evaluate them, and then to arrive at fair conclusions on the basis of those facts. Instead, we are presented with an inquiry in which facts played no part'' (quoted in Whitaker, 1974, p. 109). Editorials in the *Washington Post* and the *New York Times* and articles in the *Atlantic* and *Harper's Magazine* all denounced the committee (see also Macdonald, 1989, pp. 31–35).

Ironically, one of the charges raised by the Reece Commission was that foundations had supposedly overemphasized empirical methods of social inquiry at the expense of more deductive methods of analysis such as those of Thomas Aquinas. As a result, Reece claimed, they neglected ''Studies regarding the excellence of the American Constitution, the importance of the Declaration of Independence and the profundity of the philosophy of the Founding Fathers'' (taken from Macdonald, 1989, pp. 31–32). Curiously, a principal target of the committee was Robert M. Hutchins, famous for advocating precisely this kind of social inquiry (including Aristotelian logic and the Great Books programs) during his presidency at the University of Chicago. Dwight Macdonald, in his haste to score points against all comers, completely misses this similarity amidst the obvious political differences between Hutchins and Reece. Macdonald also misses the fact that Hutchins and Reece put forth criticisms of the social sciences similar to his own (1989, p. 81).

Subsequent treatments of the relationship between philanthropic foundations and government have few kind words to say about the Cox and Reece committees. Bremner claims, "[W]hatever disservice the Committee rendered the House, it did no serious harm to foundations" (quoted in Whitaker, 1974, p. 109). Ben Whitaker calls the Reece majority report a veiled attack on "intellectual, and especially Eastern, elitism" (1974, p. 108). Warren Weaver in 1967 writes even more contemptuously: "[I]t can be argued that the United States tolerates the expression even of absurd ideas in the interests of freedom, and then in good season gives the absurd ideas the attention they deserve" (p. 179).

Simple dismissal of Populist attacks by Weaver and others, however, fails to acknowledge the potential power of Congress to strip foundations of their legal status, since foundations are strictly a creature of tax-exempt legislation. This fact was almost fatally forgotten during the 1969 Patman hearings, which we discuss in some detail later in the chapter (e.g., Whitaker, 1974, pp. 109–17). Many scholars and foundation activists subsequently recognize such de facto political control, including philanthropoids Jane H. Mavity and Paul Ylvisaker (1977) in their congressional testimony in 1972 and John Simon (1973) in his support of foundation activism in public affairs.

Further, as Dwight Macdonald, hardly a supporter of the congressional committees, pointed out, the foundations might have avoided some of their problems with the Populist right. Foundations could have dodged such political attacks if people like Hutchins, one-time associate director of the Ford Foundation and president of the Fund for the Republic (a Ford Foundation spin-off), "were a little better instructed on Communism, say up to the high-school level" (Macdonald, 1989, p. 78).

The paradox of the fifties is that the political climate and congressional searches for subversives produced an atmosphere hostile to foundations. Despite such a hostile climate, foundations grew in number and size, and, led by the Ford Foundation, began to promote projects aimed toward massive social change in the fifties. The efforts would culminate in many noteworthy joint foundation-government projects of the 1960s.

PHILANTHROPY AS AN AGENT OF SOCIAL CHANGE

Knowledge and Social Action

We can sum up foundation ideology of the 1960s with the phrase, "the more we know and the more we do, the better off we are." Yet neither the sheer growth in the number of private fortunes nor the growing professionalism of philanthropy alone sufficiently explains major changes in the philanthropic world oriented toward the social movement activism of the sixties.

We attribute much of sixties philanthropy to a vision that combines two ideas. The first is an expansion of the notion of a "social problem." In the 1960s, cultural deprivation, bad education, widespread disease, and war were added to poverty as social problems looking for solutions rather than situations endemic to the human condition. The second belief shaping sixties philanthropy grew out of the New Deal and was further extended during World War II. This was the belief that the government had a tremendous capacity for doing good, internationally as well as domestically.

Strongly influenced by Progressive intellectuals, foundations channeled efforts to correct social evils through knowledge-based, planned reforms. This initially formed the rationale behind foundation-sponsored scientific and social science research. By the 1960s, "up-to-date" foundations believed in using social science knowledge to develop pilot programs as prototypes for much larger government-funded programs, which were thought to be more efficient and more equitable. The shift in purpose led foundations to urge the government to assume the burden of developing massive programs for social change.

The Ford Foundation of the fifties and sixties exemplified foundation-government efforts. Although a relative latecomer among large foundations, in the 1950s Ford became the most important foundation in the United States, merely by virtue of its enormous size (e.g., Macdonald, 1989). Once the anticommunist turmoil subsided, the Ford Foundation established a formal public policy agenda under its famous Public Affairs Program. The program funded projects that became the kernel for the Johnson administration's War on Poverty, and, according to Daniel P. Moynihan, "invented a new level of government, the inner-city community action agency" (1970, p. 42).

McGeorge Bundy, however, did the most to push the Ford Foundation into a prominent role in setting the national agenda. In the words of one former Ford philanthropoid, "In the United States, it is mainly in the last dozen years or so [with Bundy's accession to the Ford Foundation's presidency] that we have consciously and deliberately worked to affect public policy" (Magat, 1979, p. 84). Ford Foundation support became part of Moynihan's "professionalization of reform." Moynihan notes that by the 1950s, initiatives to change the American system came from those whose profession was to do just that (Moynihan, 1970, p. 23). In particular, the War on Poverty, the social welfare initiative of the 1960s, did not emerge from the poor. Rather, the "war" was declared in the interest of the poor "by persons confident of their own judgment in such matters" (Moynihan, 1970, p. 25).

While detailed exposition is beyond the scope of this chapter (see, for example, Levine, 1970, pp. 158–68; Moynihan, 1970; Marris and Rein, 1972, pp. 164–90; Matusow, 1984; and Lemann, 1991), we comment on the principle of the day, "maximum feasible participation" (Moynihan, 1970, p. 87), which proved to be, at once, the most innovative and controversial part of the War on Poverty.

Peter Marris and Martin Rein describe it generously as the actions of "a talented elite, with enough authority to deploy seed money, [who could then] generate a self-sustaining democratic impulse towards reform" (1972, p. 167).

This strategy of reform from the top was paradoxical. As Marris and Rein note, "[A]nyone who could hold his own in a committee of public officials, business leaders, the mayor and project directors was unlikely to be still poor and uneducated" (1972, p. 167). The Ford Foundation rejected the settlement house tradition in favor of community participation, but those at Ford were never clear exactly what this meant or what was to be put in place.

As Moynihan points out, what ensued was a good deal of conflict as some of the more venturesome community action programs (CAPs) challenged local elites. He describes the typical sequence in the life of a CAP as follows. First, the community sees a period of organization, with much publicity and fanfare. Operations then begin and mark the onset of conflict between the agency and local government. This phase is often accompanied by the radicalization of white, middle-class reformers who began the effort, which in turn leads to stirring amongst the poor. In general, the result is heightened racial antagonism between blacks and whites.

Local government and the larger white community then retaliate. Often, at this point, internal difficulties of the agency manifest themselves. Finally, established institutions are victorious, or local government and the community groups reach a stalemate, with much bitterness all around. Moynihan (1970) discusses in some detail the case of Syracuse, New York, where the local community action program advocated violence while failing to set up any useful programs. Simultaneously, it appropriated most of its $8 million grant for salaries of organization members. CAP-sponsored demonstrations against Syracuse's Republican mayor did not win the program political allies, nor did it lead to the mayor's political defeat (Moynihan, 1970, pp. 132–34).[8]

Ironically, all this activity resulted in militancy itself becoming the mark of merit (Moynihan, 1970, pp. 140–42). Members of the Newark, New Jersey, CAP participated in the 1967 Newark rioting (Moynihan, 1970, p. 156), while the notorious Chicago gang the Blackstone Rangers received federal funds "to train themselves and do other good things [sic]" (Levine, 1970, pp. 78, 85; see also Marris and Rein, 1972, pp. 254–55; and Lemann, 1991, pp. 245–49, which provides a history of the gang itself). In 1967, the Office of Education funded Chicago's Woodlawn organization and the gangs to the tune of $1 million (Lemann, 1991, p. 247). The grant was a complete failure; two gang members were subsequently arrested for murder and three more for rape, and one instructor in the program shot two of his students. The program was terminated after one year of operation (p. 248).

Moynihan (1970, p. 168) notes that the essential problem with community action is that it had four different meanings: organizing the power structure, expanding the power structure, confronting the power structure, and assisting the power structure. While it made up only a part of the government's War on Poverty, which also included the Head Start program, legal services for the poor, neighborhood health centers, and the infamous negative income tax experiments, the CAP programs were the most audaciously original and, in a sense, characteristic of the entire era (see Levine, 1970, for a complete list of programs).

While not a formal part of the War on Poverty, the National Welfare Rights Organization (NWRO) emerged as a major social movement during this same period. The ideas of social scientists Frances Fox Piven and Richard A. Cloward served as the organization's inspiration; they provide a sympathetic portrait of the NWRO in subsequent work (1971; 1979). Sociologist J. Craig Jenkins (1989) points out that, in one of those 1960s turnabouts, the organization received money from the Rockefeller Brothers Fund, while at the same time its New York affiliate was demonstrating against Governor Nelson Rockefeller, who was also a board member (p. 308). The NWRO also received much of its initial funding from the Norman, Stern, and Field foundations (p. 308).

Although almost forgotten today, the NWRO played a major role from the mid–1960s to the mid–1970s in putting people on welfare and persuading many recipients and would-be recipients that welfare is a right, not a shame, and that their problems were the fault of the system. The organization won several court fights making it easier to get on welfare and harder to be dislodged from it. Recipients were entitled to due process hearings before they could be removed from the rolls. Moynihan summarizes the entire effort in a phrase that also describes subsequent programs: "public funds, and tax-free private funds, employed on a vast scale to further what was in effect a political agenda of a fairly small group of intellectuals" (1970, p. 190). Nicholas Lemann (1991) is more sympathetic to community action because it provided jobs to upwardly mobile black leaders. He nevertheless concedes that it was both a political and a practical failure. He concludes, "There is no clear example of a community action agency in a poor neighborhood accomplishing either the original goal of reducing juvenile delinquency or the subsequent goal of reducing poverty" (p. 192).

Foundations' strategies changed even more in the late 1960s and 1970s. Funding of social movement activities and organizations increased, while scientific research funding declined even more. From the sixties experience, foundations became major institutions in the modern process of policy proposing. As we shall see in chapter eight, even today, many foundations mobilize critical resources, recruit people to develop policy ideas, and hold and publicize major conferences to diffuse these ideas and translate abstract intellectual musings into more concrete actions. In addition, based on their 1960s experiments, foundations still implement demonstration projects and aid groups that litigate, testify, and lobby against the government.

Most significant foundation funding in the 1960s and 1970s followed the model provided by the Ford Foundation. Ford continued to fund social change programs, including the school board decentralization programs (culminating in the Ocean Hill–Brownsville school controversy), minority voter registration programs, and, in the 1970s, the prisoners' rights movement and the environmental movement.

Foundation activism during the 1960s nevertheless had two major, unintended consequences. The first was yet another round of congressional hearings. The second was a massive crisis of confidence among foundation leaders themselves.

THE POPULIST BACKLASH

Populist Democrat Wright Patman of Texas had railed against foundations since 1961, accusing them of being tax-exempt shelters for "Big Corporate Capitalism." Patman's pressure resulted first in a Treasury Department investigation of big foundations. This forced the foundations to correct financial abuses, many in the form of overly close ties between the donor family, the donor's business, and the foundation (Nielsen, 1972).

Patman, however, was dissatisfied with Treasury's findings. Demanding tax reforms for a more equitable system, Patman managed to get a congressional committee to investigate the foundations. This time, however, the investigating body was the House Ways and Means Committee, headed by Wilbur Mills, one of the most powerful politicians on Capitol Hill. The hearings attracted considerable congressional attention because key witnesses claimed that foundations were altering election outcomes.

Mills called Patman himself as the first witness. Patman demanded that the foundations' tax-exempt status be cut back. "Mr. Chairman," Patman cried, "when a privilege is abused, it should be withdrawn. And the onerous burdens of 65 million taxpayers demand that Congress curb the tax-exempt foundations, which in unwitting good faith, it helped to create" (Nielsen, 1972, p. 10). The U.S. taxpayer, Patman charged, had to pick up what foundations were exempt from paying.

Other testimony drew even more attention. One congressman accused a wealthy opponent of using the latter's personal foundation to sway the election. Shortly before the election, the foundation aided such key groups as the local Puerto Rican Trade Committee, the Hispanic Society of the Fire Department, the Zion Negro Baptist Church, and the local neighborhood study club. "This time, Mr. Chairman," the congressman claimed, "it happened in my district. It can—and probably will—happen in your districts" (Nielsen, 1972, p, 10).

The Ford Foundation came under scrutiny again, for voter registration of Southern blacks; for funding a radical Mexican-American group, whose leader ran for local office; and for funding a critical voter registration drive in Cleveland. In the last case, most of the newly registered voters were black. When Cleveland elected its first black mayor, Carl Stokes, politicians of both political parties complained that Ford helped get him elected.

The most controversial project was Ford's funding of the school decentralization experiments in Ocean Hill–Brownsville, New York (see Weisbord and

Stein, 1970, pp. 161–205, and the additional sources cited therein). Bundy's idea was that community control of schools would increase cooperation among parents, teachers, and administrators, thus improving black students' education. New York State did not authorize the full "Bundy Plan." It did permit the Ford Foundation to support three new experimental programs, including the infamous one at Ocean Hill–Brownsville in the fall of 1968.

By March 1969, the Ford Foundation spent $1.4 million on the program (*New York Times*, March 2, 1969, p. 46). For the community control project, Ford gave $46,000 directly to the districts and $38,000 to assist in initial planning (*New York Times*, February 16, 1968, p. 49). Ford also gave $160,000 to SCOPE, a parent group that would eventually participate in some of the boycotts, and $101,000 to United Parents Association, another parents group with similar views (*New York Times*, May 19, 1968, p. 27). Ford later gave $905,000 to Queens College for "technical assistance" in the project (*New York Times*, May 30, 1968, p. 23) and $5,000 to finance school board elections (*New York Times*, June 13, 1968, p. 52).

The result was a disaster. Rhody McCoy, the newly appointed leader of the school's governing body, tried to remove from the districts teachers and administrators who were hostile to the experiment. After the teachers' union (the American Federation of Teachers) protested, the Central Board of Education countermanded McCoy's order, which prompted local parents to blockade the school (JHS 271) in Ocean Hill–Brownsville. The blockade prevented teachers from returning, despite pleas from the superintendent of schools (*New York Times*, May 15, 1968, p. 1).

The conflict pitted the teachers' and supervisors' unions, with predominantly Jewish leadership, against the mostly black governing board of the school district. Black parents charged the city with racism and police brutality, while the teachers' union charged the parents' groups with vigilantism and anti-Semitism. The intensity of the conflict impelled most Jewish groups in the city to support the teachers and most black groups to support the local school board. Three separate teachers' strikes further escalated the struggle.

At one point, white union teachers returning to their schools for an official orientation meeting "were told from the [black] crowd that if they came back to the district, they would be carried out in pine boxes" (Weisbord and Stein, 1970, p. 167). One of the teachers, Leslie Campbell, was suspended for harassing union teachers but later appeared on Julius Lester's radio show to read an anti-Semitic poem written by his student, "dedicated to Albert Shanker." One couplet ran: "Hey, Jew Boy, with that yarmulka on your head/ You pale-faced Jew boy—I wish you were dead" (quoted in Weisbord and Stein, 1970, p. 175). The Jewish Defense League was another direct consequence of the strikes (Weisbord and Stein, 1970, pp. 201–5). City politics would never be the same.

One Ford Foundation official claims he "[had] not counted on the fallout which had occurred" (Weisbord and Stein, 1970, p. 189). To quote from an official commission regarding the program, "an appalling amount of prejudice surfaced in and about the school controversy'' (p. 185). The official apologia for the foundation summarized the problems of Ocean Hill–Brownsville in this way: ''One danger of encouraging substantial social change is that the effort may intrude abruptly on systems in equilibrium and thereby release the sometimes considerable forces maintaining that equilibrium'' (Magat, 1979, p. 81). To the foundation's credit, Ford financed a conference bringing rabbis and black clergy together for dialogue once the damage was done (Weisbord and Stein, 1970, p. 199).

In his testimony before the House Ways and Means Committee in 1969, Bundy called the grants for school decentralization and the other grants for social change educational and nonpartisan. Nielsen thinks that Bundy's testimony actually hurt the foundations. He quotes one anonymous member of the committee, who said, ''I went into that hearing this morning basically friendly to the foundations; I came out feeling that if Bundy represents the prevailing attitude among them, they are going to have to be brought down a peg'' (quoted in Nielsen, 1972, p. 12).

John D. Rockefeller III tried to mollify the committee but caused even greater rancor. In passing, Rockefeller admitted that the unlimited deductions for charitable contributions in these years meant that he had not paid any income tax since 1961. This led to great political uproar (Nielsen, 1972, pp. 12–13).

The hearings resulted in the Tax Act of 1969, which banned funding of ''political or propagandistic activities.'' Congress had previously forbidden foundations to provide any ''substantial'' portion of their funding for such vaguely defined purposes. Now they were completely prevented from funding such activities. In Nielsen's opinion, the Tax Act served to discourage foundations from taking risks in the politically sensitive areas of race, urban politics, and education reform. More traditional foundations, which limited support to research and ''bricks and mortar'' projects, were untouched by the reforms.

Despite congressional uproar in 1969, significant nonprofit activity continued to move in a liberal, sometimes even radical, direction. While most foundation activity in the 1970s continued to be nonpolitical, some of the work of the big foundations moved into more innovative, radical arenas.

THE THIRD SECTOR AND ITS NEW MISSION

Nonprofit recipient organizations faced serious problems in the 1970s: double-digit inflation, a stock market decline, and a resulting decline in charitable donations (Nielsen, 1979). For foundations, the problem was somewhat different. Foundation leaders in the late 1960s and 1970s believed that government could— and should—''do it better.'' The concern was over the role of the foundation and nonprofit agencies, given the activist federal government. Foundation leaders feared that the nonprofit sector was rapidly becoming obsolete, to be replaced by government agencies. In 1940, according to Nielsen, the federal budget was

$9.5 billion, by 1960 it was $92 billion, and by 1979 it was $500 billion (Nielsen, 1972, p. 14).

More significant, government did not intervene in new, untested areas, but it did intervene in fields already filled with private nonprofit agencies and foundations. Nielsen cites the Peace Corps as an example: "[T]he creation of the Peace Corps in the first months of the Kennedy Administration brought into being a valuable new program and at the same time extinguished a number of small private efforts of the same character" (Nielsen, 1979, p. 15).

Secondary, other independent nonprofit agencies became highly dependent upon government largess. While such funding excluded churches, many cultural institutions, and social action movements, government supported most other nonprofit organizations. By the late 1970s, private research centers received 90 percent of their budgets from government. Voluntary hospitals received 40 percent from government. For instance, the Federation of Jewish Philanthropies raised $25 million from private institutions but spent $700 million of government money. Private colleges relied on government for about one-third of their income, and cultural institutions received about 15 to 20 percent of their budget from government sources.

By the 1970s, nonprofit recipient groups were enmeshed in a web of federal regulation and restrictions as a result of federal funding. They gave up a considerable degree of control over their operations as the number and scope of federal regulations increased considerably.

The crisis of purpose within philanthropic foundations mirrored the nonprofit recipients' dependence on government. Foundations were no longer the primary source of funds for the nonprofit sector, so, once again, the large foundations were wondering what to do. The annual report of the Danforth Foundation captures the dismay:

American philanthropy has never been healthier or more puzzled. . . . On the one hand, the calls for support from schools and colleges are more urgent than ever before, and the foundations are responding in ever-increasing measure. On the other hand, the complexities and uncertainties of education and the millions of dollars of new government money cause the foundations to wonder what they should do; and they seem to spend more time in pondering their role in general, and perhaps their particular grants, than was once their custom. (Quoted in Horowitz and Horowitz, 1970, p. 227)

Innovative foundation leaders handled the predicament by promoting the notion that donor and recipient groups that make up the nonprofit sector should help government to undertake more responsibility for society as a whole. Nonprofit recipient agencies should either become "subsidiaries of government," as one critic pointed out in 1965 (Cornuelle, 1965), or became initiators of more innovative projects that government would later adopt. As early as 1961, an ad hoc commission on voluntary welfare agencies financed by the Rockefeller Foundation made the case for a "public service cartel—this time with independent agencies reduced to [the status of] limited subsidiaries of government'' (Cornuelle, 1965, p. 68).

Bundy, president of the Ford Foundation from 1966 to 1979, deserves the credit for transforming Ford into the most active of the activist foundations (Nielsen, 1985). From 1970 to 1975, for example, Ford spent $100 million for minority higher education. It provided $15 million for research and advocacy in public education, to correct educational inequalities that Ford leaders thought were caused by economic inequalities among districts (Nielsen, 1985, p. 66). Ford, along with the U.S. Education Office of the Department of Health, Education, and Welfare (HEW), the Carnegie Corporation, and the Markle Foundation, helped create public television, most notably the Children's Television Workshop, famous for ''Sesame Street'' (*New York Times*, January 28, 1970, p. 22; February 9, 1970, p. 79; November 19, 1970, p. 95).

Although we lack the space to fully describe foundation activity of the late 1960s and 1970s in the kind of detail it deserves, two studies by sociologists provide an indication of the kind of social change activities that foundations funded at that time. Mary Anna Colwell's (1980) dissertation, on foundation public policy grants during the 1970s, shows quantitatively that Ford was the leading activist foundation. Ford made over half of all foundation public policy grants during the 1970s, the vast majority of which went to liberal causes. Colwell also found that most other large foundations followed Ford's lead. A second study by sociologist J. Craig Jenkins (1987; 1989) shows that foundations finance a lot of social movement activity. From about 1970 to 1980, philanthropic contributions to social movements came to approximately $24 million. The number of social movement grants rose more than tenfold, from 102 in 1966 to 1,266 in 1979 (1989, pp. 294–95). From 1966 to 1980, organizations representing blacks received $56.9 million; environmental groups received $25.2 million; feminist groups received $16.6 million; Mexican-American advocates received $15.8 million (from which Ford donated $5.5 million to create the Mexican-American Legal Defense and Education Fund in 1971); and consumer groups received $12.8 million (Jenkins, 1989, p. 295). Peace movement groups received $4.7 million, and prisoners' rights groups received $5.0 million in that same period (p. 297). Public interest law firms obtained more than 30 percent of their support from private foundations (1987, p. 313).

Thus Horowitz and Horowitz (1970) find the nonprofit sector expanding rather than declining in resources and numbers, as government spending increases. Their findings match Nielsen's reporting of nonprofits as increasingly dependent on government in the 1970s. Horowitz and Horowitz believe that such expansion is in part sustained by greater complexity in higher education and industry, which in turn produces a great demand for skilled researchers. Large amounts of funding in the 1970s in fact helped produce highly technical researchers.

Horowitz and Horowitz also make the point that the demand for social services outruns the ability of government agencies to provide them. Foundations are also needed here. Last, foundations support travel and research funds for those from other countries to study in the United States, as a form of international cooperation.

Horowitz and Horowitz argue that foundation-government collaboration leads to the mission of the public policy foundation in "its innovative role . . . in contrast to the more established role of the government—the cautious partner" (1970, p. 227). Foundations can take risks government cannot, for political reasons as well as fiscal reasons.

Cooperation between private philanthropy and government is in fact so entrenched that the government had to organize a commission to find out how much foundations and government worked together. According to its press release, the goal of the Commission on Foundations and Private Philanthropy was to define "new roles for foundations as the government invests unprecedented amounts in traditional areas of welfare and philanthropy" and to develop "guidelines to help determine the proper role of private philanthropy to controversial public policy issues and the political process" (quoted in Horowitz and Horowitz, 1970, p. 227). The commission never questioned the legitimacy of a new network of policy elites among foundations, nonprofit recipients, and the federal government.

That foundations have a close relationship with government leads Horowitz and Horowitz to conclude that the large foundations "have a liberalizing effect upon public policy" (1970, p. 223). The liberalism, they argue, is a result of two factors, one of which is government dependence on foundations as the innovative partner in public policy ideas. They think that foundation liberalizing of public policy is also due to major foundations having a liberal outlook, promoting liberal programs, and being associated with a liberal constituency (p. 223).

In order to be innovative, however, some liberal activists of the 1960s and 1970s took the nonprofit mission one step further. They devised an answer along the lines of maximum feasible participation—foundations should fund radical social change. As Colwell (1980) and Jenkins (1987; 1989) show, the Ford Foundation provided the model and led by example.

FUNDING FOR SOCIAL CHANGE

In the wake of the 1969 Tax Reform Act, John D. Rockefeller III organized the Filer Commission to study private philanthropy and public needs, which resulted in a "mainstream" report and a dissenting response by a self-styled group of recipients or "donees." Many in the group were members of liberal or left organizations; none was conservative.

The dissenting donees from the Filer Commission argued that philanthropic spending should provide the "venture capital of social change" in order to fulfill its tax-exempt role as a "fearless agent of social change." Philanthropic spending in turn should *not* support private institutions that deliver public services (e.g., higher education, health care, and the arts). Last, the dissenters argued for greater public (political) oversight of foundations in order to limit donor control.

Although the donee group disbanded, its dissent led to the formation of the National Committee for Responsive Philanthropy, which spread its views concerning the role of foundations and other charitable activities (*New York Times*, June 24, 1979, p. E27; Nielsen, 1985, p. 30). William A. Stanmeyer (1978) provides a detailed analysis of the successor group, the National Committee for Responsive Philanthropy, which remains quite active today. The committee challenged the United Way's claim that it "works for all of us"; it encouraged givers to fund such "innovative" groups as legal aid for the poor, the women's movement, and environmentalists. In the eyes of the committee, nontraditional but conservative groups (e.g., the American Enterprise Institute or the Heritage Foundation) were not considered "innovative."

Currently, the foundation world is debating whether grants should be given primarily to projects committed to continued social change or to support established private institutions. Many on the left advocate the former, while those on the right often encourage the latter. Some potential recipients accuse foundations of demanding safe, effective, tried-and-true projects while refusing to fund causes that are controversial, new, untested, or open-ended.

However, given the well-documented liberalism of the academy and U.S. intellectuals, and the close relationship of both to foundations, one would predict a continued preponderance of funding oriented toward liberal policy proposing. As we demonstrate in later chapters, the current concerns of many public policy foundations are increasing the political power of the poor, minorities, and women; monitoring the performance of government and industry; and remaining "open and responsive" to new currents of social change.

More important, some current writers on foundations believe that support for scientific research and knowledge-based social problem solving eroded with the rise of the New Left. During the 1960s, New Left critics associated foundation support of scientific research with the Vietnam War and the military-industrial complex, which gradually weakened the original relationship in the philanthropic world between liberalism and support for hard science. As Francis X. Sutton, sociologist and long-time staffer at the Ford Foundation, writes about his one-time employer, "[I]t took the critical populist upsurge at the end of the 1960s to weaken faith that the Foundation's prime vocation lay in helping government, great universities, and research centers" (1989, p. xviii).

In its place, the new orientation was toward social change activism. To quote Sutton again on Ford, "[A]s the Sixties wore on the values of the New Left spread through American society, an activistic spirit entered the Foundation that pulled it away from [the Ford Foundation's] original vision of solving the world's problems through scientific knowledge" (p. xv). He remarks that if Macdonald were able to see the foundation today (he died in 1982), he would probably be pleased with the direction in which it has evolved (pp. xviii–xix).

After the rise of the New Left, stories emerged in the popular press of rich heirs turning against the family dynasty and actively supporting causes of social activism. Examples include Abby Rockefeller and her financial support of *Ramparts* magazine; George Pillsbury who gave away all his inheritance to form the Haymarket People's Fund; and the establishment of the Funding Exchange, a network of rich, young philanthropists "with avowedly leftist politics using their inheritances to promote 'change not charity' " (*New York Times*, January 30, 1990, p. A–18).

These young members of the foundation elite think of themselves as at the cutting edge of social change activism. The most radical donors have relinquished control over grant making to a board of community activists representing the poor, blacks, women, and union organizers (Odendahl, 1990, pp. 164–65). While once outside the circle of mainstream philanthropy, these wealthy donors are now a part of the foundation world. In the words of George Pillsbury, heir to the baked goods dynasty, "We've grown up; we're part of the landscape of American philanthropy. We're now seen as members of the club" (*New York Times*, January 30, 1990, p. A–18).

The continued leftward drift of liberalism and liberal foundations since the 1950s produced a counterreaction. The election of Ronald Reagan, the prominence of the conservative agenda, and the increasing prominence of several conservative counterweights to the Committee for Responsive Philanthropy meant that the polarization has continued and even intensified.

Robert Payton's six examples of modern American philanthropy capture foundation polarization in action: the Ethiopia famine relief effort; war and revolution in Central America; nuclear arms control; South Africa; the Lincoln Center for the Performing Arts; and the homeless (Payton, 1988). Four of the six are directly linked to government policy (Central America, nuclear weapons, South Africa, and the homeless). Independent foundations give to activist groups seeking to alter government policy. In chapter eight, we show that most recipients of such funds are either liberal or radical leftist groups.

CONCLUSION

The 25,000 foundations in the United States today are run by numerous directors, trustees, and professional staff. The sheer number of foundations and their grant-making capacities have resulted in the emergence of a foundation elite. The foundation elite forms a link between the intellectual developments of the postwar era and the massive social change that followed. In the postindustrial United States, the foundation elite, along with new strategic elites in the media, motion pictures, prime time television, and the public interest groups, look to the intellectual elite as their primary reference group, a role which has only grown since World War II. More and more members of the American elite have since become acquainted with and influenced by the alienated stance of the intellectual. The consequences of this have worked themselves out in the politics of post–World War II America. Before examining the empirical evidence regarding foundations and the adversary culture, however, let us consider the flaws in more conventional understandings of foundation behavior in chapter three.

NOTES

1. Marvin N. Olasky provides the most extensive and sympathetic treatment of the COS groups known to the authors. He describes the COS movement, which he labels a form of Social Calvinism, as the middle way between Social Darwinism, which in his eyes lacks all sympathy for the poor, and Social Universalism, the belief that institutional changes will solve the poverty problem (Olasky, 1992, pp. 80–98). He quotes Gurteen: "To avoid these extremes, both of which are fatal, is the grand object of the Charity Organization Society" (p. 74).

2. It is noteworthy that the approach to poverty and the dole advocated by the Charity Organization Societies closely parallels the argument made by Charles Murray in his 1984 analysis of the failure of the Great Society's poverty programs, *Losing Ground*. Murray argues that government welfare is demoralizing to those who receive it, including the deserving poor (although Murray is careful not to use this language). Murray writes, "It is wrong to take from the most industrious, most responsible poor—take safety, education, justice, and status—so that we could cater to the least industrious, least responsible poor" (p. 219). Interestingly, his solutions tend to follow those of the COS, especially when he speaks of using "the network of local services" that "depend for support on local taxes or local philanthropy" as a way of dealing with the hard-core poor (pp. 229–30).

3. Walter I. Trattner (1979, pp. 84–89) provides several other criticisms of the COS movement. Several of these are not without force:

1. COS volunteers could not be friends with the people they attempted to help. This is because friendship exists among equals, moral uplift is intrinsically unequal when not reciprocal. Such help is condescending. On the other hand, it is possible to create a satisfactory professional relationship between unequals—professional to client.
2. The very emphasis placed by the COS movement on objective, factual knowledge of individual cases made the use of volunteers more difficult because they lacked both the training and the experience to interpret case records. Thus, the COS movement contributed rather directly to the establishment of professional schools of social work, the rise of the social work profession, and the weakening of voluntarism.
3. Finally, Trattner argues that poverty and dependency were not then and are not now largely expressions of individual moral perversity but often had systemic causes beyond the control of specific individuals.

An extensive discussion of the issues posed here is well beyond the scope of this modest essay. However, the experience of the COS movement with volunteers is highly relevant in light of the new importance the foundation world places on volunteering and voluntarism (see, for example, the readings in O'Connell, 1983).

4. Trolander (1987) provides an account of the decline of the settlement house in the wake of the community action radicalism of the 1960s. Ironically, while they were once critical of the COS movement for imposing middle class values on the indigent, the settlement houses themselves came under fire from 1960s radicals for the same reason. Sociological studies such as William F. Whyte's *Street Corner Society* (1955) promoted a similar critical view.

5. Unlike other founders, Rosenwald believed that foundations should not be perpetual. Thus the Julius Rosenwald Fund went out of existence in 1948 (Andrews, 1956, pp. 55–56, 103). Brian O'Connell (1983) reprints Rosenwald's original 1929 article.

6. The transformation of pre–New Deal liberalism to incorporate what we call collectivist liberalism has been often commented on (e.g., Minogue, 1963; Nash, 1976; Shils, 1980; Rotunda, 1986). Ronald Rotunda (1986) traces the change in meaning of the term *liberal* to the New Deal and, in particular, FDR's successful appropriation of the liberal label from Herbert Hoover. The philosopher John Dewey, in his manifesto for modern liberals, *Liberalism and Social Action* (1935), describes his preferred kind of liberalism as "collectivistic liberalism" (p. 20) and explicitly contrasts it to "individualistic liberalism" (p. 43).

7. This assumes both the enormous capacity of the state to raise revenues, which has become doubtful, as well as the utility and feasibility of central planning, which many other scholars challenge. Additionally, the utter collapse of communism in the former Soviet Union and elsewhere has raised fundamental objections about socialism of any kind.

8. Joseph Helfgot (1981, pp. 70–96) describes in detail Mobilization for Youth, the Ford Foundation–funded program that was the direct ancestor of and the inspiration for the CAP programs.

CHAPTER 3

FOUNDATION LEADERS AND THEIR PLACE IN THE AMERICAN SOCIAL STRUCTURE

Any study of the foundation elite must begin with a hotly debated issue: the relationship between money and power in American life. Are the foundation elite merely offshoots of the upper class in the United States, or are they a new kind of American elite? What are the differences between an upper class and an elite group, conceptually and empirically? This chapter develops in some detail the view that foundation leaders comprise a new strategic elite in the United States. Chapter four deals with the ideological cleavages and the prominence of the adversary culture in the foundation world.

We start with a summary of the ruling class (i.e., ruling elite) model of the foundation elite and examine their social backgrounds to show that many aspects of the ruling class model are not empirically supported. We then offer the notion of foundation leaders as a strategic elite and support our claim with data.

FOUNDATION LEADERS AS PART OF THE RULING CLASS

Many studies of the foundation elite emphasize the degree to which leaders in the world of philanthropy are part of a ruling class. Generally, the ruling class viewpoint holds that the United States is dominated by a small, relatively stable group, of which foundation leaders form a part. One noted social scientist summarizes the basic thesis about class and power in the United States:

[T]here is a social upper class in the United States that is a ruling class by virtue of its dominant role in the economy and government. . . . [T]his ruling class is socially cohesive, has its basis in the large corporations and banks, plays a major role in shaping the social and political climate, and dominates the federal government through a variety of organizations and methods. (Domhoff, 1983, p. 1)

The foundation elite are a part of this very close-knit group because they are from the same upper-status background and are often related by blood or marriage. These ties become evidence in support of a "unitary ruling elite" model of the foundation elite and even of national leadership as a whole. Moreover, the ruling elite share fundamental values that support liberal capitalist society—free enterprise and limited government (see, for example, Dye, 1986, p. 220).

With regard to foundations, what we call the "unitary ruling elite" (or sometimes the "ruling class") model has been around for a long time. In 1936, Eduard Lindeman wrote the pioneering study *Wealth and Culture*, characterizing the foundations as part of the ruling elite. Lindeman believes the foundation to be the consequence of "surplus wealth" and an unfair distribution of income in this country. He states: "Taken as a group the trustees of foundations wield a power in American life which is probably equaled only by the national government itself, and by the executives in our dominant financial and industrial corporations" (Lindeman, 1936, p. 33).

To show that foundation decision makers are part of "that successful and conservative class that came into prominence during the latter part of the nineteenth and early twentieth century, the class whose status is based primarily upon pecuniary success" (1936, p. 46), Lindeman examines the social background of the roughly 400 trustees of 70 of the richest U.S. foundations in 1930. The typical foundation leader was an older, rich man, who was a part of a network of the richest and most powerful men in the country. He was a graduate of an Ivy League college or university, with a background in the liberal arts. He belonged to the most prestigious social clubs and was most often an Episcopalian or Presbyterian.[1] In short, the trustee was part of the American upper class.

Lindeman's study is, in fact, a critique of free-market capitalism. He views the foundation as the outcome of a "faulty distribution of wealth and income" (1936, p. 3). Foundations, he argues, are the consequence of surplus wealth—that is, wealth not needed for reinvestment and that should be redistributed. The philanthropist, however erroneously, defines the money as private wealth to be dispensed in whatever manner the donor so chooses. The donor ignores the reality of foundation power and that foundations, in Lindeman's eyes, are "semi-public institutions" (p. 6).

In his extensive study of power in the United States, G. William Domhoff (1971) says that there is a governing class in this country. This class is generally cohesive in action, conscious of itself as a ruling elite, and relatively self-contained. Domhoff shows that foundation leaders are a part of this governing class, given their role in backing certain kinds of projects and not others and their extensive ties to those in government and business (1971, pp. 325–27).

Sociologist Lewis Coser shares a similar view of the foundation elite, arguing for foundations as "brokers of ideas and . . . cultural transmission belts" (1970, p. 337). Through their control of funds, foundations exert significant power over intellectuals and U.S. culture generally, Coser believes. Assuming that social background reflects ideology, Coser argues that the narrow backgrounds from which foundation executives and trustees are drawn result in "[f]oundation trustees [being] an elite group representative of certain 'establishment' values and traditions" (1970, p. 339). Then status quo orientation is reinforced by the ties between business, government, and foundation elites.

The view of "the foundation leader as part of the ruling elite" is also articulated within the foundation world itself. Former foundation executive and researcher Teresa Odendahl (1990) is the latest in a long line of critics. She proclaims, "Elite American philanthropy serves the interests of the rich to a greater extent than it does the interests of the poor, disadvantaged, or disabled" (p. 3). It supports primarily elite culture, elite art, and elite education. By doing so, it "assists in the social reproduction of the upper class" (p. 232).

Recently, a more complex argument has emerged concerning the relationship between the philanthropic foundation and social control. Donald Fisher (1980; 1983) among others, contends that the cultural relations and forces embedded in such institutions as the philanthropic foundation and the large-scale research university, rather than the capitalist class and the capitalist economy, are the primary forces maintaining the hegemony of the system. This perspective (which could be labeled neo-Gramscian) explicitly rejects the notion that the capitalist class directly and overtly rules through the coercive power of the state. Maintaining the social order is not accomplished simply through the blatant use of threat or force. Instead, class rule exists because the cultural, political, ethical, and intellectual elite articulate a world view that everyone, ruling and ruled, comes to uphold. Adoption of the supporting world view occurs through its embodiment in social processes, organizations, and institutions. Given the assumption of ongoing class struggle, the dominant class constantly seeks new cultural vehicles by which it can offset the revolutionary impulses of the working class; in colloquial parlance, it looks for new and better ways to "cool out the mark."

Thus Fisher argues that foundations seek to maintain rather than change society by supporting the existing class structure as "participants in both the reproduction and production of cultural hegemony" (Fisher, 1980, p. 206). Foundations provide the resources for those ideas, values, and attitudes—produced by intellectuals—that support the ruling capitalist class. As an example, the support provided by the Rockefeller Foundation for the professionalization and "objectivization" of the social sciences from 1910 to 1940 was not disinterested support for the growth of knowledge. The foundations, "objective social science," and the rise of the welfare state through New Deal legislation reformed society enough to reduce class tensions until the 1940s, taking the evolution of capitalist class domination in yet another direction.

Robert Arnove (1980, p. 1) takes a similar critical point of view. He argues that foundations:

serve as "cooling out" agencies, delaying and preventing more radical, structural change. They help maintain an economic and political order, international in scope, which benefits the ruling-class interests of philanthropists and philanthropoids—a system which . . . has worked against the interests of minorities, the working class, and Third World peoples.

Mary Anna Colwell (1980) describes the foundation world as a type of exclusive private club that thrives on secrecy and is controlled by an "inner group" of the elite—the white, Anglo-Saxon, Protestant (WASP) establishment. Marvin G. Dunn (1980) goes so far as to describe this inner group as part of a kinship network. The "family office" coordinates activities with its foundations, corporations, holding companies, and political action committees. Each group has members with kinship ties to the family office. Whitaker (1974) believes that the predominance of the WASP in the foundation world creates "a self-perpetuating system that militates against the very impetus for social change that foundations argue they exist to supply" (p. 91).

What unites these ruling elite critics is the belief that no matter what changes foundations support, they ultimately reflect a conservative, business-oriented view of the world. Thus Fisher (1980) quotes Dean Rusk, then president of the Rockefeller Foundation: "[The Foundation] reflects the application to philanthropy of the principles of private initiative and free enterprise, under public policies which have long recognized the benefits of such activity to a free society" (p. 257). Fisher best articulates the premises that tie together radical critics of philanthropists. He argues that when foundations speak of furthering "free society," the term basically means "capitalist democracy," and that foundations are consciously organized to preserve capitalism. He refers to the ideology of foundation leaders as a "sophisticated conservatism" (1980, p. 256). They were in favor of changes "that contributed to a more efficient industrial productive system; to a more efficient functioning of colonialism; to ways of controlling the trade cycle; and to the preservation or spread of free, democratic political systems" (p. 256).

Ruling elite theorists argue that the interests and values of foundation, government, and business elites are identical. "That the Rockefeller foundations had objectives which pertained to the distribution of power in American society and served the interests of the economic elite should not come as a surprise" (Fisher, 1980, p. 258). This is due to the fact that foundation leaders and the business elite share the same social background. If foundation leaders and corporate leaders are drawn from the same class, and if their interests are identical, then the interests of foundations and business are identical. "Philanthropy becomes capitalism's way of distributing surplus wealth, which might otherwise go to the state in taxes, in its own interest" (Fisher, 1980, p. 258). In this view, disagreements among foundation managers, trustees, and corporate business leaders are over specific project items, not general orientations.

Political scientist Thomas Dye (1986) directly addresses this issue of conflict and consensus among ruling elites. His textbook *Who's Running America?* also presents the leaders of the foundation world as part of a fairly cohesive, conscious, and self-contained civic elite. In his view, these foundation elites form part of an interlocking network among foundations, major corporations, leading financial institutions, the mass media, universities, policy think tanks, and the federal government (Dye, 1986, pp. 140–59).

Dye contends, moreover, that *all* American leadership groups share certain fundamental values, such as "private property, limited government, separation of church and state, individual liberty, equality of opportunity, advancement based on merit, and due process of law" (1986, p. 220). Like Fisher, Dye believes the conflicts within and among U.S. elites stem from differences over specific policy questions (1986, pp. 219–20).

The question raised by ruling class arguments, however, is strictly an empirical one. How restricted is entry into the foundation elite, and is it primarily based on ascriptive criteria? A comparison of the social background of foundation leaders with that of other American elites shows them to be much less the closed upper-class, Anglo-Saxon, Protestant strata, although they are not as open at the top as are some other elite groups.

ASSESSING ASCRIPTION VERSUS ACHIEVEMENT AMONG AMERICAN ELITES

Social background characteristics are of two types: ascribed and achieved (Keller, 1963).[2] Ascribed characteristics are those that cannot be changed through individual effort; they are "accidents of birth." Ascribed characteristics include one's personal family ties (e.g., being born into the Rockefeller family) but also such features as one's gender and race. Achieved characteristics result from individual effort. This includes a person's level of education and, for the most part, a person's current occupation. A doctorate in the social sciences, for example, is an achieved characteristic since it requires effort on the part of the individual and cannot be simply inherited from one's parent. Similarly, most occupations, especially the professions, cannot be passed down through generations as a trust fund can.[3]

We assess social mobility into the foundation elite by examining the relative importance of achievement versus ascription. Empirically, greater mobility into an elite is indicated by careers open more to persons with the objective characteristics of achievement. By contrast, a closed social system requires conformity to ascriptive criteria for recruitment and membership. That is, in order to get to the top, where you come from and whom you know are more important than what you can do. Thus, little mobility at the top is one indicator that the upper strata have coalesced into an upper class.

We explore these questions by examining the social origins of our philanthropic elite. Are they mostly from well-off business families, or are they socially mobile? We also examine the role of ascribed attributes among top foundation personnel. How much do race, religion, ethnicity, and gender matter?

On both counts, the business elite (and, where relevant, other elite groups) serve as a standard of comparison. Keller (1963) describes the U.S. business elite as an elite of achievement because members of the business elite do not inherit their positions. Performance ideally determines one's salary and promotion. The business elite, however, retain important elements of ascription in recruitment and promotion, at least in terms of sex and race. The group is, on the whole, white, male, and middle-aged.

Using the business elite as a model of a strategic elite, the closeness of fit between the mobility profiles of business leaders and philanthropy leaders provides an approximation of how open the philanthropic system is and, conversely, how closely the philanthropic elite resemble an upper-class model.[4]

Our examination of the social origins of the foundation elite uses several unique bodies of data. Other studies of the foundations are individual case studies of a few people and foundations (except for Odendahl, Boris, and Daniels, 1985); our analysis relies on an extensive quantitative survey of the foundation elite. Moreover, none of the other foundation studies systematically compare foundation leaders to any other elite group or to the public at large. We compare them with other leadership groups in the United States, using comparable survey data taken from a larger project on U.S. elites (see Appendix 2 for a description of the other elite groups).[5]

SOCIAL DIVISIONS WITHIN THE FOUNDATION ELITE

The Ascriptive Categories: Race, Gender, Ethnicity, Religion, and Class Origins

The "upper class" stereotype of foundation leaders fits only if we limit it to the most all-inclusive categories of gender and race. There are proportionately more whites among the foundation elite (98 percent) compared to all other elite groups, except for business leaders.[6]

There are proportionately more women members of the foundation elite (20 percent) than of other elite groups except for the media and public interest groups, but we believe in this case the proportion of women is actually an ascriptive indicator. Women members of the foundation elite are probably related to the original donors. This speculation is supported by evidence that women foundation leaders grew up in much wealthier surroundings and yet have less education than both their women counterparts in other elite groups and their male philanthropy colleagues.[7]

The ethnic composition of the foundation elite is more varied than might be expected of the citadel of the WASP establishment. Only one-third of the foundation elite list their ancestry as "English, Scottish, or Welsh." Twenty-eight percent list their ancestry as divided among several groups. Ten percent list their ethnicity as Jewish.[8]

This diversity also extends into the area of religion. The standard ruling class analysis of U.S. society predicts the foundation elite to be overwhelmingly

Protestant. While this may have been the case thirty or more years ago (see Baltzell, 1964), there are fewer Protestants in the foundation elite (53 percent) than in the American public (63 percent); 16 percent are Catholic, and 12 percent are Jewish. In contrast, 25 percent of the general public are Catholic, and 2 percent are Jewish (National Opinion Research Center, 1990, p. 144).

On the other hand, a slightly larger proportion of the foundation elite are Protestant than of the other elite groups, except for military leaders, where 60 percent are Protestant.[9] Protestants constitute nearly half of the membership of the business elite (48 percent) and of federal judges (47 percent). They are even more sparsely represented in the civil service (32 percent), labor unions (33 percent), corporate law (28 percent), and the media elite (22 percent).

The foundation elite, while less religious than the general public, is more religious than are members of most other elite groups. For example, only 19 percent of the foundation elite claim no religious affiliation. Only the business elite (13 percent) and the military (8 percent) are less likely to deny a religious affiliation. In contrast, most of the media elite, movie makers, 41 percent of public interest leaders, and the same proportion of the television elite profess no current religious affiliation.[10]

Moreover, the foundation elite attend church as often as traditional elites and the general public and much more frequently than nontraditional leadership groups.[11] Almost half (47 percent) of the foundation elite raised as Catholic or Protestant currently go to church once a month or more, compared to 51 percent of the general public (National Opinion Research Center, 1990, p. 146).

Labor leaders and the military are more religious; 62 percent and 68 percent, respectively, attend church at least once a month, and roughly the same proportion of non-Jewish civil servants and business leaders attend church (45 percent and 51 percent, respectively). At the other extreme, Catholic and Protestant members of new elite groups (the media, the public interest leaders, the television and movie elites) seldom go to church. Only 21 percent of elite journalists, 28 percent of the public interest leaders, 13 percent of the creators of prime time television, and 7 percent of the motion picture elite attend church on a monthly or weekly basis.

Education: An Indicator of Achieved Status

The foundation elite are better educated than the business elite, but not more so than many other groups. All members of the foundation elite attended college, and 96 percent received at least a bachelor's degree. In contrast, 13 percent of business leaders, one-fourth of the television elites, one-third of movie makers, and 61 percent of labor leaders are not college graduates. The best educated elite are lawyers, federal judges, military officers, public interest group leaders, and religious leaders; they all attended college, and almost all hold at least bachelor's degrees.

A greater proportion of the foundation elite (40 percent) than other groups attended the most selective U.S. colleges and universities.[12] Only among public interest leaders (45 percent), federal judges (47 percent), and corporate lawyers (68 percent) were there more graduates of these institutions. In contrast, only one in four business elites graduated from these schools.

While the selectivity of an undergraduate institution measures the intellectual quality of its student body, as E. Digby Baltzell (1964) and others point out, some institutions of higher education, especially the Ivy League and the Seven Sisters colleges, confer a high degree of prestige on their graduates. One in four of the foundation elite attended an Ivy League or Seven Sisters college as an undergraduate. Unfortunately, similar information for the rest of our elite samples is not yet available.[13]

SOCIAL MOBILITY

The large percentage of non-Protestants among the foundation elite raises the issue of general upward mobility. How much opportunity is there for those to rise from lower socioeconomic backgrounds? To what extent must one be born and raised in these wealthy circles to become part of the foundation elite?

To answer these questions, we asked our respondents about their parents' background. Based on their recollections, a sizable number rose from the lower socioeconomic classes as measured by their parents' education, occupation, and income while they were growing up.

Father's Education

The foundation elite are far more educated than were their fathers. While 66 percent of them went beyond an undergraduate degree, only one in four had fathers who did the same. The fathers of 37 percent of them never went beyond high school.

Furthermore, mobility is not restricted only to those with smaller salaries. While 27 percent of our respondents with incomes over $100,000 had fathers who went to graduate or professional school, 36 percent of this same wealthy group had fathers who had a high-school-level education or less.

Other elite groups are split. Bureaucrats, business, and the military have higher rates of educational mobility than do foundation leaders. The fathers of over half the members of each group had high school educations or less (56, 62, and 59 percent respectively). However, corporate lawyers and public interest leaders had proportionately *fewer* fathers with comparable education (34 percent of lawyers and one in four public interest leaders). Of those with advanced training, 36 percent of lawyers and public interest leaders and one-third of the judges had fathers who went to graduate school—a larger percentage than foundation leaders.

Father's Occupation

There is also occupational mobility among the foundation elite. A total of 12 percent had fathers in lower white-collar occupations (salesmen, draftsmen, clerical workers); 14 percent had fathers in blue-collar jobs. The fathers of one-third were high-status professionals, and 36 percent who were in business.

Members of the foundation elite are as occupationally mobile as corporate lawyers. They are less mobile than business executives but more mobile than public interest leaders. Twenty percent of the businessmen had fathers who came from the professions; and 27 percent had fathers with business backgrounds; 30 percent came from blue-collar backgrounds. Thirty-eight percent of corporate lawyers had fathers who were high-status professionals, and 18 percent had fathers who were managers or businessmen, while 14 percent came from blue-collar backgrounds. Fifty-seven percent of the public interest leaders grew up in the homes of professionals, one in five grew up with fathers in business, and only one in ten had blue-collar fathers.

Class Origins

Family income while growing up is another measure of social mobility. Compared to other elite groups, the foundation elite come from the wealthiest of families. More have been raised in families with high income, despite considerable entry by members of lower socioeconomic strata. In contrast, considerably fewer members of business and military elites come from the upper classes (4 and 2 percent respectively).

Twenty-seven percent of foundation leaders recall growing up in families with below average incomes, although most of the foundation elite (54 percent) remember growing up in families that were somewhat or very well-off. Moreover, 23 percent of those that earn over $100,000 come from families with well below or somewhat below average incomes.

Roughly the same proportion of the foundation elite rose from relatively poor backgrounds as those from other elite groups. For example, 29 percent of the business elite recall growing up in poor families, as do one in five corporate lawyers. Public interest leaders (along with congressional aides) have the smallest percentage rising from poor backgrounds (14 percent; 13 percent for congressional aides).

Despite the fact that the foundation group is partly composed of an upper-class elite, their group is also quite open. For these reasons, the foundation elite should be called a "strategic" elite, and U.S. society should be thought of as guided by "strategic elites" rather than a "ruling class." We use the term *strategic* in reference to the foundation elite in the same sense that we have in the past referred to media and business elites. The next section examines the concept in application to the foundation elite.

STRATEGIC ELITES AND AMERICAN SOCIETY

The concept of "strategic elite" is not nearly as well-known as that of the ruling or upper class, so some elaboration is in order. Keller (1963) and Baltzell (1979) both argue that social systems presided over by ruling classes need to be carefully distinguished from those ruled by strategic elites. Strategic elites consist of the top leadership of the leading organizations in strategic sectors of society (Keller, 1963, pp. 20–21; Baltzell, 1979; Rothman, Lichter, and Lichter, forthcoming). Keller defines strategic elites as "the minority of individuals responsible for keeping the organized system, society, in working order, functioning so as to meet and surpass the perennial collective crises that occur" (1963, p. 23).

Stated slightly differently, every society has norms that generate authority relationships. The persons in authority—the superordinates—are, by virtue of their authority, societal elites. These may or may not be integrated into a single ruling class. In essence, while "strategic elites have existed in some form in every organized human society; ruling classes have not and need not. A society may thus have strategic elites without having a ruling class" (Keller, 1963, p. 58).

The implications of the strategic elite concept can be better understood by examining in more detail the differences between strategic elites and ruling classes. They can be distinguished as follows. First, a ruling class constitutes a single entity in a given society at a given time, while strategic elites are multiple and plural. Second, the scope of authority of a ruling class is "diffuse and wide," while the scope of authority exercised by any given strategic elite is "special and limited" (Keller, 1963, p. 58). Baltzell captures the differences in authority relations when he equates class authority, which we call the rule of a ruling class, with Max Weber's concept of traditional authority (Baltzell, 1979, p. 21). Where class authority is strong, he states, traditional authority tends to reign and vice versa. Conversely, the weaker the traditional authority, the greater the amount of bureaucratic authority (or charismatic authority) required in order to govern. A society dominated by multiple and competing strategic elites is one that alternates and mixes bureaucratic and charismatic governance.

These disparities between strategic elites and ruling classes also manifest themselves in differences in their internal organization, degree of occupational specialization, and patterns of recruitment (Keller, 1963).[14] A particular strategic elite consists of individuals who occupy one or more distinct social categories or, at best, a set of role-positions. It need not be a self-conscious, organized grouping. More significant, the collection of a society's strategic elites taken together does not form such a self-conscious group (e.g., Merton, 1968).

A ruling or upper class is different. An upper class is a self-conscious, cohesive group. It is, thus, a structured collectivity, often with a name everyone knows (e.g., the Communist Party of the Soviet Union). A true ruling class is a self-conscious and cohesive unit capable of common collective action. Strategic elites, on the other hand, are not usually capable of such collective action. This is generally true for a particular strategic elite and is especially the case when considering all of a society's strategic elites taken together as a group. Baltzell contrasts strategic elites and ruling classes in a similar manner: "Elite individuals come from a wide variety of social backgrounds, but an upper class is . . . a more or less endogamous subculture" (1979, p. 32). The upper class is, thus, a *"sociological* and *historical*, rather than a natural aristocracy. It is nothing more or less than a group of consanguine families whose ancestors were elite members and family founders one or more generations earlier" (p. 25). Like Baltzell, Domhoff and Ostrander among others identify members of the upper class as those listed in the *Social Register*, who attended one or more exclusive boarding schools and day schools, and/or who have membership in one of the exclusive social clubs (Domhoff, 1983, pp. 44–47; Ostrander, 1984).

Baltzell's use of the term *class* is not idiosyncratic. While the term *class* often has Marxian or neo-Marxian connotations, one can use the term more generally. For example, Joseph Kahl (1957) defines social class (in this broad sense) in terms of six variables: (1) personal prestige; (2) occupation; (3) possessions; (4) interpersonal interaction; (5) degree of class consciousness; and (6) value orientations (pp. 8–10). (For still other closely related discussions of class differences including differences of time horizons and work flexibility, see Banfield, 1974; and Kohn, 1973.)

Having little in common also means that members of different strategic elites do not share "old school" ties, whether it be the same network of private boarding or day schools or the Ivy League schools and the Seven Sisters colleges. "Old school" connections, however, are critical for the founding and reproduction of an upper class, as they serve as an important mechanism for inculcating the exclusive and distinctive upper class subculture. Put in somewhat different terms, an upper class is a status group in Weber's sense of the term. Upper classes possess a distinctive style of life and abide by restrictions on social intercourse with non-upper-class members, precisely as Weber (1947) describes.

Unlike an upper class, strategic elite members do not partake of a culture distinct from that of the larger society. Or, in Keller's words, "the President of the United States, the president of a giant corporation, the top atomic scientist, and the leading writer of an era have little in common beyond their general cultural background and their achievement of prominence" (1963, p. 83).

Strategic elites also differ from an upper or ruling class occupationally. Members of ruling classes can be and are often required to be leisured individuals living off inherited wealth. Keller, in fact, defines members of aristocracies as those who must *not* work for a living (1963, p. 31).[15]

In contrast, members of strategic elites must work full-time at their occupations for a long period of time in order to reach the top levels. Strategic elites are not amateurs exhibiting a generalized "gentlemanly" or "lady-like" competence but are professionals who are "specialists in excellence" (Keller, 1963, p. 32). Keller describes the interpersonal relations characteristic of societies with multiple, competing strategic elites by quoting the Texas banker Clint Murchison who, when asked to describe national leadership, stated, "Bankers know bankers, scholars know scholars, utility men know utility men, and [only] politicians know everybody" (1963, p. 110). So far as we are aware, Weber never uses the term *elite*. However, his analysis of the occupational bases of modern democratic politics in his essay on politics as a vocation (1947) parallels our discussion.

The differences between the upper class and strategic elite are also systematically related to differences in how new members of each group are recruited. "A ruling class consists of groups of families who have more or less monopolized access to elite positions . . . who are able to transmit their rewards and opportunities to their descendants" (Keller, 1963, p. 57). In contrast, strategic elites are "composed of individuals selected on the basis of individual motivation and capacity. . . . [T]he recruitment of strategic elites is not confined to any specific group or class" (p. 57).

Our own sociodemographic data on the foundation elite support Keller's notion that most sectors in U.S. society (in this case, philanthropic foundations) are dominated by strategic elites, not a ruling class. The foundation elite today is not quite the repository of the WASP establishment that scholars often picture it to be. While there are very few blacks or Hispanics in our sample, one-fifth are women, roughly one-tenth are Jewish, and only one-third are white, Anglo-Saxon Protestants.

While roughly the same proportion of philanthropy leaders graduated from college as those of other elite groups, proportionately more graduated from elite colleges and universities except for judges, lawyers, and public interest leaders. A quarter of the foundation elite graduated from Ivy League colleges.

Many members of the foundation elite are socially mobile, although generally less than those in business. Substantially more of the former grew up in families with well above average family income compared to businessmen and businesswomen. Foundation leaders are more mobile than corporate lawyers and the public interest elite. While fewer fathers of the foundation elite are from modest backgrounds than business leaders, more are more upwardly mobile than public interest leaders. Similarly, with education, foundation leaders are less mobile than business leaders and the military but are more so than lawyers and public interest group leaders.

At the same time, while philanthropy leaders are a considerable distance away from the ideal type portrayed in Baltzell's *The Protestant Establishment* (1964), they more closely resemble the ideal upper class type than do most of our other samples. This is because the roles of foundation staff, officer and trustee are less well defined than that of business executive or those of other strategic elites. One can become part of a foundation board either by being a general notable or simply because of a family relationship with the donor, and there are few or no widely shared measurable standards of success in the philanthropic enterprise, either in the sense of a competitive marketplace or in the sense of educational credentials necessary for achievement.[16]

Nevertheless, other studies complementary to ours show that the more "professional" foundations are the more established and larger ones. Even in the case of the foundation elite, research shows that power is sometimes held by foundation employees, particularly the chief executive officers (CEOs) of the largest foundations, and not by the board of trustees.

Odendahl, Boris, and Daniels (1985) and Nielsen (1985) contend that the distribution of such power varies with both foundation and issue. They define *power* as the ability to influence the choice of recipients and to decide who gets what within the foundation. They studied decision making within foundations in some detail by conducting an extensive set of open-ended interviews of foundation career professionals. They find that grant-making powers are distributed along a continuum, "from situations where trustees run most aspects of grant-making programs to those where employees have almost complete control" (Odendahl, Boris, and Daniels, 1985, p. 13).

According to Odendahl and colleagues (1985), professional staff-trustee relations fall into one of three types: the presidential model, the administrator model, and the director model. In the first case, the presidential model, the foundation staff run the organization, with trustees delegating their power to the CEO, who, de facto, becomes the most powerful person (p. 13). These foundations are most dependent on the foundation professional, not on family members. Most of the largest foundations fall into this category. The second type of professional staff-trustee relation, the director model, depends on collegiality. The CEO acts as consultant to trustees, who give weight to his recommended grant proposals. Decision making, however, still rests with the trustees. In the third case, the administrator model, trustees dominate decision making and sometimes involve themselves in the actual day-to-day operations of the foundation. This is most common in small foundations.

Like Odendahl, Boris, and Daniels, we define the foundation elite in terms of the organizational roles within the most important U.S. foundations. These include professional staff as well as trustees. Importance in the foundation world need not be necessarily based on "old family" ties or ties to the corporate business class. We reject the view that the most powerful in the United States are only those who are members of the upper class or the corporate class. Instead, we believe that it is more fruitful to view foundation leaders as one of many competing strategic elites contending for power and influence in advanced industrial society.

The last, but no less significant, reason for thinking of the foundation elite as a strategic elite is that the strategic elite, as opposed to the notion of a ruling elite, accounts for polarization of political ideology among U.S. elites as a function of current occupation.

RULING CLASS, STRATEGIC ELITE, AND IDEOLOGY

The ruling class view of foundations and U.S. elites in general assumes elite commitment to upholding the sanctity and strength of traditional institutions and,

thus, to some type of elite conservatism. Even C. Wright Mills (1956), who sub-
stituted a power elite for a class model, argued that this unified group comes from
a common milieu and shares common values. While Mills's own formulation of
the power elite thesis (a product of the early Eisenhower years) is clearly untena-
ble, Dye's defining the traditional philosophy of America's elites as ''liberal''
(1986, p. 221) is equally so; the view is ahistorical in the extreme.

Prior to the New Deal, as Baltzell points out, many members of the American
upper class were deeply conservative in their attachment to traditional U.S.
institutions and to the rugged individualism of *laissez-faire* capitalism. During
the Great Depression, members of this ''caste'' exhibited great hostility to FDR
personally as well as to the reforms of the New Deal, which created countervailing
institutions of governmental power (Baltzell, 1964, pp. 226–59; Sitkoff, 1985).
The New Deal ''revolution'' succeeded to the extent that the mildly liberal world
view described by Dye became widely accepted among elites prior to the late
1960s. The rise and institutionalization of the adversary culture has, as we argued
in chapter two, put an end to this consensus.

The strategic elite model, unlike the ruling class model, assumes that different
elites are socialized to different and conflicting values. This occurs primarily
through differential recruitment to and socialization within occupational groups.
Societies such as ours, with multiple and competing strategic elites, have more
trouble attaining social cohesion than societies dominated by a ruling class
(Keller, 1963, p. 141).

Although society expects its elites to support its norms, each elite group,
Keller notes, ''has its own special definitions and criteria of these virtues'' (1963,
p. 141). This moral diversity, as a result of elite specialization and differentiation,
leads to conflicting outlooks regarding what society as a whole should seek to
accomplish.[17] In support of Keller's argument, Allen H. Barton (1975) reports
that current occupation is the most important and perhaps even the only predictor
of current ideological beliefs. Similarly, in our studies of elites, we found sharp
differences between the political, economic, and social views of different elite
groups (Lerner, Nagai, and Rothman, 1990).

The implications of moral diversity for elite political socialization and, thus,
for overall political stability (which is something largely not considered by Keller)
can be seen by more systematically considering the varieties of ruling classes
and strategic elites. Societies can be divided not only into their respective types
of rule (class versus elite) but also by degree of conflict or consensus they exhibit
at any particular time (see Table 3.1).

Cross-classifying these two dimensions yields the four types denoted in Table
3.1. The first is cohesive upper class rule, which we call the Marxian model. This
is the view summarized at the beginning of the chapter. It emphasizes common ascriptive roots and upper class ties as primary conditions for elite recruitment. The
second type, conflicted upper class rule, characterizes class societies on the verge
of revolution or civil war, where the upper class is split and in conflict. Type three
is cohesive rule by strategic elites, which can be described either as dominance by

Table 3.1
A Typology of Power and Ideology

	Ideology	
Unit of Rule	Consensus	Conflict
Class	Upper Class Rule	Civil War
Elite	Power Elite	Adversary Culture

the society's political class or by its power elite. Mills's power elite, describing the United States as dominated by a small circle of elites and written during the Eisenhower years, fits this type. Political power in contemporary Japan would best fit this model, whereby a tripartite group of elites dominates. These elites are drawn from the ruling Liberal Democratic Party, the Japanese civil service, and the large Japanese corporations. While Japanese recruitment and mobility within the political party, civil service, and large corporations are based on achieved rather than ascribed criteria, the common ideology held by the ruling party, the national bureaucracy, and big business and the consensus-oriented decision-making style within and among these three groups make a good case for a ruling elite model of Japanese power. Finally, type four is characterized by conflicted strategic elites or, in extreme form, "culture wars" (e.g., Bell, 1992). We believe it is characteristic of contemporary U.S. society.

This leads us to introduce the conservative critique of contemporary philanthropy, which argues that the philanthropic elite—like the media elite, the Hollywood elite of film and television, and the leaders of the public interest movement—take a decidedly adversarial stance toward U.S. moral values.

The growth and spread of the adversary culture among some segments of the U.S. elite mean that some elites hold to a belief system in conflict with generally established national norms. In its stronger form, the adversary culture view implies that some elites (such as the Hollywood elite and the media elite) seek to erode the status of traditional elite groups (usually business and the military), who they believe hold too much power.

The growth and spread of the adversary culture are both a result of the existing degree of moral diversity among elites in our advanced industrial society and a cause of its perpetuation and extension among conflicting elites. A number of noted conservative critics of foundations argue that the foundation elite are a part of this adversary culture. They claim that the leaders of the foundation world oppose the values held by more traditional groups, especially business.

Chapter four turns to the conservative critique of the foundation elite, followed by survey evidence demonstrating that a significant proportion of the foundation elite hold attitudes commonly associated with the adversary culture.

NOTES

1. The Episcopalian and Presbyterian churches are associated with the upper class in U.S. society.

2. Suzanne Keller (1963, p. 175) includes a third category of elite traits—their functional attributes—and associates these with particular elite roles (business, politics, the judiciary). Thus, the business elite possess the functional attribute of efficiency insofar as the business elite manage large-scale production of goods and services and, we add, succeed in the competitive marketplace. That competitive success is not a foreordained conclusion is shown by the fate of the Big Three American automobile manufacturers. While in the 1950s they were kings of the hill, in the 1980s they had to fight hard to survive.

3. The exception to inherited occupations might be the head of the family firm, where the owners could pass the business down to their children.

4. Unfortunately, because of confidentiality requirements, our data do not permit us to undertake an exploration of the extent of family and kinship ties.

5. The data used in these elite comparisons are taken from a larger, unpublished project, "Leadership and Social Change," directed by Stanley Rothman and sponsored by the Center for the Study of Social and Political Change.

6. Percentages are calculated among whites and blacks only. There are almost no Hispanics or Asians within U.S. elite groups. Ninety-eight percent of business leaders and 96 percent of the media elite are white; 94 percent of bureaucrats, 89 percent of federal judges, 94 percent of labor union leaders, and 89 percent of religious leaders are white.

7. For example, almost half (44 percent) the female foundation leaders grew up in rich families, compared to only one in five male foundation leaders, 14 percent of elite women journalists, and 19 percent of female public interest leaders.

In terms of education, roughly 12 percent of foundation women received an undergraduate education from a select institution, compared to roughly 31 percent of women public interest leaders and one in three women members of the media elite.

8. This figure includes the lone individual who lists his ethnicity as half German-Jewish and half East-European Jewish, but not the person who gives Mexican-American as his or her ethnic origin but Jewish as his or her current religion and the two persons who list their ethnicity as Russian but their current religion as Jewish.

9. The relatively large percentage of Protestants in the military is *not* related to a disproportionate number of blacks. Only 5 percent of the military elite are black.

10. According to the 1989 General Social Survey, 2 percent of the American public give "none" as their religious affiliation and an equal percentage give "other" (National Opinion Research Center, 1990, p. 144).

11. We have excluded Jewish elite members because religiosity among Jewish Americans cannot be measured by temple attendance (Cohen, 1983).

12. These schools include Ivy League colleges but also such highly competitive schools as Oberlin, Stanford, and MIT. We base the ranking of school selectivity on a scale of one to seven, with seven being the most selective, as defined by the mean combined SAT

score of a school's first-year class to be 1200 or better (see Ladd and Lipset, 1976, for a detailed discussion).

13. The Ivy League colleges are Dartmouth, Princeton, Yale, Harvard, Columbia, Cornell, and the University of Pennsylvania, according to the Encyclopedia Americana. The Seven Sisters are comprised of Smith, Wellesley, Bryn Mawr, Barnard, Mount Holyoke, Radcliffe, and Vassar (Zophy, 1990).

14. Keller's own list, which we have modified slightly, consists of eight criteria: (1) number; (2) size; (3) duration; (4) modes of entry; (5) modes of exit; (6) scope of authority; (7) cultural bonds; and (8) accessibility (Keller, 1963, p. 58).

15. Peter Laslett (1971, p. 30) demonstrates the importance of leisure in the making of the English gentleman. His work provides a detailed empirical discussion of the English aristocracy of Stuart England and illustrates in great detail how different a society governed by a ruling class is from a society like ours, which is governed by multiple and competing strategic elites (pp. 23–54). William Manchester (1988) provides an example of the failure of the descendants of this aristocracy to act effectively when he quotes Winston Churchill's despairing quip: "We take our weekends in the country, Hitler takes his countries during weekends" (p. 481).

16. This argument is elaborated on in considerably more detail in subsequent chapters.

17. The term *moral diversity* is taken by Keller from Emile Durkheim's *Division of Labor* (1947). A more extended development of her essentially Durkheimian perspective is beyond the scope of the present work.

CHAPTER 4

OTHER VIEWS: PLURALISM VERSUS THE ADVERSARY CULTURE

As we showed in chapter three, social background and elite status bear little correlation. The foundation elite in the United States is not part of a cohesive, autonomous, and homogeneous group that holds power over the nation, based on a common pattern of upper class socialization.

From a somewhat different point of view, foundation leaders and others in the nonprofit sector criticize the ruling class view, claiming that it does not capture the activities of the foundation world. These foundation pluralists see U.S. philanthropy as diverse in focus and varying in action, and not merely furthering the power of the upper class.

The argument in support of philanthropic pluralism is analogous to views about U.S. pluralism in general. The basic premise of the philanthropic pluralist is that some members of the philanthropic elite exercise their power over certain issues but not others, much like the medical elite involve themselves in health, business elite in tariffs, the Hollywood elite in free speech, and so on. Foundation action is varied, and foundation leaders often act with neither cooperative nor conflictual relationships. In fact, some say, each foundation frequently acts with no relationship to any other organization at all.

The problem with the pluralist view is twofold: first, there is a lack of conceptual and intellectual rigor, and second, there is a lack of empirical testing. With regard to its analytical imprecision, philanthropic pluralism's meaning and implications are seldom reflected upon, although there are a few exceptions (such as Douglas and Wildavsky, 1978). In fact, many nonprofit pluralists repeat, almost as an incantation, that philanthropic foundations exhibit value pluralism, a capacity for experimentation, and an organizational flexibility not found elsewhere in the society. For example, Brian O'Connell, president of Independent Sector, says, "[T]here are many roles and values that philanthropic institutions represent," but he argues that "the largest contribution is the independence they provide for innovation, excellence, criticism, and, where necessary, reform" (1988, p. 31). O'Connell also believes advocacy for reform has been and should be a fundamental aim of all third-sector action because "most of the best voluntary efforts in our history are related to those efforts which advocated most of the public programs we take pride in today" (p. 34).

Paul Ylvisaker states even more forcefully the diversity of philanthropy: "Every cause, every constituency, every discipline, every point on the philosophical continuum somehow finds a niche no matter how tiny in the dispensation of foundation monies" (1987, p. 367). Much of the substantive pluralism in grant making is due to the individualistic interests of the donors, "which range from bird feeding to world hunger, from neighborhood parks to global pollution, from juvenile delinquency to schistosomiasis" (p. 367).

More important, Ylvisaker does not think that government activism necessarily reduces the role of philanthropy. On the contrary, he argues that foundations complement and challenge government action, on both a short-term and a long-term basis. They articulate the needs of groups locked out of the voting arena, and they support innovations that would never survive the partisan debates in the governmental process. They can afford to look at the long-term impact of projects, and they need not deal with the problem of short-term accountability as faced by the politician.

Clearly, neither O'Connell nor Ylvisaker openly addresses the conflict between advocating reform and "a pluralism of roles and values." There is little discussion regarding funding of opposite sides of the ideological battlefield, nor do they discuss the implications of such a conflict, both for the nonprofit world and for the larger society. What happens when foundations support programs promoting policies hated by the American public or, at least, by some prominent members of Congress?

These questions highlight the amorphous role of foundations and the nonprofit sector in U.S. society. The general argument regarding philanthropic pluralism appeals to many nonprofit elites, precisely because it rests on the uniquely American solution to public problems. At the same time, as we see in chapter two, the lines between the private (market) sector, the public sector (government), and the nonprofit sector are not clearly drawn.

Despite the fact that government today provides many public services, Americans still believe that large portions of the public interest are not best served by the state. At the same time, Americans believe that there must be a buffer against the harshest aspects of free-market capitalism, hence our reliance on private philanthropy. As Michael Novak (1988) observes, promoting the common good solely through government action has many drawbacks for Americans. One drawback is that taxes would have to be raised to provide for public goods. The second problem is that "public goods" would be defined monolithically—by government and through laws. The corollary is that where government is silent, by definition, there would be no "need" (Novak, 1988, p. 11).

Americans believe that more things get done by private philanthropy because private philanthropy comes from free citizens acting on their own. Novak argues that such action is possible only in a society that values individualism, freedom, and association. The habit of association, Novak argues, "is an original and powerful principle of the common good" (1988, p. 12).

In essence, private philanthropy represents the American notion that between the state and the individual is civil society, which Novak defines as "a zone of social living in between . . . the pole of the autonomous individual, on the one side, and the state or large collective, on the other" (p. 17). Novak further believes that private philanthropy, which is private action for public purposes, is the means by which Americans deal with this limitation of government.

Because civil society is the arena in which there is no formal authority (i.e., government) with the monopoly to define "the public good," it follows then that private action for public purposes (i.e., private philanthropy) must be pluralistic. There must be multiple perspectives on thinking about social problems, and multiple skills to carry them out. Pluralism as a central concept also runs through Peter Berger and Richard Neuhaus's (1977) view of the role of social institutions mediating between the individual and the state. They argue that such U.S. institutions as churches, local communities, and voluntary associations have served as alternatives to the state. Modern practices, however, have reduced reliance on these mediating institutions in favor of the welfare state with a concomitant increase in government intrusion into, and regulation of, individual lives. This in turn has led to atomization and alienation from the larger public order. Berger and Neuhaus argue that pluralism is provided in large part by relying on private philanthropy and the nonprofit sector to carry out tasks elsewhere performed by the central government. Foundations, by providing an independent source of financial support, are crucial in developing and sustaining the third sector (1977, p. 38).

Berger and Neuhaus firmly believe that the hostility of the Populist attack on foundations (e.g., the congressional tax reforms of 1969; for further discussion, see chapter two) from both the right and the left needs to be blunted if this country is to retain an important support of its pluralism. Revoking tax-exempt status, the government's means of controlling nonprofits, has become tied to the notion that foundations and other nonprofits cost the government a certain amount of revenue because they are tax exempt. Berger and Neuhaus declare this concept to be "incipiently totalitarian," insofar as it assumes that all wealth "really belongs to the government and that the government should therefore be able to determine how all wealth—including the wealth exempted from taxation—should be used" (1977, p. 38).

In short, Novak and Berger and Neuhaus think philanthropic pluralism is the natural mission of the nonprofit sector, a thesis based on the view that Americans on the whole do not want government action and government solutions. They all see private philanthropy and nonprofit activity as a better alternative than dependence on the welfare state.

Notwithstanding the virtues of relying on private philanthropy, the problems that come with philanthropic pluralism must be addressed, for example, as Douglas and Wildavsky (1978) have done. In an essay on the future of foundations, these authors start with the understanding that pluralism is central to the institutional mission of foundations. However, they distinguish several types of foundation pluralism: a pluralism of problem-solving procedures; a pluralism of policies directed at types of problems; and last (and most neglected), a pluralism of values in the foundation world.

Procedural pluralism is basically foundation support for many applicants for projects directed at the same problem. While any given project will probably not succeed, supporting many applicants raises the odds that one approach will work. This type of pluralism, they argue, requires a massive commitment of financial resources to the same area—in other words, a redundancy of effort over a narrow range of interests and a low rate of return. Clearly, it is the rare foundation that can commit large resources to a multitude of approaches in the same area (each with a high probability of failure), given the constraints of foundation portfolios.

Closely related is an approach of policy pluralism with different approaches to the same policy, between private philanthropy and the national government. In Douglas and Wildavsky's words, foundations could adopt the principle of big government—"the bigger the better—big foundations and even bigger government" (1978, p. 37), with the foundation gently nudging expanding government to go in the direction the foundation sets rather than in another direction. The problem, however, is that close relations between foundations and the political party in power (i.e., "government") lead to partisan backlash, as occurs periodically in Congress. The mirror of policy pluralism with regard to government is what Douglas and Wildavsky call "the policy perversity approach." This approach encourages foundations to tackle areas in which government fears to tread. The problem with policy perversity is political backlash, as described in chapter one, of funding politically unpopular causes.

The third type of pluralism is, according to Douglas and Wildavsky, "values pluralism and a concept of balance." They argue that it should be the role of the third sector "to take special interest in the balance between the other two sectors [government and industry] and citizens in society at large" (1978, p. 39). The foundations' role is to call for redress when either government or industry becomes too powerful. When industry threatens to overwhelm U.S. society, they suggest foundations look for ways in which government can be built up as a countervailing force. Likewise, as government grows exponentially while the private sector declines in power, the focus should be on finding ways to reduce government dominance. Most important, Douglas and Wildavsky argue that foundations, as neither business nor government, can support many types of alternative associations in pursuit of the public good.

While Douglas and Wildavsky's typology covers much of what foundations do, they too neglect a fundamental problem of foundation pluralism. Simply stated, foundation pluralism is not the same as interest group pluralism in government, nor is it like the competitive free market. There is no inherent "corrective" mechanism for the foundation world as a pluralist system. The laws of supply and demand constrain firms; the invisible hand guides the free market. In government, elections and public opinion constrain elected officials. All other things being equal, a politician captured by an interest group working against the electoral majority risks losing his office.

Foundation pluralism lacks such a constraint, except in the most egregious violations of the IRS tax code. As we note in chapter one, political involvement in foundation and other nonprofit activity has meant changes in tax laws. In addition, revoking tax exemption status and deductibility is what John G. Simon, law professor, scholar, and former foundation head, calls "uncharted territory" (1987, p. 79).

While the tax code makes nonprofits broadly accountable, the larger empirical question remains: How much foundation pluralism, especially policy and value pluralism, exists in the foundation world? It is only after establishing the type and extent of pluralism that one can raise the next question: Under what conditions does foundation pluralism conflict with majority preferences exhibited in markets and elections? This leads us to the third question: When they are in conflict, particularly with national government policy, what are the consequences of such conflicts?

Our survey of foundation leaders' attitudes and analysis of public policy grant making directly addresses the first two issues. We believe an important example of philanthropic pluralism, foundation involvement in public affairs advocacy, can conflict with the majoritarian principle of popular government. Over the past thirty years, foundation policy advocacy has proved to be of paramount importance and has produced the greatest public controversy.

David Sidorsky argues that political pluralism "assumes and requires mechanisms for negotiation of consent" (1987, p. 95). In politics, conflict between political groups is settled through the internal politics of the budgetary, legislative, and electoral processes.

Foundation pluralism, on the other hand, lacks corrective mechanisms of negotiation, consensus, and resolution among foundations in conflict. What keeps philanthropic pluralism from resulting in the creation and funding of programs in direct opposition to each other? To the extent the foundation world is genuinely pluralistic and to the extent it truly embodies a variety of values, there is no guarantee that some philanthropic "invisible hand" necessarily will produce beneficent results. At best, these programs in conflict cancel each other out with no net gain for any side; at worst, conflict is heightened.

Despite the lack of some systemwide mechanism to assure that philanthropic funding produces beneficent results, many foundation leaders assume that foundations should play a role in public affairs funding. Probably the most widely cited discussion of the public affairs role of philanthropic foundations is the testimony before the 1970s Commission on Private Philanthropy and Public Needs, better known as the Filer Commission, by Jane Mavity and Paul Ylvisaker (1977). Mavity and Ylvisaker see philanthropy as part of the system of large-scale endeavors through which societal problems are defined and addressed. In their view, philanthropy is a private version of the legislative process by which goals are targeted and resources distributed, and foundation recipients are the private counterpart of public bureaucracies. In each case, the private and public mechanisms for redistributing society's resources work in tension and in tandem (Mavity and Ylvisaker, 1977, p. 795).

Mavity and Ylvisaker identify several factors that contribute to the increasing tendency of foundations to engage in public affairs. First is the increasing wealth of foundations. Such wealth has allowed the expansion of benevolence beyond personal, one-to-one charity. The second factor is the increasing professionalization of philanthropic giving. Professionalization has meant that more donor organizations and donee groups are run by paid professionals who serve as intermediaries between philanthropists and recipients. This contributes to the third factor encouraging public policy giving, which is the belief among foundation professionals that the goal of philanthropy is to engage in societywide change rather than to solve individual social problems.

American philanthropists, especially when professionally trained, have increasingly come to realize that isolated acts of personal charity are not enough to cure basic social ills or to reshape the larger forces that give rise to them. More and more, their efforts have turned toward understanding, and getting the public to understand, these basic forces, circumstances, causes, and possible cures. (Mavity and Ylvisaker, 1977, p. 797)

The philanthropist systematically encourages government to deal with victims of larger social forces "by identifying programs and policies, such as social security, income maintenance, and educational entitlements that convert isolated and discretionary acts of private charity into regularized public remedies that flow as a matter of legislated right" (pp. 797–98). This step from individual acts of charity to social welfare as a public right, if viewed as defining philanthropic activity, makes the foundation the handmaiden of the welfare state and forecloses debate on questions raised by conservatives since the end of the nineteenth century.

Mavity and Ylvisaker believe private philanthropy should fund four types of public affairs activity: to improve the government process; to tell government what the important issues are; to expand rights, participation, and resources of those perceived as lacking them; and to improve private institutions' responsiveness to public pressure. With this as its guiding culture, philanthropy becomes a form of private government, minus the political control exercised by the public through elections. Mavity and Ylvisaker recognize this and acknowledge that it is a difficult charge to rebut, urging only that private philanthropy has always played such a role.

PERSPECTIVES ON PHILANTHROPIC FOUNDATIONS: PHILANTHROPY AND THE ADVERSARY CULTURE

The Mavity-Ylvisaker view of the public policy role of foundations is novel only in its explicit formulation. It has quickly become part of the foundation world's conventional wisdom. At the same time, the widespread acceptance of the idea that philanthropic foundations, in the words of the trade publication *Foundation News*, "ought to recognize their obligation to bring about constructive social change" (quoted in Kristol, 1978, p. 132) has been challenged since the late 1970s by a number of conservative critics, who claim that the foundation world is dominated by liberals and that constructive social change is "always something that government does to and for people" (Kristol, 1978, p. 132). Given the lack of political (i.e., electoral) restraint on foundation activities, conservative critics assert that foundations and their recipients play a role largely unaccountable to the public.

In the late 1970s, Henry Ford II resigned as a trustee of the Ford Foundation, charging that the foundation had turned too far toward undercutting the very system that allowed its growth. "I'm not playing the role of the hard-headed tycoon who thinks all philanthropoids are socialists and all university professors are Communists. . . . I'm just suggesting to the trustees and the staff that the system that makes the Foundation possible very probably is worth preserving" (Nielsen, 1985, p. 72). In asserting that Ford was not "suffering from delusions of persecution," neoconservative social critic Irving Kristol writes, "the majority of the large foundations in this country, like most of the major universities, exude a climate of opinion wherein an anti-business bent becomes a perfectly natural inclination" (1978, p. 132). While he qualifies this statement by noting that foundations are not homogeneous institutions, he considers the generalization to be indisputably true. In a separate essay, he includes "staffs of the larger foundations" as one component of the "new class," along with the media and intellectuals. Today the "new class" challenges the legitimacy and power of the traditional capitalist classes to rule (Kristol, 1978, p. 25).

A decade later, William Simon, president of the John M. Olin Foundation, leveled similarly harsh criticism at corporate philanthropy: "[L]eaders of the American free enterprise system—or people acting in their name and with their corporate profits—are financing the destruction of their own system and ultimately of our free society" (quoted in Meiners and Laband, 1988, p. iii).

With few exceptions, the literature on foundations has not clearly presented, much less analyzed, the conservative view of foundations. The argument is basically that the foundation elite is one of a number of new elites in certain strategic sectors of society (see Keller, 1963). The emergence of new elites, a process described by some as the rise of the "new class," has led to extensive and sharp ideological divisions in U.S. society.[1] As Suzanne Keller argues in *Beyond the Ruling Class* (1963), a modern society based on the principles of specialization and division of labor places little premium on elite consensus. Socialization occurs primarily through one's occupation, and, while we all expect our elites to support general American values, Keller notes that each elite group holds its own world view of life in the United States.

The conservative argument regarding the "adversary culture" is based on the thesis that an unprecedented proportion of cultural elites are exposed to the ideas of postmodernist intellectuals, through affluence, leisure, higher education, newspapers, television, films, and books. This has resulted in a distinctive "public-interest" liberalism, which has been described by many different labels. It has been called the "adversary culture" (Trilling, 1965; Kristol, 1978; Hollander, 1988) but also "postmaterialism" (Inglehart, 1977) and "the egalitarian culture" (Wildavsky, 1982; 1991). No matter how characterized, the critics argue that this new culture serves as the adversarial platform from which members of new strategic elites criticize U.S. society.

Previous research shows that these new elites—notably the media elite, the makers of prime time television, the makers of top grossing movies, and public interest group leaders—are considerably more politically liberal than members of traditional leadership groups and less inclined to support both capitalism and traditional moral perspectives (e.g., on abortion or nonmarital sex).[2] Most significantly, quantitative analysis shows that members of new strategic elites are significantly more alienated from the U.S. system than elites in business, corporate law, and the military (Lerner, Nagai, and Rothman, 1990).

The exact description of the positions and the persons who hold such views in general remains, however, a matter of considerable dispute despite the popularity of the term *new class*. For example, Daniel Bell (1980) and Steven Brint (1984) argue that the new class is not a class in any economic sense at all but a group of "social-cultural specialists which shares no common position in the labor market . . . that is also not shared by other professionals" (Brint, 1984, p. 42). In contrast, Peter L. Berger (1986) and John McAdams (1987) contend that while imperfect, the new class formulation retains considerable explanatory utility. In either view, however, the meaningful conjunction of two social facts is accepted as significant: (1) the emergence of new occupations and professions based on large-scale bureaucracies and expanded knowledge; and (2) the diffusion of a new adversarial world view critical of traditional U.S. society and of traditional religious, moral, economic, and political values (e.g., Bell, 1976).[3]

Why, in this view, have foundations come to reflect the adversarial liberal views of foundation professionals and their intellectual-academic advisors? Conservative intellectuals contend it is because most professional philanthropic foundations now rely on experts with scientific backgrounds and firsthand experience with important problems to guide their granting activities. The great donors, believing in such principles as scientific management, the division of labor, and reliance on professional expertise, have ceded the day-to-day management of the most prominent foundations to professionals in the nonprofit sector. The composition and philosophy of the boards of trustees of the most "professional" foundations have changed even more with the proliferation of professional social workers, lawyers, administrators, academics, civil servants, and social movement activists.

This process has snowballed in importance because, since World War II, the number of foundations and their explicit involvement in the formulation of public policy have grown exponentially.[4] Today, roughly 25,000 foundations are supervised by many directors, trustees, and professional staff who have emerged as a philanthropic managerial elite by virtue of the sheer numbers and grant-making capacities of these institutions and despite management patterns that vary widely.

Thus, conservatives argue, the professionalization of philanthropy provides the historical explanation for the supposedly adversarial posture taken by the foundation elite. While social critics on the right have come to assume that members of the foundation elite partake in the adversary critique of the American system, the proposition itself has not been put to systematic empirical test.

Cast in a somewhat different light, the next chapter asks the following questions: How much pluralism is there in organized private philanthropy? Does the adversary culture permeate the foundation world? If foundation pluralism is a primary virtue in philanthropy, and, as we argue in chapter three, foundation leaders are a strategic elite, then we would expect to find considerable tolerance for "value" diversity.

We, thus, must add the following corollary to our analysis of strategic elites. If the United States is dominated by strategic elites, and if some elites are advocates of the adversary culture, elite groups should be characterized by ideological dissensus. More important, the foundation elite, given the norms and structure of modern philanthropy, should exhibit less ideological cohesion than other elites. Lacking the corrective mechanisms of conflict resolution available to other social sectors, we would expect ideological diversity to be even more pronounced than in other elite groups.

Keeping these issues in mind, the next three chapters look at the empirical evidence regarding the ideology of the foundation elite, its impact on the philanthropic ethos, and actual public affairs giving in the 1980s. Chapter five examines in detail the ideological world view of the philanthropic elite.

NOTES

1. The following is based on an extensive quantitative analysis of elite dissensus by Robert Lerner, Nagai, and Rothman (1990). See also Rothman, Lichter, and Lichter, forthcoming, for a more accessible discussion.

2. Other important new strategic elites whose views are strongly influenced by the adversary culture include academics (Ladd and Lipset, 1976), the intellectual elite (Kadushin, 1974), and publishers and editors of major publishing houses (Coser, Kadushin, and Powell, 1982, p. 113).

3. It is beyond the scope of this book to determine whether a person's ideology is derived from his or her membership in any "new class" occupation or whether, in fact, a person's ideological views and identifications determine their choice of occupation. There appears to be some evidence for both positions (e.g., Lerner, Nagai, and Rothman, 1989; Macy, 1988).

4. The historical statistics on foundations may be found in Ann D. Walton and F. Emerson Andrews (1960, pp. x–xi).

CHAPTER 5

IDEOLOGICAL DIVISIONS WITHIN THE FOUNDATION ELITE

This chapter more closely examines the propositions put forth in the previous chapters. The pluralist's view of foundations suggests a diversity of values, but not to the extent that there is open antagonism toward traditional liberal-capitalist society. The conservative view is that the foundation world is dominated by the values of the adversary culture.

Our survey of the ideology of the foundation elite shows, first of all, that the foundation elite are ideologically divided among conservatives, moderates, and liberal left. Second, foundation executives are the most polarized of all elite groups. Third, and finally, their ideology influences their views on political events, leaders, and news sources.

We shall examine in greater detail the issues that make up "conservatism" and "liberalism" among the foundation elite. First, we shall look at how members of the foundation elite ideologically label themselves.

Before we proceed, we should note that our use of the terms *liberal* and *conservative*, while consistent with general usage in political science, differs from that of such critics of foundations as Waldemar A. Nielsen (1985, p. 420 and *passim*). Nielsen defines as conservative any foundation that supports basic institutions such as hospitals and universities, while he defines as liberal any foundation that "conceives of itself as primarily an instrument of social change in behalf of justice and equity" (1985, p. 421).

As examples of this difference, Nielsen cites the Andrew W. Mellon and Ford foundations as conservative and liberal, respectively, characterizations we believe are misleading. Aside from its built-in value bias (that assumes that non-liberals are against justice and equity), this analysis ignores the role of genuinely conservative organizations like the John M. Olin, Sarah Scaife, and Smith Richardson foundations, which Nielsen relegates to a brief introductory discussion.

Supporting existing nonpolitical societal institutions, as Mellon does, is neither conservative nor liberal in any conventional understanding of these terms. Support for an ideologically based program, whether liberal or conservative, is obviously different from support for established cultural and educational institutions, even though these institutions (especially artistic and academic institutions) may operate in a manner that supports liberal or conservative ideologies.

SELF-IDENTIFIED IDEOLOGY

Conservative, *moderate*, and *liberal* are the standard categories by which U.S. politicians, the media, social scientists, and general intellectuals talk about political opinions. Today, they are a standard part of public opinion polls. We posed this conventional question to the foundation elite (and twelve other American elite groups), asking them to describe their political views on a seven-point scale, from one (conservative) to seven (liberal), with four labeled as "middle of the road."

Based on this question, foundation leaders are strongly politicized and ideologically split. When asked to rate themselves on an ideological scale, 42 percent of the foundation elite label themselves as ideologically conservative, while 37 percent call themselves liberal; 21 percent call themselves moderate (see Figure 5.1).

The foundation elite stand in contrast to the general public, where moderates comprise the largest ideological group (39 percent). Foundation leaders are also proportionately more conservative; 32 percent of the public label themselves conservative, compared to 42 percent of the foundation elite.[1]

In addition, foundation leaders are among the most polarized of U.S. elites.[2] Most elite groups swing either toward the right or to the left. More than three out of four military leaders, for example, and two-thirds of the business elite label themselves conservative. At the other end of the ideological continuum, nine out of ten public interest leaders call themselves liberal.

While discussion of self-identified ideology is important, it does not present a complete picture of the views of foundation leaders. A thorough discussion of the ideology of the philanthropic elite requires more attention devoted to the nature of ideology per se than has been provided so far. The next sections look at the specific opinions that make up a conservative versus a liberal world view among the foundation elite (see Table 5.1).

Economic Issues

Members of the foundation elite hold some beliefs in common. The overwhelming majority of conservative, moderate, and liberal members of the foundation elite do not support a radical restructuring of capitalism in the United States. As one would expect, no conservatives and very few moderates and liberals support the public ownership of large corporations. Moreover, only one

Figure 5.1
Self-Identified Ideology and the Foundation Elite

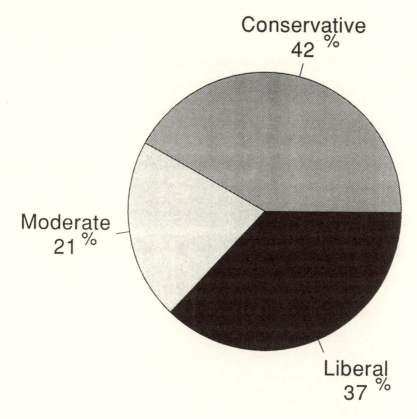

in five liberals supports a move toward socialism. Large majorities of all three ideological groups also support a balanced federal budget and believe in a version of the merit system (that those with more ability should earn more money).

The ideological gaps on economic policy questions occur between liberals and the others. Most conservatives and moderates support a version of *laissez-faire* capitalism, while liberals support policies encouraging the welfare state. For example, while more than four out of five liberals agree that the government should reduce the income gap between rich and poor, roughly three out of four conservatives and three out of five moderates disagree. Two-thirds of liberal foundation leaders believe that government should insure a good standard of living for everyone, and roughly three out of five believe that government should guarantee jobs for all. Not surprising, two out of three liberal philanthropoids oppose less regulation of business.

Table 5.1

Social, Political, and Economic Attitudes by Self-Identified Ideology (percentage)

QUESTION WORDING	IDEOLOGY		
	Con.	Mod.	Lib.
Economic Questions			
Less government regulation of business is good for country	98	76	33
The American private enterprise system fair to working people	98	92	57
More ability should earn more	98	88	82
It is not the proper role of government to insure that everyone has a job	84	85	39
America offers security for all those willing to work	80	64	36
The federal budget should be balanced even if it means raising taxes	71	80	73
People are poor because of circumstances beyond their control	31	56	80
The government should insure good standard of living for all	29	28	67
The government should reduce income gap between rich and poor	24	38	84
The U.S. should move toward socialism	0	4	23
Big corporations should be taken out of private ownership	0	4	7
Social Structure			
There is too much concern in the courts for the rights of criminals	86	48	33
America should retain death penalty	92	60	47
In general, blacks don't have the motivation or will power to pull themselves out of poverty	51	36	16
Special preference in hiring should be given to blacks	38	28	67
In general, blacks don't have the chance for the education it takes to rise out of poverty	35	52	80
Our environmental problems not as serious as people led to believe	35	8	9
Woman with children should not work	34	40	20
U.S. needs to restructure basic institutions	27	23	47
Special preference in hiring should be given to women	24	24	62
The American legal system mainly favors the wealthy	22	52	75
Social structure causes alienation	10	25	36
Gains by blacks come at whites' expense	8	0	0

Table 5.1 (continued)

Social Issues			
Woman has right to abortion	80	79	93
Adultery is wrong	84	75	73
Homosexuality is wrong	70	71	24
Lesbians and homosexuals should not teach in public schools	51	31	7
Religious prayer should not be allowed in the public schools	31	64	78
Foreign Policy			
It is sometimes necessary for CIA to undermine hostile governments	76	67	36
America should have strongest military, no matter what it costs	49	28	7
The United States has a moral obligation to prevent the destruction of Israel	43	48	53
We should be more forceful with the USSR even if increases risk of war	41	16	9
The main goal of U.S. foreign policy has been to protect business interests	16	46	56
Ns	51	26	45

The liberal position on economic policies reflects an underlying belief that unrestricted capitalism produces massive problems. Thus, only 57 percent of them (compared to almost all conservatives and moderates) believe that U.S. capitalism is fair to workers. Most do not think that a willingness to work guarantees security, and roughly eight in ten believe that people are not personally responsible for their poverty.

Self-identified conservatives and moderates are more openly supportive of a free-market economy. Almost all conservatives and three-fourths of moderates support less regulation of business. Most conservatives and moderates do not believe in government narrowing the income gap between rich and poor. They do not support government guarantees of a good standard of living or jobs for all.

Their confidence in free-market capitalism is reflected in their belief in the American dream: that the United States offers financial security to those willing to work; and that being poor is *not* a function of external circumstances. It is no surprise that the overwhelming majority of conservatives and moderates among the foundation elite believe in the essential fairness of the American private enterprise system.

Social Structure

Polarized beliefs regarding U.S. capitalism, however, do not readily generalize into support versus criticism of U.S. society in general. The majority of conservatives, moderates, and liberals do not believe that the social structure of U.S. society causes alienation; and most do not think that U.S. institutions need a basic restructuring (although 47 percent of liberals think so). More than half of conservatives, moderates, and liberals believe that women with children should be allowed to work and that environmental problems are serious (although 35 percent of conservatives do think that environmental problems are not as serious "as people have been led to believe").

Liberals, moderates, and conservatives disagree, however, on issues of race and crime. While almost all reject the claim that black gains come at whites' expense, half of the conservative foundation leaders and one-third of moderates believe that blacks lack the will power to rise from poverty. Conversely, only one in three conservatives agree that blacks lack educational opportunities. As expected, most conservative and moderate foundation leaders do not support special hiring programs for blacks. In contrast, two-thirds of the liberal foundation elite favor affirmative action programs for blacks (and roughly the same proportion support affirmative action for women). Eighty-four percent of liberal philanthropoids reject the notion that blacks lack the motivation to pull themselves out of poverty; four in five believe that black poverty is due to a lack of educational opportunities (as do more than half the moderates).

Ideological labels also translate systematically into beliefs about the U.S. legal system. As a group, liberals are the most critical, followed by moderates and then conservatives. Three-fourths of foundation liberals and a slight majority of moderates think that the legal system favors the wealthy. More than three-fourths of foundation conservatives, however, disagree. At the extreme, the overwhelming majority of conservatives believe that courts are too concerned with criminals' rights, a notion supported by less than half of moderates and rejected by two out of three liberals. Similarly, nine of ten conservatives and six of ten moderates support the death penalty, a position rejected by most liberals.

Foreign Policy

Although proportionately more self-labeled liberals are "doves" compared to the other two groups, the conservative-liberal split is not especially prominent within the foreign policy arena; most notably, the issue of the United States' moral obligation to Israel is not related to ideological labels. It receives support from a bare majority of liberals but from less than 50 percent of moderates and conservatives.

In fact, conservatives and liberals are sharply polarized on only two issues in surveys conducted before the end of the Cold War. Three-fourths of the conservatives support the proposition that it is legitimate for the Central Intelligence Agency (CIA) to undermine hostile governments, while two of three liberals disagree. On the other hand, while most liberals believe that the main goal of U.S. foreign policy is to protect big business, more than eight in ten conservatives disagree.

On other issues, the foundation elite takes more dovish positions than the public at large. More than nine in ten liberals and roughly seven in ten moderates do not believe that the United States should have the strongest military regardless of cost, and roughly the same proportion reject the notion that we should be more forceful with the Soviet Union. Even conservatives do not whole-heartedly support these positions.[3]

While there is evidence of ideological polarization among the foundation elite, particularly in economics and certain issues related to race and crime, are the foundation elite significantly more polarized than other elite groups? To address this question, we performed a statistical analysis of the above attitude questions and compared the answers of the foundation elite with those of other elite groups.

The Structure of American Ideology

Our data show six independent dimensions of American ideology, despite the fact that the words *conservative* and *liberal* are casually used in everyday conversation matters and imply a single ideological dimension. Considering ideology as consisting of several independent dimensions allows us to accommodate the possibility that an individual can hold liberal opinions on some issues and conservative opinions on others.

The Dimensions of Ideology

For most members of the foundation elite, ideological labels of conservative, moderate, and liberal translate into predictably conservative, moderate, and liberal responses to specific questions. When comparing self-identified conservatives, moderates, and liberals, we find a polarized foundation elite over several different types of issues.

We asked our respondents about various political, social, and economic issues. Responses were in the form of a four-point Likert scale: "strongly agree," "somewhat agree," "somewhat disagree," and "strongly disagree."

We group our discussion of the responses according to a classification system derived from our earlier studies of elite ideology (e.g., Lerner, Nagai, and Rothman, 1990). These studies rely upon the statistical technique of factor analysis to extract the key attitudes that surround several core beliefs. The technique enables us to group these responses into six underlying dimensions of ideology: moral Puritanism versus expressive individualism; *laissez-faire* individualism versus collectivist liberalism; system support versus system alienation; "hawks" versus "doves" in foreign policy; law and order versus rights of the accused; and support for and opposition to affirmative action (e.g., Lerner, Nagai, and Rothman, 1989; Nagai, Lerner, and Rothman, 1991). These represent certain underlying core values that link otherwise seemingly disparate attitude questions into what we generally call modern conservatism versus modern liberalism. The dimensions are ideal-type abstractions meant to represent and partially explicate the underlying link between otherwise disparate issue positions. (We also include responses to some questions not part of the earlier factor analyses under the headings that seemed most appropriate *a priori*.)

• The first dimension pits the traditional Puritan ethic of self-restraint on the right against expressive individualism on the left. The term *expressive individualism*, coined by Bellah and colleagues (1985), refers to the free expression and satisfaction of individual desires in the pursuit of the good life.

Expressive individualism has as its core the priority given to free, unfettered expression of impulses, assumed to be good in and of themselves, and is characterized by a shift in the concept of the individual from a "being" (part of a great chain of being) to a "self." Historically, it marks a shift from traditional Puritan restraint to the free expression of impulse and rejection of the traditional for the new and avant-garde.

The difference between representatives of these views can be seen by comparing the reasoning used by prochoice activists and their prolife counterparts. Kristen Luker (1984) finds that proabortion activists are believers in situation ethics, in part because they are moral relativists, secularists, and utilitarians. The right to choose has often been stated in precisely these terms: a woman, not society or her family, has a right to "control over her own body" and, thus, the right to decide whether or not to have an abortion. In contrast, Luker describes prolife advocates as traditionally religious and committed to a transcendent view of human action which restricts the possibilities of human choice and emphasizes human frailty and capacity for error. Thus, they reflect the traditional Western view of human nature. In classical, Catholic, and traditional Calvinist thought, all human beings possess a common nature related to their humanity and their place in the cosmos; and their common nature ties them to, even as it separates them from, other species as part of a "great chain of being." This "natural law" view provides a strong set of moral guidelines, and to flout them is to risk committing sin.[4]

Liberals, moderates, and conservatives among the philanthropy elite agree on these issues more than on any others, but in surprising ways. Overwhelming majorities of all ideological groups are prochoice; 93 percent of liberals and roughly eight of ten conservatives and moderates agree that a woman has the right to decide whether or not to have an abortion.

Ideological divergence emerges on issues of homosexuality and school prayer. Roughly seven in ten conservatives and moderates believe that homosexuality is wrong. A slight majority of conservatives and roughly seven of ten moderates think that lesbians and gays should not teach in public schools. In contrast, only one in four liberals believes homosexuality to be wrong, and more than 90 percent disagree that lesbians and gays should not teach.[5] On the issue of school prayer, roughly 70 percent of the conservatives believe that school prayer should be allowed, while two-thirds of the moderates and almost 80 percent of liberals believe that school prayer should be banned. The foundation elite, however, are surprisingly conservative on the issue of adultery. A large majority of liberals, moderates, and conservatives believe that adultery is wrong, as compared, say, to the journalists we sampled. Over 50 percent of the latter group believe that adultery is not wrong (Lichter, Rothman, and Lichter, 1986).

• The second dimension places "rugged" *laissez-faire* individualism, derived from America's Calvinist heritage, on one end and collectivist liberalism on the other. Max Weber (1930 trans.), Louis Hartz (1955), and Seymour Martin Lipset (1963) all observe that this country's uniqueness lay in her religious-cultural ethos. The Protestant ethic gave rise to a previously unknown degree of personal autonomy and a remarkable discipline of the passions that enabled the individual to achieve the goals of this world; and the autonomy and self-restraint arising from a Puritan ethos that fostered the development of a strong but disciplined sense of self provided the psychological foundation of modern American liberalism and capitalism. Persons holding this position favor hard work, diligence, self-discipline, frugality, will power, and rational foresight over the environment as the correct way to relate to the world. They stress sobriety over playfulness, restraint over expression, and reason over emotion.

Collectivist (or welfare state) liberalism emerged from the Great Depression (see, for example, Shils, 1980) and is often seen as the major domain of contemporary ideology (see, for example, Verba and Orren, 1985; and Feldman, 1983). This concept rests on the belief that the central government should ameliorate the economic inequalities of the capitalist system, as opposed to the traditional "rugged individualist" view that economic well-being stems from individual effort and personal achievement. Collectivist liberals support the expansion of the welfare state, favor more government-induced economic equality, support government regulation of business "in the public interest," and hold that those who are economically unsuccessful are not ultimately responsible for improving their own condition. Interestingly, although it is not usually thought of as one of its components, we find support for environmental regulation of business to be another indicator of collectivist liberalism (see, for example, Lerner, Nagai, and Rothman, 1989; 1990).

• The third dimension situates traditional patriotism against system alienation, another strand of contemporary ideology that emerged during the 1960s. (An example might be the formula "Screw God Bless America," cited in Rothman, 1979.) System alienation rests on the belief, expressed in its pure form by the New Left, that the social order of bourgeois liberal society is inherently dehumanizing and repressive and its structures of authority inherently suspect. Feelings of system alienation are closely tied to a critique of American capitalism, although feelings of general alienation and beliefs about the welfare state are separate ideological dimensions. One can be patriotic, for example, and also believe in the welfare state, as did many New Deal liberals before the Vietnam War. The opposite of system alienation is simply traditional patriotism, the belief that the United States is a good or even great society.

The following attitudes reflect this underlying "core value" of alienation versus patriotism:

A belief that the U.S. legal system mainly favors the wealthy.

Agreement that the U.S. private enterprise system is generally unfair to working people.

Agreement that the United States needs a complete restructuring of its basic institutions.

A belief that big corporations should be taken out of private ownership and run in the public interest.

Agreement that the structure of our society causes most people to feel alienated.

A belief that the main goal of U.S. foreign policy has been to protect U.S. business interests.

• The fourth dimension involves foreign policy and has structured opinion along an isolation-interventionalist axis. For simplicity's sake, and because we have not reached agreement yet among ourselves as to what to call it, we treat foreign policy and crime issues as separate dimensions. However, our research results on a larger sample of U.S. elites show that these issues taken together constitute a single dimension of ideology (see Lerner, Nagai, and Rothman, 1992 for more discussion).

In the 1980s, conservatives, or "hawks," were suspicious of the motives of the rulers of the former Soviet Union and were more likely to be in favor of increased defense spending, support for anticommunist regimes, and general support for military intervention against communist insurgencies.

Liberals, or "doves," tended to view the conflict between the United States and the Soviet Union as relatively less significant and to emphasize human rights as a standard by which to judge other governments. Following from this set of beliefs, examples of liberal foreign policy attitudes salient in the 1980s would include less defense spending, increasing arms control, increasing ties to the Sandinistas, cutting aid to El Salvador, and increasing external pressure on South Africa until it abolished apartheid.

• The fifth dimension involves positions on issues relating to crime and law and order. Conservatives here are those concerned with rising crime rates and the problem of establishing law and order, a core belief which manifests itself as support for capital punishment, long prison sentences for criminals, and a minimum of procedural rights for criminal defendants. It also leads one to think that the courts are too lenient toward criminals.

Liberals believe the opposite. Moreover, a liberal would favor increasing intervention by the courts in most matters (judicial activism), while a conservative would believe in the contrary position, usually identified as "judicial restraint."

• The sixth dimension, which forms a completely separate dimension in our extended factor analyses, is social equality for women and minorities. Conservatives tend to oppose affirmative action and "goals" for blacks and women, regarding them as quotas, while liberals tend to support such programs.

Considering contemporary ideology to be multidimensional allows for the possibility that an individual could be a *laissez-faire* (economic) conservative but heavily supportive of issues that constitute what we call expressive individualism. In fact, this particular combination is generally the model for contemporary libertarianism and is embodied in the policies of the Weld Administration

Figure 5.2
A Comparison of Philanthropic Elites with Other American Elite Groups:
Expressive Individualism

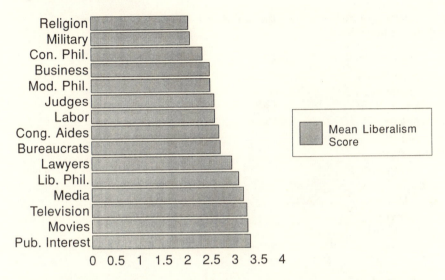

in Massachusetts. In other cases, such as Catholic religious leaders, those who are conservative on issues of expressive individualism take positions in support of collectivist liberalism.

We present the data in two parts. The first compares conservative, moderate, and liberal foundation leaders to other elite groups specifically along these independent ideological dimensions. The second presents the responses of foundation leaders on their ratings of individual political figures and groups, their goals for the United States, and the perceptions of power in society.

Ideology among Foundation Elites and Other Leadership Groups

To simplify comparisons between the philanthropic elite and the other elite samples, we computed mean ideological scores for each elite group for each dimension. This was done by recoding individual responses to each question so that scores range from 1.00, which is the most conservative response, to 4.00, which is the most liberal response. Each respondent received a mean score for each dimension. We then computed group mean scores for self-identified conservatives, moderates, and liberals (see Figures 5.2 to 5.7).[6]

Expressive Individualism

On this dimension of liberalism that pits the traditional Puritan ethic of personal self-restraint on the right against expressive individualism on the left, we find

Figure 5.3
A Comparison of Philanthropic Elites with Other American Elite Groups: Collectivist Liberalism

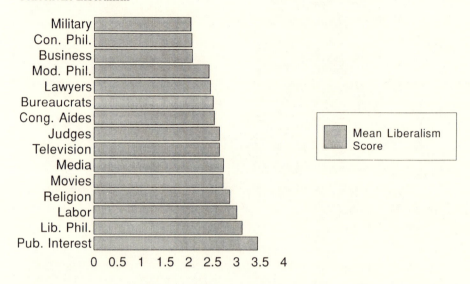

Figure 5.4
A Comparison of Philanthropic Elites with Other American Elite Groups: System Alienation

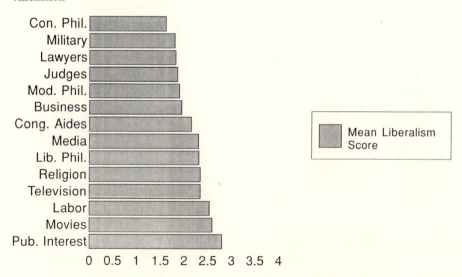

Figure 5.5
A Comparison of Philanthropic Elites with Other American Elite Groups: Foreign Policy

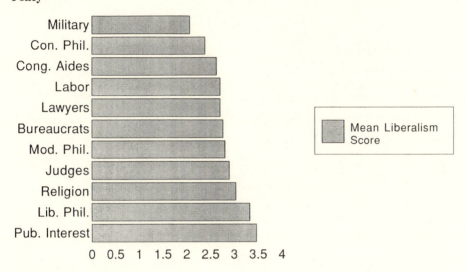

Figure 5.6
A Comparison of Philanthropic Elites with Other American Elite Groups: Crime

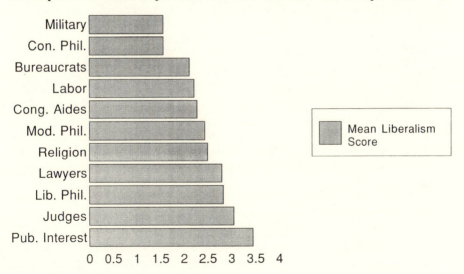

Figure 5.7
A Comparison of Philanthropic Elites with Other American Elite Groups:
Affirmative Action

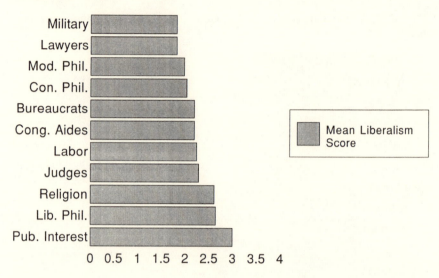

that self-labeled conservative and moderate philanthropic leaders are among the more conservative of U.S. elites, closely resembling business leaders. At the other end of the ideological spectrum are liberal members of the foundation elites, who are far from the most liberal. They are clearly to the right of new cultural elites such as those in the media, television, movies, and public interest groups.

Collectivist Liberalism

The second dimension places "rugged" *laissez-faire* individualism, derived from this country's Calvinist heritage, on one end and collectivist (welfare state) liberalism on the other. Philanthropic leaders are sharply polarized on questions of collectivist liberalism. Only issues of crime divide the sample more. The conservative foundation leaders are one of the most conservative groups ideologically, resembling business leaders and the military, while foundation liberals score nearly as highly as the most liberal elite group in our sample, the public interest group leaders.

System Alienation

The third dimension situates traditional patriotism against system alienation. The philanthropic leaders are split on the dimension of system alienation, but the gap is not as large as for the collectivist liberalism dimension. The conservative foundation elite is the least alienated of the U.S. elites, while the military, judges, and corporate lawyers are the only elite groups less alienated than the moderate members of the foundation elite. Liberal foundation elites are more alienated, but they are far less alienated than many other elite groups. The most alienated are the public interest elite, followed closely by the elite film makers and labor leaders.

Foreign Policy

The fourth ideological dimension deals with positions taken on how to best deal with the Soviet Union, structuring opinions along a "hawk-versus-dove" axis.[7] Both the self-styled moderates and liberals are quite liberal in comparison with other elites, where only the public interest leaders are more dovish than are self-defined liberal philanthropic leaders. However, the five years between the philanthropy survey and the other surveys may account for these differences. At the same time, the conservatives are the most hawkish, next to the military, and the gap between conservatives and liberals on this issue is greater than on the dimensions of alienation and expressive individualism. It is only slightly smaller than that of collectivistic liberalism.

Crime

The fifth dimension involves positions on issues relating to crime and law and order. Issues of crime divide the philanthropic elite more than any other set of issues we surveyed, including collectivist liberalism. Self-identified conservative foundation leaders are as conservative as any of our other elite groups, while moderate and elite foundation leaders are only somewhat less liberal than are the most liberal elite groups: judges and public interest leaders.

Affirmative Action

The sixth dimension, which forms a completely separate dimension in our extended factor analysis, concerns socioeconomic-political equality for women and minorities. While liberals and conservatives disagree on questions of affirmative action, these issues divide the philanthropic elite less than any other dimension. Foundation conservatives are substantially less conservative than the most conservative groups (the military and lawyers) although they do rank as the third most conservative, while liberal philanthropic leaders are more liberal, although somewhat less so than the public interest leaders.

Summary

To sum up our findings, despite the overwhelmingly elite status of philanthropic leaders, and while conservatives slightly outnumber liberals, they are not the most conservative elite group we studied: business and the military elite are consistently much more conservative than are foundation leaders. Equally important, philanthropic leaders are more ideologically divided than other elite groups. Self-identified liberal foundation leaders and self-identified conservative foundation leaders are sharply split in their opinions on issues of collectivist liberalism, foreign policy, and crime and are somewhat less split on issues of system alienation, expressive individualism, and affirmative action.

Moreover, conservative and liberal foundation leaders often fall on the opposite ends of the ideological spectrum. The difference in mean scores between conservative and liberal foundation leaders is only somewhat less than the difference in average scores between our most conservative groups (business and the military) and our most liberal ones (public interest leaders), especially on collectivist liberalism, foreign policy, crime, and affirmative action. There is somewhat more consensus among foundation elites only on system alienation and expressive individualism, compared to the most conservative and most liberal of the U.S. elite groups. Even here, however, liberal foundation leaders are quite liberal.

NOTES

1. Figures for the general public are from *General Social Surveys* (National Opinion Research Center, 1990, p. 107).

2. Our samples of corporate lawyers and congressional aides are ideologically most like our philanthropic elite. The percentages of conservatives and liberals are roughly the same, and each group is far larger than the middle.

3. In fact, less than half of them do.

4. For more on the abortion issue and the related questions comprising the expressive individualism dimension, see Lerner, Nagai, and Rothman (1990).

5. It is a testimony to the rapid change taking place in U.S. society that current elite responses to questions of homosexuality have probably changed dramatically since our 1980s surveys of various leadership groups.

6. In our past writings on the U.S. elite, we analyzed three dimensions of ideology, using the eighteen questions asked of all twelve elite groups. We also did a subsequent factor analysis based on the thirty questions asked of the eight elite groups surveyed in the mid–1980s. The three subsequent factors did not emerge in the twelve-group analyses because the relevant questions were not asked of the first four groups, for example, on affirmative action, crime, and foreign policy. The discussions of ideology combine the results of both factor analyses.

While our prior work used factor scores for elite groups, we chose in this case to use a slightly different analytical technique based on group mean scores for each ideological dimension. Mean scores for dimensions correlate highly with factor scores. For the elites data, the correlation between factor scores for system alienation and mean scores for alienation is 0.96; the correlation between factor scores for collectivist liberalism and mean scores is 0.88; and the correlation between expressive individualism and mean scores is 0.96. A separate factor analysis performed on the foundation elite data produced five factors with a nearly identical pattern of rotated factor loadings to those derived from factor analyses done on the larger sample of U.S. elites. To maintain comparability, we used the mean score indices as described in the text. The one exception to this was the crime index, which included an additional question on capital punishment. This question loaded on both the second elite factor analysis and the subsequent philanthropy factor analysis. See Appendix 3 for a list of questions loaded on the elite factor analysis.

7. Positions on Cold War issues, in fact, are highly correlated with positions taken on crime. These taken together make up a factor we tentatively label the "outside threat" factor (Lerner, Nagai, and Rothman, 1992). However, we decided to treat these separately to simplify matters for purposes of this chapter.

The collapse of Soviet communism and subsequent ending of the Cold War may call the composition of this factor into question. What is surely true is that positions on this underlying dimension can no longer be measured by attitudes toward the Soviet Union. However, we suspect that the interventionist-isolationist division of opinion will continue for some time as demonstrated by the Persian Gulf War and by the persistence of differences on how much money should be spent on defense. Those who opposed U.S. intervention and those who are most strongly in favor of reducing defense spending are more likely to be on the liberal left than elsewhere on the political spectrum, though there are important exceptions.

CHAPTER 6

THE IMPACT OF IDEOLOGY

DEFINING AND MEASURING IDEOLOGY

Ideology has several meanings, but in this study we use the term to describe a set of related political opinions and ideas that frequently come together.[1] The definition does not imply a perfect degree of convergence between attitudes and behavior, nor does it require fully conscious articulation. It does not require a person to have a coherent philosophical system of thought and a logically derived agenda for action supporting it. Last, this definition of ideology does not imply that ideology is a thought system held only by extremists.

Ideological views among the foundation elites are generally consistent and extensive. Their political opinions are in line with their ideological self-identification. The question is, however, how extensive is their ideological thinking? Does it extend to other arenas? In studies of other elite groups, Stanley Rothman and others (e.g., Rothman and Lichter, 1984; Lichter, Rothman, and Lichter, 1986) show that political ideology affects perceptions of reality. A widely held world view, after all, defines what is the conventional wisdom within a particular occupational elite. Even in the case of the media elite, where professional ethics demand factual or balanced reporting, ideology slips in. At the same time, we find in other research that some elite groups are more ideologically sophisticated than others (Lerner, Nagai, Rothman, 1990). This means that some individuals and groups hold more cognitively consistent opinions than do others. Among the general public, more education results in greater political information and more coherently held political opinions. Among elites, where most elite groups have on average a college education or better, ideological consistency is more characteristic of those who work with abstract concepts and ideas, not merely those who deal on a day-to-day basis with political matters. For example, U.S.

Figure 6.1
Leaders and Movements

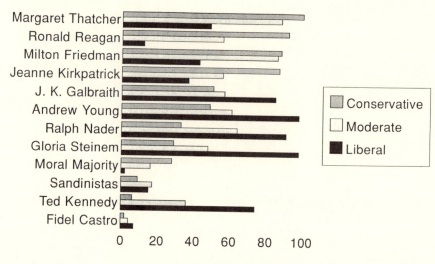

% of Foundation Leaders Approve

religious leaders are one of the most ideologically sophisticated of elite groups, and more so than the media elite or federal bureaucrats, notwithstanding the latter groups' daily involvement in political matters.

How extensive is ideological thinking among the foundation elite? We find their ideological thinking to infuse their evaluations of various prominent individuals, their goals for U.S. society, their impressions of power in society, and their appraisal of various sources of news and opinion. Their ideological self-labels are proxies for their responses on a host of more general questions.

Prominent Figures

We gave the foundation elite a list of prominent individuals and groups and asked them how strongly they approved of each person or group. The scale of approval runs from one to four, where one means "disapprove strongly" and four means "approve strongly" (see Figure 6.1).

Large majorities of each ideological group disapprove of two cases: Fidel Castro and the Sandinistas. It is notable that there is more consensus among liberals and conservatives on ratings for the two groups than we found on foreign policy issues abstractly considered in the previous chapter. This suggests that liberal disillusion with Castro and the Sandinistas as specific personalities does not generalize to more abstract considerations of foreign policy.

Moreover, it is consistent with the underlying argument made by Paul Hollander in his *Political Pilgrims* (1981) that suspicion of U.S. motives for foreign military intervention is a more general disposition. This interpretation is supported by noting that, by and large, liberals were much more likely to be opposed to military intervention in the Persian Gulf than were conservatives.

Similarly, many of the conservative foundation leaders are not ''moral'' conservatives. A majority disapprove of the Moral Majority, although 28 percent do approve of them, compared to 16 percent of moderates and only 2 percent of liberals. This is consistent with the finding that one-third of conservatives are against allowing prayer in schools.

The approval ratings for the rest are bifurcated along the expected conservative versus liberal divide. In economics, almost nine in ten conservatives and moderates approve of free-market economist Milton Friedman, compared to less than half the liberals. Liberals clearly prefer economist John Kenneth Galbraith, who also receives support from most among the other two groups. Not surprisingly, 91 percent of liberals also approve of consumer advocate Ralph Nader, compared to roughly three in five moderates and only one-third of conservative foundation leaders.

In the realm of foreign affairs, all conservatives and almost nine in ten moderates approve of Margaret Thatcher; the majority of liberals disapprove of her. Almost 90 percent of conservatives (and a slight majority of moderates) also approve of former U.N. Ambassador Jeanne Kirkpatrick. In contrast, more than three in five liberals disapprove of her. Liberals overwhelmingly prefer Andrew Young, U.N. ambassador during the Carter presidency; 61 percent of moderates and 49 percent of conservatives also approve of him.

Ronald Reagan, Ted Kennedy, and Gloria Steinem are the most polarizing cases. Roughly nine in ten conservatives approve of Reagan, while roughly nine in ten liberals do not; the moderates fall right in the middle. At the other end of the ideological spectrum, three of four liberals approve of Ted Kennedy, compared to 37 percent of moderates, while more than nine of ten conservatives disapprove of him. Similarly, almost all liberals approve of Gloria Steinem, as do 48 percent of moderates. Roughly seven in ten conservatives disapprove of her.

Goals for the United States

We then asked the foundation elite about their visions of U.S. society, in the form of the most important and least important goals for this country. We then asked the foundation elite to pick the most important, the next most important, and the least important goals for the United States in the next decade (see Figures 6.2 and 6.3).

Consistent with their sharp ideological differences, there is little consensus among the foundation elite about the goals this country should aim for and avoid. In accord with their favorable attitudes toward free-market policies, conservatives and moderates overwhelmingly believe that a high rate of economic growth is far and away the most important goal for the United States, while 16 percent

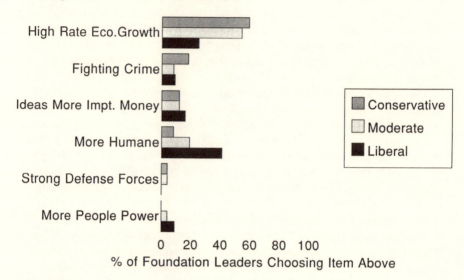

Figure 6.2
Most Important Goals for the United States

High Rate Eco.Growth

Fighting Crime

Ideas More Impt. Money

More Humane

Strong Defense Forces

More People Power

Conservative
Moderate
Liberal

0 20 40 60 80 100
% of Foundation Leaders Choosing Item Above

For exact wording of questions, see Appendix 4.

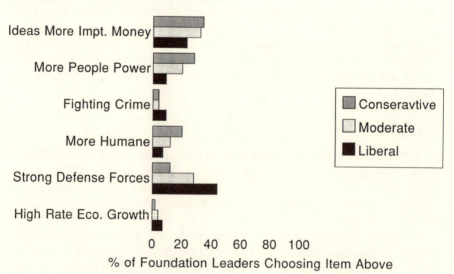

Figure 6.3
Least Important Goals for the United States

Ideas More Impt. Money

More People Power

Fighting Crime

More Humane

Strong Defense Forces

High Rate Eco. Growth

Conseravtive
Moderate
Liberal

0 20 40 60 80 100
% of Foundation Leaders Choosing Item Above

For exact wording of questions, see Appendix 4.

more conservatives and 23 percent more moderates make it their second most important goal.

A plurality of liberals, however (41 percent), think the country should work toward a less impersonal, more humane society as its most important goal; and an additional 30 percent believe this should be the United States' second most important goal. Yet one-fifth of conservatives think it the least important. Another difference between liberals and conservatives is that while only 9 percent of liberals list more power to people at work and in communities as the most important goal, one-quarter list this goal as the second most important goal. By contrast, no conservatives select this as their most important goal, and a scant 4 percent list this as their second most important goal for the United States.

Liberals oppose conservatives and moderates on the issues of national defense and reducing the crime rate. A total of 44 percent of liberals believe it to be the least important goal for this country. Only 28 percent of moderates and 12 percent of conservatives agree. While conservatives, moderates, and liberals give little support to fighting crime as the most important goal, 31 percent of conservatives and 19 percent of moderates think it the second most important goal, while only 11 percent of liberals feel similarly. No conservatives, moderates, or liberals value progressing toward a society where ideas are more important than money. However, one-third of conservatives rate this as their least important goal, while only 23 percent of liberals do likewise.

Power in America

We asked the foundation elite to rate the position in U.S. society of a number of different groups and institutions on two different scales. Respondents were first asked to describe how much influence they thought each group does have and, second, how much influence they believed each group *should* have. Groups were rated on a scale ranging from one to seven, where a score of one means having very little influence and a score of seven means having a great deal of influence (see Figures 6.4–6.6).

With some notable exceptions, perceptions of who *has* power are not affected by ideology. Thus, nearly all conservatives, moderates, and liberals alike believe that the news media are the most highly influential institution in the United States. Conservatives, moderates, and liberals alike also generally believe that religious leaders, intellectuals, black leaders, and feminists lack influence (although conservatives and liberals view them as having significantly less power than do moderates). They all view foundations (i.e., themselves) as having little power. This modest view should not be taken as disingenuous. Rather, it is the mark of strategic elites in modern democratic society, as opposed to traditional ruling classes, to view themselves as relatively powerless in the face of other competing institutions. There is a second reason for this apparently modest estimation. Generally the differences that exist among conservatives, moderates, and liberals are due to the fact that all groups tend to perceive institutions they support as

Figure 6.4
Influence in the United States: Views of the Conservative Foundation Elite

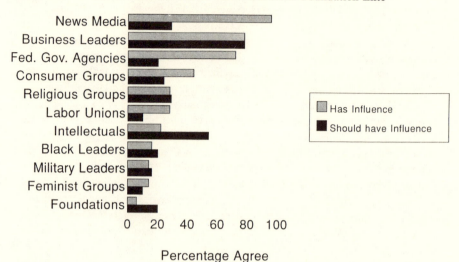

Percentage Agree

Figure 6.5
Influence in the United States: Views of the Moderate Foundation Elite

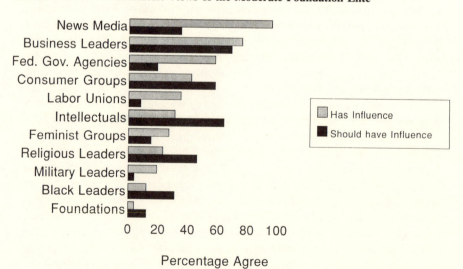

Percentage Agree

Figure 6.6
Influence in the United States: Views of the Liberal Foundation Elite

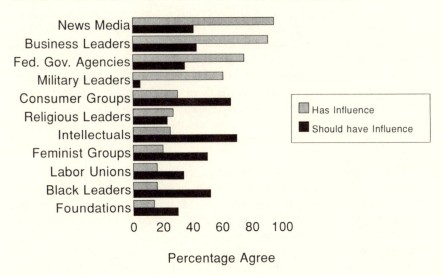

Percentage Agree

less powerful than institutions they oppose. For example, conservatives view consumer groups and labor unions as more powerful than do liberals, while the latter are more likely to view business as powerful than are either conservatives or moderates. Thus, considerably more liberals (91 percent) than conservatives (78 percent) and moderates (76 percent) see business leaders as highly influential. Roughly 40 percent of conservatives and moderates see consumer groups as powerful, while only 30 percent of liberals agree. Conservatives and moderates view labor as wielding more power than do liberals.

The widest gap in the perception of great influence concerns the place of the military. While only 14 percent of conservatives and 19 percent of moderates view the military as having a great deal of influence, 61 percent of liberals believe the same.

Perceptions of who *should* have power are more closely related to ideological belief. We expect liberals to devalue those groups associated with foreign policy hawkishness and with unrestricted capitalism (the military and business) and to favor, more than conservatives, strengthening those groups supportive of egalitarian social reform movements: consumer groups, feminists, and blacks. By and large, this is what we find. Thus, two-thirds of the liberals believe that the military should have so little influence in the United States that it becomes the least influential group in society. By contrast, conservatives see the military as having little influence and want them to remain that way, but they want the military to have somewhat more influence than do liberals. Not surprisingly, conservatives and moderates would prefer federal government agencies to be significantly less influential than they are now. Liberals are more sympathetic to government power.

As expected, large majorities of conservatives and moderates think that the business elite has a great deal of power and that it should continue to do so. Conversely, most liberals want business to have significantly less influence than it does at present.

Conservatives differ from moderates and liberals on the ranking of consumer groups. Most conservatives would prefer them to continue to have little influence, while a majority of moderates and liberals would prefer consumer groups to have a great deal of influence. Conservatives and moderates would also like to see labor become significantly less influential, while liberals would give labor a bit more power.

The three groups exhibit the same pattern of preferences for black leaders and feminists, with liberals wanting blacks and feminists to have much influence, ranking them behind only consumer groups and intellectuals, while conservatives and moderates prefer that they have less, although moderates would give blacks more power than they think they have now.

Conservatives, moderates, and liberals generally agree that religious leaders should not have much influence in the United States, and they all want to see media influence significantly decline, although liberals are less likely to feel this way than are conservatives and moderates. All three groups, however, believe that intellectuals should have significantly more influence than they presently have. Liberals desire to make intellectuals the most influential group in this country, while moderates and conservatives rank them second. Finally, all three groups wish that foundations had somewhat more influence, but none desire to substantially increase the power of foundations.

Rating the Media

We asked the foundation elite to rate the reliability of various news sources and journals of opinion on a scale of one (not at all reliable) to seven (very reliable). We also report the percentages of those who regard themselves as unfamiliar with the news outlet or journal of opinion in question (see Figures 6.7–6.8).

Almost all members of the foundation elite have some opinion on the standard media outlets (PBS, television news, the *New York Times*, the weekly news magazines, and the *Washington Post*). An interesting finding, not anticipated, is that conservatives are less likely to be familiar with the intellectual journals of opinion, even those like *Commentary* or *The Public Interest* that are sympathetic to their point of view, than are either moderates or liberals. Most conservatives are only familiar with the *National Review*. Ironically, significantly more conservatives could rank the reliability of the *New Republic* and the *New York Review of Books* than could rate *Commentary* and the *Public Interest*. In

Figure 6.7
News Sources: Familiarity

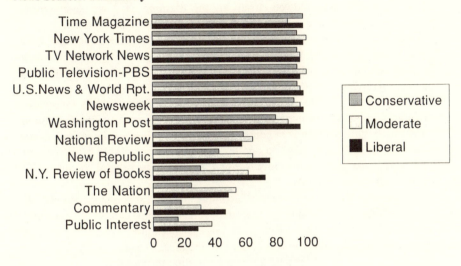

Percentage Familiar with Source

Figure 6.8
News Sources: Reliability

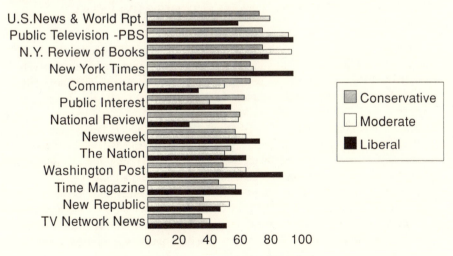

Percentage Think Reliable Source

every case, more liberals and moderates than conservatives could rank these opinion magazines.

Of the more popular media sources, almost all liberals and moderates believe PBS to be a reliable news source, and almost all liberals think the same about the *New York Times*, followed closely by the *Washington Post*. Most conservatives agree about the *Times* and PBS, but in far smaller proportions.

Large majorities of all three ideological groups also believe the *New York Review of Books* and the three weekly news magazines to be reliable, although more conservatives than liberals think U.S. News to be reliable. More liberals than conservatives favor *Newsweek*.

As we expected, more conservatives and moderates than liberals favor conservative journals of opinion, while the opposite is the case of liberal opinion journals. Roughly two-thirds of conservatives and half the moderates think *Commentary* is reliable, compared to one-third of liberals. A total of 60 percent of conservatives and moderates think *National Review* to be reliable, compared to roughly one in four liberals.

The *Nation* and the *Public Interest* are interesting cases. A majority of liberals and conservatives believe both journals to be reliable. Some conservatives clearly assume that the *Nation* is a conservative journal of opinion, while some liberals assume the *Public Interest* to be liberal, thus the more unusual results. Very few members of the foundation elite are familiar with either journal.

Television network news ranks at the very bottom. Most moderates and conservatives think television news to be an unreliable source of information, and only a bare majority of liberals think it reliable.

IDEOLOGY, THE RULING CLASS, AND THE ADVERSARY CULTURE

The polarized ideology of the foundation elite suggests that neither a simple model of the ruling elite (where the foundation elite would be more cohesively conservative) nor of the rise of philanthropic leaders as a new adversarial elite (where they would be, on the whole, ideologically liberal) gives us a complete picture.

The weaknesses of the ruling elite model are multiple. It fails to take into account the liberalism of a substantial percentage of the foundation elite.[2] Moreover, there is, at best, a weak relationship between social mobility and political ideology. Those born in higher status families are *not* more conservative. If we use mean attitude scores, we find no relationship between current ideology and either father's occupation or family income while growing up. If we use self-identified ideology, we find a weak relationship between family income when growing up and ideology ($r = -.16, p \leq .05$) but none between current ideology and father's occupation.[3]

The relationship between current income and ideology further depends upon whether we use current personal income or current family income. Personal income and ideology are weakly correlated for both self-identified ideology and mean ideological score ($r = -.16$, $p \leq .05$; $r = -.21$, $p \leq .01$). Neither measure of ideology, however, correlates with current family income ($r = .00$, $r = .01$). In short, the results of the eight relationships examined here are consistently weak enough to conclude that socioeconomic status is not significantly related to ideology.

The adversary culture model, however, is also incorrect on several points. As discussed earlier, it consists of two parts. The first is that the foundation leaders are to be thought of as a strategic elite, while the second is that its members are permeated by the adversary culture. The weaknesses of the ruling class model of philanthropy provide additional support for the view that philanthropic leaders are a strategic elite. However, the attitudinal data at least partly confute a simple adversary culture model. First, a plurality of the sample are self-identified conservatives, and a clear majority do not define themselves as liberals. Second, none of the conservatives, moderates, or liberals espouse a high degree of system alienation. However, it is true that the substantial polarization of the foundation elite along with the collectivist liberalism, foreign policy, and crime dimensions shows a substantial minority who embrace some aspects of the adversary culture.

At best, there seems to be a considerable degree of value pluralism within the foundation elite, at least at the level of political opinions. Moreover, the foundation leaders shape their views of various leaders, news and information, goals for society, and perceptions of power along the lines of their political attitudes.

To what extent does political ideology structure their visions of the philanthropic mission? Is the ethos of the foundation professional colored by political ideology? As we stated earlier it would be naive to think that foundation work remains distinct from members' values. On the other hand, a profession's mores can check political biases. Professional mores, for example, keep most journalistic endeavors either objective or balanced. The media data do show however that bias occurs, and when it occurs, news stories almost always slant in a liberal direction—thus fitting the conventional (and liberal) world view of the media elite (see Lichter, Rothman, and Lichter, 1986).

The next chapter looks at a relatively unexplored topic, a quantitative analysis of the attitudes that make up the philanthropic ethos. Because the issues vital to the foundation world are almost totally unknown to those outside it, we first look at what these critical issues are. We then show the aspects of the foundation ethos that exist independent of ideology and those that are merely projections of one's political views. Clearly, if most philanthropic principles substitute for political views, then the foundation leaders are a highly politicized elite.

We elaborate upon three dimensions of the professional ethos of foundations: the ideology of the independent sector; the ideology of voluntarism-progressivism; and the ideology of foundation innovation. These dimensions have their roots in the historical changes described in chapter two and, as we show, are associated with the spending preferences of the foundation elite. We shall also explore the relationship among these three dimensions and the staff-trustee relationship within our sample.

NOTES

1. "Ideology also can mean visionary speculation and idle theorizing" (*Webster's Third International Dictionary*, definition of "ideology"), and *ideologist* can imply one who is utopian, dogmatic, impractical, and coercive in thought and behavior (Geertz, 1973, p. 194). *Ideology* can also mean a well-integrated set of political assertions, ideas, and goals, forming an explicit party program. An example is the programmatic platforms of notably "ideological parties," often found among European party systems but less so in the United States.

2. Due to the confidentiality requirements of our survey, we were unable to ask respondents to identify their exact position and duties within the foundation. All we know is that every respondent was either an officer or a board member of one of the foundations in our sampling frame.

3. We asked for father's occupational status (recoded into upper white-collar, lower white-collar, and blue-collar) and respondent's family income when growing up (well below average, below average, average, above average, and well above average).

CHAPTER 7

FOUNDATIONS, PROFESSIONALISM, AND THE ORGANIZATIONAL DILEMMA

The New Deal broke the near monopoly of private benevolence. From then on, philanthropy became the handmaiden of the welfare state. By the mid-sixties, the conventional wisdom viewed philanthropy as creating pilot programs for government to take over.

The fiasco of the Reece Commission destroyed any possibility of a cogent conservative response to liberal philanthropy. Richard Cornuelle's *Reclaiming the American Dream* (1965), generally an unknown book, is the only conservative analysis of philanthropy written during that period. Cornuelle argues that the conservative response to the liberal foundations was mostly negative. Despite articulate opposition to big government and the expanding welfare state, conservatives offered no ideas to replace it. Waldemar Nielsen summarizes the condition of conservative philanthropy: "Most conservative donors did not give to public policy work at all. As one fund raiser for right-wing causes complained at the time, 'H. L. Hunt would invite you to lunch and give you a ham sandwich out of his desk' " (1985, p. 43).

This changed in the late 1970s and 1980s with a new twofold conservative response. The first was (and is) to encourage private philanthropy as a substitute for government funding. The second was (and still is) to fund research and activities supportive of the conservative cause, in such fields as economics, public law, human rights, and foreign policy.

Despite the conservative revival, many prominent scholars and professionals in the foundation world still view foundation activism as funding pilot programs for government action. In the search to be programmatically innovative, many foundations have come to fund projects that seek massive changes in U.S. society. The irony is that foundations are the products of the U.S. capitalist system, created by wealthy individuals or as adjuncts to large corporations. While many have commented on this irony, none has explained it satisfactorily.

This chapter begins by examining the different components of the philanthropic ethos and the spending priorities of the foundation elite. We find significant differences in how conservatives, moderates, and liberals view foundation culture and what they think should be funded. Statistically we find three dimensions of foundation culture: independent sector, voluntarism-progressivism, and foundation innovation. We also find three dimensions of spending priorities: research spending, health and welfare spending, and spending for social change.

We then examine the relationship among foundation ethos, funding priorities, and political ideology. We find that political ideology lies at the core of foundation members' beliefs about foundation norms and spending preferences. The more liberal respondents favor more foundation innovation and spending for social change. Last, we examine the relationship between these concepts and the internal organization of foundations. We find that the more liberal leaders are associated with foundations where staff have more power.

This chapter demonstrates how a politically liberal, significant number among the foundation elite are on the cutting edge of social change. They challenge traditional foundation culture and advocate major reforms in the foundation world itself. They also favor increasing funding for social change, in terms of direct aid to marginal groups (e.g., blacks, gays, women) and, more important, increasing their power (e.g., through improving access to legal services).

Their inclination to rely on foundation professionals is the result of their political liberalism, but only because a trusted staff taps into their attitudes of alienation, collectivist liberalism, anti–law and order, and pro–affirmative action. Their attitudes toward giving are not related to their views on issues of expressive individualism or foreign policy.

The next section begins with a discussion of foundation mores. We first look at what conservative, moderate, and liberal foundation leaders think about foundations.

THE ETHOS OF FOUNDATIONS

Despite much writing on the concept of philanthropy, the "culture of philanthropy," and the "professionalization of foundation work," there have been few systematic attempts to survey those in the foundation world about these matters. How many of them hold to these norms? Do they hold a unique set of attitudes and beliefs that set their work apart from individual charity?

To see if our respondents hold these beliefs about foundations, we presented them with a series of statements drawn from the scholarly and professional literature on foundations. For each item, we asked them to select the choice that corresponds most closely to their opinion: strongly agree, somewhat agree, somewhat disagree, or strongly disagree. We first present our results in the form of individual questions. We follow it with our results of a more complex statistical analysis, which yields three distinct dimensions of foundation culture.

Before we present these results, however, we must address another more basic issue. The guiding assumption of this study is the importance of the adversary culture to the foundation elite. This runs contrary to the idea that working in a foundation as a "philanthropoid" is an emerging profession.

The conventional wisdom regarding U.S. professions is that the mores of any professional group (e.g., medicine, law, science) are independent of its members' political views. The qualities that make a good lawyer, doctor, or scientist are not due to the person's political liberalism or conservatism. For the most part, that is such an unquestioned assumption regarding the traditional professions that most scholars do not even ponder any causal connection between the two.[1]

Robert Lerner and Stanley Rothman (1989; 1991), however, find that journalists' professional self-conceptions are influenced at least in part by their political views. If journalists' political views affect their professional beliefs, are foundation leaders influenced by their political views when thinking about philanthropy? Table 7.1 shows the distribution of opinion about foundations, at points comparing ideological conservatives, moderates, and liberals.

Foundation Autonomy

Despite their political differences, foundation leaders generally agree on questions of foundation autonomy. Nearly all respondents think foundations do a reasonably good job; only 6 percent of conservatives and liberals, and 4 percent of moderates think that most foundations do more harm than good.

Additionally, the foundation elite as a group have a coherent "third-sector ethos." Most foundation leaders see the role of foundations as providing a safety net against the harshness of *laissez-faire* capitalism. A majority of conservatives and moderates and two of three liberals believe that foundations ought to make up for the shortcomings of the private sector. A majority of each group also think that foundations should do the same for government programs. As proponents of philanthropic autonomy, most members of the foundation elite dislike the idea of greater government regulation of foundations. However, 9 percent of the liberals support such regulation, while none of the conservatives are sympathetic.

Foundation Mores

Personal voluntarism is an integral part of the U.S. tradition but is no longer thought to be the best way of handling massive societal problems. Foundation leaders still think that personal giving and community service are good things to do, but roughly one in three surprisingly do not think the practice should be demanded of their employees. About two-thirds of each group believe that those who work for foundations should also do volunteer work on their own time.

Table 7.1
Ideology and Philanthropic Ethos

	Percentage Agree		
	con	mod	lib
Philanthropic foundations should make up for the shortcomings of the private sector.	58	50	68
Philanthropic foundations should make up for the shortcomings of government programs.	52	46	53
There should be greater government regulation of philanthropic foundations.	0	4	9
Today, most philanthropic foundations support the status quo.	29	38	64
Philanthropic foundations should primarily fund projects that have the potential for large societal impact.	55	65	67
When funding academic projects, philanthropic foundations should support only those that are objective and unbiased.	50	72	57
On the whole, most philanthropic foundations do more harm than good.	6	4	6
Philanthropic foundations should primarily fund projects where the philosophical orientation of the grantee matches that of the foundation.	61	35	36
In making grants, the intentions of the original donor should be strictly followed.	84	73	47
There should be minimum standards of philanthropic giving for foundations.	61	65	80
Foundation assets should be invested only in companies that are socially responsible, even if it results in smaller earnings.	24	35	58
Foundation employees should be encouraged to do volunteer work on their own time.	63	66	76

Liberals are somewhat more likely to agree to this than are conservatives or moderates, but the difference is not statistically significant.

Despite their aversion to government regulation, most members of the foundation elite also support the issue of minimum standards for giving, which noted liberal "philanthropoids" have encouraged since the mid–1960s. James Joseph, the current president of the Council of Foundations (the trade organization for foundations), argues for minimum standards for foundation administration and grant making. Marvin N. Olasky, historian and professor of journalism, describes Joseph as "to the political left of his liberal predecessors" (1985, p. 23). In 1980, a statement entitled "Recommended Principles and Practices for Effective Grantmaking'' was adopted by the council's board of directors. By 1983, adhering to the statement became a condition for foundation membership in the council (see Olasky, 1985, for a long discussion of the Council of Foundations and capsule biographies of its leaders, past and present).

Olasky writes extensively about the issue of foundation standards. He contends that minimum standards of performance established by the council would most probably result in converting philanthropic foundations into private governments. For example, one likely standard would be the proportional representation of minorities and women among board members.

When the Council of Foundations attempted to impose standards in the 1980s, the John M. Olin Foundation objected to council requirements. In particular, the foundation rejected adoption of the stated principle that ''each individual foundation must serve the public interest'' (Olasky, 1988, p. 2). According to Michael Joyce, Olin's executive director at that time, the principle invites someone to define the public interest and force those who do not conform into a particular mold. ''If like government, they must serve the public interest, there is no reason why their funds should not be disbursed by government'' (quoted in Olasky, 1988, p. 2). The foundation withdrew from the council but later rejoined when the issue was dropped.

Proportionately more liberals support the notion that the foundations should support the public interest than do either conservatives or moderates. Conservative support for standards of giving, however, is an unexpected finding. We believe they have not thought through the implications of such requirements, especially if not imposed by the foundation itself but by an outside body such as the Council of Foundations or the federal government.

Foundations as Social Problem Solvers

Wealthy donors originally created foundations to find solutions to large-scale social problems rather than merely to offer charity. Our sample of foundation leaders plainly supports the notion of philanthropy as enabling massive social change rather than merely providing charity and amelioration. For example, 55 percent of conservatives and two of three moderates and liberals want to fund projects that have large-scale impact.

Many foundation leaders no longer hold to the Progressivist conviction of using university-based knowledge to solve problems. Only a bare majority of conservatives and liberals support unbiased research (our own bias is such that we expect nearly all respondents to claim to support it). This is a clear departure from the 1950s. At that time, the famous liberal foundations (e.g., Carnegie, Ford, and Rockefeller) gave enormous sums for research in both the natural and social sciences to further societal problem solving, while the more conservative foundations supported such projects as buildings and libraries.[2]

Democratizing the Foundations

Conservatives, moderates, and liberals are sharply polarized on the questions we group together under the rubric "democratizing the foundation from within." For example, conservatives and moderates disagree strongly with liberals on whether foundations support the status quo. Reflecting the polarization within the foundation world, roughly two out of three liberals believe that foundations support the status quo, compared to only 29 percent of conservatives.

The issue of "socially responsible investment" also sharply divides conservatives from liberals. Socially responsible investment is another key issue raised among foundation leaders in the 1980s, especially concerning divesting from companies that invest in South Africa. Following the lead of many universities and corporations (e.g., Ford, Coca Cola, and IBM), the Council of Foundations and its president, James Joseph, encouraged foundations to do the same (Olasky, 1988). Joseph also suggested ten guidelines for those choosing to get involved with opposition South African groups. In his own words, such efforts "may provide the matrix out of which the ingredients of a new political regime will be formed"(Joseph, 1988, p. 49).

On the conservative side of the debate, and in reference to corporate philanthropy, Milton Friedman argues that only individuals, not corporations, have social responsibilities. In a free-enterprise system, the social role of business should be to increase profits (so long as it is done without fraud or deceit), not to engage in "socially responsible behavior" (Friedman, 1970). Following his logic, then, the conservative position would be that the purpose of investing foundation assets would maximize the rate of return on investment assets, not further a political agenda. Not surprisingly, nearly three-fifths of liberals but only 35 percent of moderates and 24 percent of conservatives support the idea that foundation investments should be socially responsible.

The third issue that produces conflict along ideological lines is the issue of donor intent. A full 84 percent of conservatives and 73 percent of moderates but less than a majority of liberals believe that in making grants, foundations should follow the original intent of the donor. This large difference between conservatives and liberals, 37 percentage points, is statistically significant.

The issue of original intent creates more uproar in the foundation world than possibly any other point of contention. The recent Buck Trust case, which the Capital Research Center called "the SuperBowl of probate" (*Organization Trends*, 1986, p. 1), is perhaps the most notorious. The donor, Beryl Buck, stipulated that funds were solely for residents of Marin County, California, and named the San Francisco Foundation as its executors. With the trust, the San Francisco Foundation became the sixth largest foundation in the country. The foundation, however, sought to drop the "Marin only" clause. The public interest law firm, Public Advocates, representing potential recipients from outside Marin County, joined the suit. The courts ruled that the San Francisco Foundation could not change the terms of the will. The court ordered the foundation to petition to resign as the distributor of the trust and ordered Marin County to create the Marin Community Foundation to administer the trust. The bequest reverted to its original purpose: to be used in and for the benefit of Marin County (*Organization Trends*, 1986, p. 1).

The Buck Trust case is unique, however. Other cases do not involve attempts to change the conditions of the will. Had the San Francisco Foundation won its suit, the foundation world would tilt even more to the left.

Most disputes over interpreting donor intent are the result of the vagueness of donors' wills. Although such vagueness allows executors to change with the times, it also allows them to violate the spirit if not the letter of the endowment bequest. For example, Andrew Carnegie granted the trustees of the Carnegie Corporation "full authority to change policy or causes hitherto aided, from time to time, when this, in their opinion, has become necessary or desirable. They shall best conform to my wishes by using their own judgment" (Wooster, 1990). Carnegie was, according to Martin Morse Wooster, "an articulate champion of free enterprise and opponent of government" (1990, p. 1).

By the mid–1980s, the Carnegie Corporation, in the spirit of the times, was at the cutting edge of funding social change. Nielsen describes the Carnegie Corporation as "the quintessential liberal, activist, entrepreneurial foundation: more a combat force than a conventional charity" (1985, p. 134). Its grant recipients include the Children's Defense Fund, the National Council of La Raza, the Council on Economic Priorities, and the Arms Control Association (Wooster, 1990, p. 2; Foundation Center, 1988, p. 69)—groups hardly in favor of reducing the power of government and supporting free-enterprise capitalism.

Trustee fights led to a similar leftward shift in the John D. and Catherine T. MacArthur Foundation. John MacArthur was a noted antigovernment businessman. According to Joshua Muravchik, "to the extent he was [interested in politics], he was known as a conservative with a jaundiced view of taxes and government spending" (1992, p. 35). He left his foundation, however, with no guidelines; "I figure out how to make the money. You fellows will have to figure out how to spend it" (Wooster, 1990, p. 2).

The MacArthur Foundation started out with a few recognized conservatives on its board, including William E. Simon and popular radio commentator Paul Harvey, whose radio broadcasts MacArthur "had sponsored for decades" (Muravchik, 1992, p. 35). Internal battles led to resignations of those trustees who reflected the donor's conservative, antigovernment views. As we see in the next chapter, the MacArthur Foundation, while supporting some conservative recipients, prefers recipients with a liberal or even radical left orientation.[3]

In both the Carnegie Corporation and the John D. and Catherine T. MacArthur Foundation, the trustees today are not going against the terms of the will, just perhaps against the spirit of the donor. That liberals on the whole do not favor adhering to original intent supports Wooster's (1990) contention that the donor's passing liberalizes the foundation.

Conservatives are also much more likely to adhere to the spirit of the donor in yet another way. A total of 61 percent of conservatives think that donees should match the views of the foundation. Most moderates and liberals disagree.

Next we use a more sophisticated statistical analysis to show that some attitudes statistically "coalesce" to form three distinct dimensions of foundation culture: one about the independent sector, one encapsulating the ideals of voluntarism-progressivism, and the third dealing with the issue of foundation innovation. These results parallel our statistical analysis of political attitudes. We use a factor analytic strategy to discern an underlying opinion structure of the "philanthropic ethos" (see Table 7.2).[4] The technique uncovers distinct dimensions that form the central values within the foundation world.

We call the first factor the "independent sector" dimension. It describes the role of foundations vis à vis business and government. The two questions that make up this factor are: (1) foundations should make up for the shortcomings of government and (2) foundations should make up for the shortcomings of the private sector. If an individual receives a high score on this dimension, this means that he or she strongly holds to the creed of the nonprofit sector. A low score suggests some other conception of foundations (perhaps rejecting the notion that foundations should be independent of government).

We call the second factor the "voluntarism-progressivism" dimension. The questions taken as a whole capture the conscientiousness, earnestness, and public spiritedness that came into being during the early part of the 1900s. The Progressive Era orientation of the original philanthropists is manifest here. Items include the belief that foundations exist to solve societal problems and the conviction that philanthropists should set a good personal example besides only bequeathing money. This dimension also expands the early progressivist notion of societal-problem solving and service in the public interest. It incorporates the newer issues of socially responsible investment and developing minimum standards of giving. Both issues indicate a strong desire to act in the proper public spirit.

We call the third factor the "foundation innovation" dimension. The three items loading on this factor are: the intentions of the original donor should (not) be followed in making grants; foundations today mostly support the status quo; and there should be greater government regulation of foundations. If an individual receives a high score on this dimension, he or she strongly believes that philanthropic foundations require massive internal change to be effective agents of social progress. A low factor score conveys the respondent's belief that foundations operate as they are supposed to.[5]

Foundation norms, however, are only one part of our inquiry. In the next section, we turn to what foundation leaders think foundations ought to fund. We first examine differences in priorities as a function of political ideology.

FOUNDATION SPENDING

We asked our foundation executives and board members in which areas they thought foundation spending should be increased, maintained at the same level,

Table 7.2
Dimensions of Foundation Ethos

	Factor Loading
Factor One: Independent Sector	
Foundations should make up for shortcomings of private sector.	.93
Foundations should make up for shortcomings of government.	.83

	Factor Loading
Factor Two: Voluntarism-Progressivism	
Foundation employees should do volunteer work.	.63
Foundation assets should be invested only in socially responsible companies.	.55
Minimum standards of giving for foundations.	.38
Foundations should fund projects with large societal impact.	.36

	Factor Loading
Factor Three: Foundation Innovation	
Most foundations support status quo.	.61
Intentions of original donor should (not) be strictly followed.*	.43
Greater government regulation of foundations.	.42

Questions That Did Not Load

Foundations should only fund academic projects that are objective and unbiased.

On the whole, foundations do more harm than good.

Foundation should fund projects where the philosophy of grantee matches foundation's.

*Question recoded for factor analysis.

or decreased. We presented them with twenty-five different subject areas, some pertaining to research, some not. For each case, the respondent decided whether a certain area (e.g., medical research) should receive more funding, receive the same funds as it does now, or less (see Table 7.3).[6]

Only a few programs elicit support from foundations leaders for increased funding. Most conservatives, moderates, and liberals support more funding for

Table 7.3
Spending Preferences

	con	mod	lib
Medical research			
More	52	43	30
Same	42	43	51
Less	6	13	19
Access to health care			
More	35	56	66
Same	57	34	34
Less	8	9	0
Health care cost containment			
More	51	57	57
Same	39	39	39
Less	10	4	4
AIDS research			
More	36	25	52
Same	56	58	43
Less	8	17	5
Birth control research			
More	25	33	52
Same	58	54	48
Less	17	13	0
Programs for women			
More	16	22	59
Same	54	70	41
Less	30	8	0
Programs for blacks			
More	28	30	70
Same	60	60	30
Less	12	9	0
Programs for gays			
More	4	9	32
Same	34	48	57
Less	62	43	11
Programs for the disabled			
More	36	48	55
Same	60	48	45
Less	4	4	0
Programs for the aged			
More	50	50	59
Same	44	46	32
Less	6	4	9
Access to legal services			
More	10	23	64
Same	68	64	27
Less	22	14	9
Problems of the homeless			
More	54	67	73
Same	32	29	27
Less	14	4	0
International student exchange			
More	10	0	16
Same	68	65	64
Less	22	35	20

Table 7.3 (continued)

```
Initiatives
      More                               14    30    37
      Same                               54    52    56
      Less                               32    17     7
Arms control
      More                               14    30    42
      Same                               48    61    49
      Less                               38     9     9
Human rights
      More                               20    43    59
      Same                               58    48    41
      Less                               22     9     0
Environmental problems
      More                               58    63    77
      Same                               38    33    23
      Less                                4     4     0
Mathematics
      More                               26    26    14
      Same                               58    61    74
      Less                               16    13    12
Genetics research
      More                               29    26    19
      Same                               55    52    72
      Less                               16    22     9
IQ research
      More                                6    17     7
      Same                               50    48    44
      Less                               44    35    49
Nuclear energy
      More                               30    17    19
      Same                               52    48    40
      Less                               18    35    41
Economics
      More                               28    30    20
      Same                               52    60    63
      Less                               20     9    15
Women's studies
      More                                4    13    19
      Same                               52    60    63
      Less                               44    17    19
Sociology
      More                                4     9    14
      Same                               66    65    60
      Less                               30    26    26
Afro-American studies
      More                                2     9    12
      Same                               38    48    65
      Less                               60    44    23
```

health care cost containment, problems of the homeless, the environment, and the aged.

The foundation elite, regardless of ideology, believe the following programs have the right amount of support: international student exchange programs, programs for peace, programs for arms control, and funding for all academic fields except medical research and African American studies. A majority of conservatives support increased funding for medical research, while most moderates and liberals think funding is adequate. A majority of conservatives want to cut funding for African American studies, while moderates and liberals think funding should remain as is.

Other issues also split the foundation elite along ideological lines. Two-thirds of liberals and most moderates favor increasing spending for health care access; a majority of conservatives believe it sufficient. Most liberals favor more funds for AIDS research, birth control research, and programs for women, blacks, and the disabled, compared to much smaller proportions of conservatives and moderates. Almost two-thirds of liberals also support access to legal services, while two-thirds of moderates and conservatives believe support for such programs is currently just about right. More liberals also support human rights programs than do conservatives and moderates.

Three Categories of Spending Preferences

For further analysis, we performed another factor analysis on these spending questions and came up with three spending dimensions (see Table 7.4). The first factor, spending for social change, is comprised of ten different spending programs: spending on blacks, African American studies, women's affirmative action programs, women's studies, human rights, arms control, peace, gays, improving access of the poor to legal services, and sociology.

The second factor is a health and social welfare factor. It is associated with seven different programs. These include spending on the disabled, access to medical care, health care cost-containment, the aged, the homeless, AIDS programs, and spending on the environment. We erroneously assumed that the AIDS programs and spending on disability (especially in the form of a disability rights movement) would also load on the spending-for-social-change dimension. They did not; clearly these are seen as health, not civil rights, issues.

The third factor, research, is a hard science research factor. Five programs appear on this factor. These are mathematics, IQ research, genetic research, nuclear energy, and economics.[7]

Given these three categories of spending preferences (and three dimensions of foundation culture), to what extent then does political ideology affect views on foundations and philanthropic spending? We address this question in the form of a more complicated statistical analysis.

Table 7.4
Dimensions of Foundation Spending

	Factor Loading
Factor One: Spending for Social Change	
Programs for women	.66
Programs for blacks	.63
Programs for gays	.63
Access to legal services	.62
Peace Initiatives	.59
Arms control	.55
Human rights	.66
Women's studies	.62
Sociology	.52
Afro-American studies	.75
Factor Two: Health and Welfare Spending	Factor Loading
Access to health care	.59
Health care cost containment	.40
AIDS research	.38
Programs for the disabled	.66
Programs for the aged	.53
Problems of the homeless	.58
Environmental problems	.43
Factor Three: Hard Science Research	Factor Loading
Mathematics	.55
Genetics research	.61
IQ research	.68
Nuclear energy	.54
Economics	.52

Items that did not load: International student exchange programs, birth control research, medical research.

IDEOLOGY, FOUNDATION NORMS, AND SPENDING PRIORITIES

We first examine the simple relationship between political ideology and each dimension of foundation ethos. We then examine the relationship between political ideology and each dimension of foundation spending. Last, we impose statistical controls to see if ideology has an independent effect upon biases in spending. When we do so, we find that political liberalism is the guiding value behind the professional norms of voluntarism-progressivism and of foundation innovation. Political liberalism is also central to increasing support for social change funding while decreasing support for hard science research.

Creating an Ideology Score

Before we analyze the data (using a multivariate regression equation), we need to simplify the number of variables, especially in the case of political ideology. As discussed in chapter five, we discovered six independent dimensions of political liberalism. To sum up the findings of these dimensions for each survey respondent, we calculated individual "ideology scores" for each respondent. These scores were computed as follows.

We used only those attitude questions that make up the dimension of liberalism. We gave the most liberal responses for each attitude a high score of 4 and gave the most conservative response a 1. For example, on the question of abortion rights, a response that strongly agrees with a woman's right to choose was given a 4; one that somewhat agrees received a 3; somewhat disagree received a 2; and strongly disagree received a 1.

To obtain a respondent's overall mean score, we summed the scores of all the questions for each respondent and then gave him or her an overall mean score, which we computed by dividing that respondent's sum by the number of questions used. Thus, a respondent's mean score of 1.00 means that our respondent gave the most conservative response on every question, while the "pure" liberal respondent would receive a score of 4.00.

We use an individual's mean score of political ideology for the rest of the analysis. These ideological scores correlate highly with respondents' self-picked ideological labels ($r = .76$).[8] Such a high correlation between labels and specific attitudes is relatively rare. For the general public, ideological labels have little to do with political attitudes. This means that the public on the whole is non-ideological and politically unsophisticated (e.g., Converse, 1964). They are unable to attach specific beliefs to general ideological labels. In the case of the foundation elite, however, their ideological labels match extremely well with positions on particular issues. Compared to the general public, they are very ideologically sophisticated.

The next section looks at the simple relationship among ideology, the three dimensions of foundation culture, and the three types of spending priorities.

Bivariate Relationships

Political liberalism is associated with two of three dimensions of foundation culture. It is not related to the independent sector dimension but correlates with increasing foundation innovation and voluntarism-progressivism. In the former case, the more liberal one is, the more one believes that the foundation world itself must be changed. This includes the belief that the original intentions of the foundation donor need *not* be binding, that foundations mostly support the status quo, and that there should be greater government regulation of foundations.

Increasing political liberalism also correlates with increasing voluntarism-progressivism. That is, the more liberal a person is, the more he or she thinks that foundation employees should be encouraged to volunteer on their own time, that foundation assets should be invested in socially responsible companies, that there should be minimum standards of philanthropic giving, and that foundations should primarily fund projects with potentially large-scale societal impact.[9]

In terms of spending biases, increasing political liberalism positively correlates with spending for social change, but negatively with spending for hard science research. In other words, the more liberal a person is, the more he or she favors increasing spending on women, blacks, gays, and peace, but the more he or she also wants to cut spending on mathematics, nuclear energy, genetics, IQ research, and economics.

The dimensions, voluntarism-progressivism and foundation innovation also correlate with a preference for social change spending. These findings raise the possibility that the more one believes in the ''foundation ethos,'' the more one desires to increase spending for social change. In other words, does merely being an integral part of the foundation world raise the chances of someone favoring massive social change?

This brings us back to the question raised at the beginning of this chapter. Recall that political liberalism correlates with voluntarism-progressivism and foundation innovation, while all three independent variables correlate with wanting to increase social change spending. Does increasing political liberalism make one hold a more progressivist world view, favor change within the foundation world, and thus advocate increasing spending for large-scale change? Or does commitment to a progressivist orientation and an orientation toward change in foundation work first lead to being liberal and, in turn, to favoring foundation spending for social change? The next section presents our statistical treatment of these three correlates of social change spending.

Multivariate Analysis: Liberalism and Social Change

Table 7.5 presents a regression equation that looks at the combined effects of political liberalism and each of the dimensions of foundation culture upon social change spending, spending for hard science research, and spending for health and welfare. When controlling for all three foundation ethos factors, we find that political liberalism still has a strong, independent effect on favoring social change spending. Moreover, political liberalism is the underlying variable that leads to the linking of both voluntarism-progressivism and foundation innovation to social change spending.

The converse, however, is no longer true. Voluntarism-progressivism and foundation innovation do not influence beliefs about social change spending independent of one's political views. When controlling for political liberalism, the correlation of both voluntarism-progressivism and foundation innovation with social change spending disappears (i.e., they are no longer statistically significant). In sum, political liberalism makes one more inclined to hold progressivist

Table 7.5
Political Liberalism, Foundation Ethos, and Spending Preferences (bivariate correlations)

	Political Liberalism	Indep. Sector	Progres-sivism	Found. Innov.	Social Change	Health& Welfare
Liblism.						
Ind.sec	-.1488					
Progrsm.	.2796*	-.0601				
Innovation	.5278*	.0007	.0927			
Soc.Chn	.6523*	.0116	.2337*	.3587*		
H&Welfare	.1367	-.2149*	.1796	.1436	.1124	
Research	-.2257*	-.0906	.1578	-.1205	.0105	.0117

*N*s range between 100 and 117 depending on which two variables are correlated.
*$p \leq .05$

beliefs about foundations, to advocate change in the foundation world, and to desire more funds for social change.

While they focus solely on public policy funding by the big foundations, Irving Louis Horowitz and Ruth Leonora Horowitz (1970) are correct to associate liberalism and risk-taking behavior among foundations. A relationship between political liberalism and foundation innovation, however, suggests that political liberalism drives organizational as well as programmatic risk taking in the foundation world.

Conservative critics of foundations are, thus, right to talk about the more liberal to radical underpinnings of such instances as the Buck Trust case. Our analysis shows that a desire for institutional innovation pushes the foundation into areas and practices that many original donors (who are ideological conservatives) may find questionable, if not abhorrent. The more politically conservative members of the foundation elite in our statistical analysis do not like change, whether it be organizational structure or foundation grant making.

Ideology, Foundation Culture, and Support for the Sciences

In a second regression analysis, we find that the more politically conservative members of the foundation elite do not automatically reject the world view of modern, scientific philanthropy, although political ideology does correlate with voluntarism-progressivism at the simple bivariate level. We ran another regression equation using our variables, political ideology, and the three dimensions

Table 7.6
Determinants of Spending Preferences (unstandardized regression coefficients)

| | Spending Preferences | | |
	Soc.Chn	Research	Health & Welfare
Political Liberalism	1.0926*	-.5071*	.2671
Foundation Ethos			
Progressivism	.1120	.2767*	.1541
Independent sector	.1125	-.1309	-.1574
Foundation Innovation	.1081	.0559	-.0237
R^2	.4228*	.1121*	.0881

$N = 95$
*$p \leq .05$

of foundation ethos. This time, we examined their impact on increased funding for hard science research.

Controlling for the foundation ethos variables, political ideology is related to funding for hard science research, but the relationship is an inverse one. The more politically liberal a person is, the less likely he or she is to promote funding of scientific research.

The negative relationship between support for hard science research and political liberalism deserves some additional comment. Additional analyses show that political liberalism is also *negatively* related to the belief that foundations should support only unbiased, objective research, when controlling for the foundation ethos dimensions.

At the simple bivariate level, support for unbiased academic research is somewhat, albeit not statistically significantly, negatively correlated with liberalism (see Table 7.6). However, when we control for voluntarism-progressivism, a strong, negative, and statistically significant relationship between liberalism and support for unbiased and objective research emerges.[10]

We believe this finding reflects the historical changes of the 1960s and their impact on foundation practices. Many case histories of the large foundations before the 1960s discuss the extensive large-scale support for the hard sciences and social sciences by the large, liberal foundations, most notably Ford, Carnegie, and Rockefeller foundations, while conservative foundations stay away from funding research (e.g., Nielsen, 1972; 1985).

More generally, the foundation case histories show that leaders of liberal foundations of the 1950s and 1960s worked alongside those in government and various nonprofit groups. They were strong believers in improving the human condition through the growth of scientific knowledge.

This orientation toward public policy formation was epitomized by the New Deal and reached its height during the Great Frontier and the early Great Society eras. Such support is very much a part of the history of modern foundations. It goes back to the early part of this century, with the early foundations helping to create the modern research university. Our survey shows that those who wish that foundations would move back to more ameliorative spending have little support among the foundation elite, even among its politically conservative members.

The tradition of progressivism, independent of political beliefs, also leads foundations to support research in the hard sciences. As discussed above, statistically the simple bivariate relation between progressive orientation and spending on hard science research is not significant (see Table 7.7). However, when controlling for political ideology, the relationship becomes statistically significant. In other words, political ideology acts as a suppressor variable with respect to the true, positive relationship between the foundation ethos variable voluntarism-progressivism and support for hard science.

Ideology, Philanthropic Culture, and Spending on Health and Welfare

The relationship among political ideology, foundation ethos, and spending on health and welfare programs has its own distinctive pattern. Like the independent sector dimension of foundation culture, favoring increasing spending for health and welfare is not related to any other variable. Political liberalism, progressivism, or foundation innovation does not show any relationship to a desire to increase health and welfare spending. This is true when we simply correlate these independent variables with health and welfare spending and when we enter these variables into a more complex regression equation.

This suggests that support for health and social welfare programs does not come from political beliefs or any of the beliefs associated with foundation culture. Increasing spending for health and welfare programs cuts across ideological lines.

Summary: The Politicization of Foundation Culture

The foundation innovation factor, thus, reflects in pure form the entry of the 1960s adversary culture into the foundation world. As recounted anecdotally (e.g., Nielsen, 1985; Odendahl, 1990, pp. 163–208), many foundation leaders with these beliefs are highly dissatisfied with what they see as the complacent foundation establishment. They seek dramatic change not only in terms of what foundations support, but also in terms of the philanthropic institution itself.

Table 7.7

A Statistical Analysis of Progressivism, Political Ideology, and Support for Unbiased Research

	Bivariate Correlations	
	Progssvsm.	Political Liberalism
Progressivism		
Liberalism	.2796* (n=107)	
Unbiased Res.	.3850** (n=117)	-.1376 (n=110)

Regression Coefficients between Progressivism, Political Liberalism, and Unbiased Research	
	Unbiased Research
Progressivism	.5943**
Liberalism	-.5542**
R^2	.2487**

$n = 107$
*$p \leq .05$
**$p \leq .001$

A desire for dramatic change expresses itself in support for programs such as those for gays, blacks, women, access to the legal system, and the peace movement. As Teresa Odendahl (1990) discovers, most donors do not advocate such funding, preferring traditional civic projects such as university buildings and hospitals, the arts, and well-known charities or what Waldemar Nielsen (1985) derisively calls the "bricks and mortar" approach to philanthropy.

Odendahl (1990) among others is correct when she claims that long-time participants in philanthropy are not radical opponents of the status quo. Our quantitative results support her contention. A preference for social change spending is *not* the outcome of a progressivist belief system. It is the outcome of contemporary liberal attitudes. Many individuals are liberals, hold beliefs about philanthropy that we label voluntarism-progressivism, and favor social change spending. So the true (non)relationship between voluntarism-progressivism and social change spending only emerges when statistically controlling for ideology. This is why the relationship between voluntarism-progressivism and social change spending, like that between foundation innovation and social change spending, vanishes when controlling for political liberalism.

There is other evidence of an independent dimension stemming from the progressivist tradition. First, the voluntarism-progressivist dimension itself exists independent of political ideology. Second, those liberals and conservatives who share this view of the philanthropic mission support hard science research.

Given the relationship between political liberalism and an orientation toward social change spending, the question is how does such a viewpoint come into being? Nielsen (1985), Horowitz and Horowitz (1970), and Dwight Macdonald (1989) in the mid–1950s all note that the great donors and later the prominent foundations become captive of the wise men around them. In the 1980s and 1990s, this translates into counting on the foundation's professional staff and outside grant reviewers. We believe that the more liberal respondents in our sample are more influenced by their professional staff. The next section examines this general thesis.

POLITICAL LIBERALISM AND TRUSTING STAFF

Critics of foundations, on the left and on the right, often contend that foundations are "naturally" liberal. The causes of foundation liberalism, however, have never been systematically investigated in a large-scale quantitative study.

Why would foundation leaders be responsive to foundation professionals and academic advisors? Some argue that donors are unduly influenced by staff and advisors, hence the foundation moves in a liberal direction. Dwight Macdonald claims that "the great foundations have proved more responsive to the values of the professionals who run them and of the academic community on whose borders they operate than to those of the rich men who founded them" (1989, p. 24). Horowitz and Horowitz also claim that foundations are liberal primarily because they are mainly associated with a constituency "holding attitudes that have been opposed by political groups showing markedly right- or left-wing characteristics" (1970, p. 223).

In our previous work (Nagai, Lerner, Rothman, 1991), we argue, like Horowitz and Horowitz, that foundation liberalism is due to the general structure of foundations. Foundation boards rely upon staff and advisors, who are liberal, for advice and direction in grant making. Additionally, the pool of grant applicants is predominantly liberal. In order to further the public good through private means, which is, after all, the institutional mission of big foundations, foundation executives find themselves coopted into supporting increasingly liberal and sometimes even left-wing projects.

Case studies of particular foundations, however, suggest that political liberalism of trustees, particularly after the death of the donor, is the key factor in foundation liberalism. Trustees rely upon their more liberal advisors and staff because they are already ideologically inclined to do so. The Joan Kroc foundation, which supports peace groups and the environmentalist movement among others, reflects the values of Joan Kroc, widow of Ray Kroc, the founder of the McDonald's fast food chain. The network of alternative foundations for social change reflects the radical beliefs of many postsixties heirs to family fortunes. Odendahl, scholar and former foundation professional, believes that professional staff and advisors exert as much influence as donors (or trustees) allow them to have. "Though they wield much influence, their persuasiveness is dependent on the authority and whims of their employers. Advisers and retainers walk a fine line between the role of servant and that of expert" (Odendahl, 1990, p. 209). Following this line of argument, then, the more liberal trustees are, the more dependent they become on their staff. Which view is correct?

Staff Influence and Ideology

To test the competing views of staff influence, we asked our respondents how much influence officers, trustees, and staff had when deciding which grant proposals their foundations should fund. Respondents based their answers on a seven-point scale, ranging from no influence at all (1) to a great deal of influence (7). An overwhelming majority of respondents (85 percent) claim that their foundation officers are influential (scores of 5, 6, or 7) in deciding who receives funds, including 53 percent who rate their foundation officials as having a great deal of influence (a score of 7). A total of 77 percent also rate board members as influential, although only 38 percent think of them as having a great deal of influence. Last, 57 percent think staff to be influential, and 13 percent think they exert a great deal of influence.[11]

Proportionately more self-identified liberals think their foundation staff to be influential, compared to conservatives and moderates. Also, 71 percent of liberals believe that staff have influence within their foundation, compared to 50 percent of conservatives and 48 percent of moderates. More important, 21 percent of liberals believe that staff exert a great deal of influence over deciding who gets funding, compared to only 6 percent of conservatives and 12 percent of moderates.

We then correlated staff influence with respondents' mean ideology scores.[12] According to Table 7.8, the degree of staff influence positively correlates with political ideology, as measured by these scores. Staff influence also correlates with self-labeled ideology. The more liberal persons among the foundation elite belong to foundations in which staff are more influential in deciding who gets grants.

This finding substantiates a major point made by both views of staff influence. Liberalism and reliance on professional staff institutionally go together. The question remains, however, does relying on staff cause persons to be liberal, or does being liberal incline one to rely on staff? We address the question in a later

Table 7.8
Staff Influence and Its Relationship with Other Variables

Variable	Correlation w/Staff Influence
Political Liberalism Score	0.1672*
Self-labeled Ideology	0.2406*
Independent Sector	0.0686
Voluntarism-Progressivism	0.1575*
Foundation Innovation	0.2132*
Research Spending	-0.1421
Health-Welfare Spending	0.0533
Social Change Spending	0.0385

*$p \leq 0.05$

section. However, let us first outline the relationship between influential staff and foundation ethos.

Staff Influence and Dimensions of Foundation Culture

Critics of foundations cite the need to rely on professional staff so that grant making and other foundation activities will become more professional. For example, the Council of Foundations (the trade association in the foundation world) and the Foundation Center regularly offer programs, provide computerized services, and publish materials on such areas as professional guides for funding by subject area, improving investments and foundation portfolios, and "how to" books on working for a foundation, running it, and serving as a trustee.

Nielsen uses the Robert Wood Johnson Foundation as an example of a large, professional, well-run foundation. The Johnson Foundation was formed in the 1960s and relies on its professional staff's scientific and technical expertise in health care. The donor was the head of the Johnson & Johnson company, which does extensive business in health care. Instead of the common practice of appointing family members, the donor appointed Johnson & Johnson executives, who presumably had some expertise (albeit from the corporate side), to the board of trustees. The foundation appointed as its president the former dean of the Johns Hopkins University Medical School and recruited its technical staff from experts in health care.

The donor and board narrowly define the mission of the foundation as helping set the national health care agenda. The foundation's statement of its beliefs and goals reflects its professionalism: "In pursuit of [its] goals [of bringing better health and medical care to the nation], the Foundation remains flexible in its thinking and closely attuned to society's current health care needs. This confers a timely and significant purpose on its decisions. The Trustees set policy and give approval; the staff searches for and evaluates programs eligible for support" (Robert Wood Johnson Foundation, 1988, p. 1).

Partly as a result of such organization, Nielsen thinks the foundation to be the best around.

[T]he Johnson foundation, judged by the standards of performance normally applicable to foundations, is virtually in a class by itself.

In the clarity and ambitiousness of its purposes, in the intellectual power that has governed its strategy and grant making, in the social sensitivity and political skill by which its programs have been shaped, in the able and creative way in which its programs have been managed, and in the general qualities of integrity and independence that have characterized all it has done, the Robert Wood Johnson Foundation is the best of the big foundations today. (Nielsen, 1985, p. 132)

Odendahl, Elizabeth Troccoli Boris, and Arlene Kaplan Daniels (1985) delineate three models of working in a foundation. In the administrator model, trustees dominate all decision making, and donor wishes decidedly control funding. Employees provide only routine help and information. Trustees examine all grant requests, and only they decide which projects get funded. The director model treats the CEO as a consultant of the board of trustees, but the donor and family still retain much control. Trustees still examine all proposals and allocate funds. The last type, the presidential model, relies on staff; it is the most "professional." Trustees delegate day-to-day operations to foundation employees. They set policy and oversee general programs but do not involve themselves with the bulk of foundation work, which includes funding, except for very large projects. The CEO runs the foundation and sets the organizational tone (e.g., McGeorge Bundy of the Ford Foundation).

This typology yields the following hypothesis: foundations that are more reliant on their staff (i.e., the professional or presidential model) are foundations whose leaders hold more strongly to the philanthropic norms than do other foundation leaders. To test this hypothesis, we correlated staff dependence with our three dimensions of foundation culture: the independent sector dimension, the voluntarism-progressivism dimension, and the foundation innovation dimension.

The hypothesis is partly right. The simple bivariate analysis in Table 7.8 shows that those respondents from foundations more dependent on staff also believe more strongly in voluntarism-progressivism and foundation innovation. Trusting staff does not correlate with the independent sector dimension. Staff reliance, moreover, does not correlate significantly with any dimension of spending preference.

Entering the degree of staff reliance into the regression equation, however, still finds political liberalism to be the single "core" value behind all other relationships (see Table 7.9). Even when controlling for staff influence (along with dimensions of foundation ethos), political ideology is still related to spending favoring social change. More liberal persons strongly favor spending for social change.

The relationship between staff dependence and voluntarism-progressivism van-

Table 7.9

Impact of Ideology, Staff Influence, and Foundation Ethos on Spending Priorities (unstandardized regression coefficients)

| | Spending Priorities | | |
	Research	Health-Welfare	Social Change
Political Ideology	-0.545	0.712	1.060*
Staff Influence	-0.074	0.340	-0.003
Independent Sector	-0.129	-0.168	0.109
Voluntarism- Progressivism	0.312*	0.218	0.135
Social Change	0.103	0.010	0.123

*$p \leq 0.05$

Table 7.10

Relationship Between Staff Influence and Dimensions of Political Ideology

Ideological Dimension	Correlation with Staff Influence
Alienation	0.2074*
Collectivist Liberalism	0.1567*
Expressive Individualism	0.0409
Affirmative Action	0.1909*
Foreign Policy	0.1159
Crime	0.1684*

*$p \leq 0.05$

ishes when controlling for political liberalism. The same is true for staff dependence and foundation innovation. Furthermore, staff dependence still has no relationship with the three types of spending (research, health and welfare, and social change).

In Table 7.10, we break political ideology into its component parts and correlate these dimensions with staff dependence. We find that staff influence is related to some but not all dimensions of liberalism. In foundations with a greater percentage of staff dependence, foundation leaders are more supportive of collectivist liberalism and affirmative action. They are more likely to reject a law-and-order view of the world and are more alienated from the U.S. system.

Our survey clearly shows that among foundation leaders, there are some who indeed support what has been called the adversary culture, and many in the foundation world are quite open about their ideological allegiance. The president of the John Simon Guggenheim Foundation, in fact, proudly proclaims "How I'm PC" (*New York Times*, July 12, 1991, p. A–29). According to Wildavsky, this type of egalitarian culture spreads primarily because an increasing number of political activists, not the general public, hold egalitarian beliefs. These activists now hold these beliefs more intensely than ever before and spread radical egalitarianism by creating new groups and institutions and/or by taking over increasing numbers of established ones.

Our survey shows that some members of the foundation elite are indeed participants in the "egalitarian culture" and think of themselves as needing to be on the cutting edge of societal change. Other (ideologically conservative) foundation leaders plainly oppose it. The question, however, is: do these views get translated into actual funding?

The next chapter deals directly with foundation grant making and ideology. We shall see that only a small proportion of foundations fund politicized grants. Most funding even among these foundations is not derived from an ideological agenda, despite the fact that the foundation elite are an ideologically sophisticated group. However, when the typical foundation gets involved in public policy matters, it most often supports a liberal project (such as reproductive rights) and sometimes prominent liberal recipients such as the American Civil Liberties Union.

NOTES

1. This is not to say that some professionals do not engage in interest group politics on behalf of their profession. They clearly do. However, the degree of political involvement is segmental, is limited to areas of immediate professional concern, and is normally not a requirement for entrance into the profession itself (for a summary of literature on the professions, see Bledstein, 1976, pp. 87–92). It should be added, however, that the politicization of some academic disciplines since the 1960s makes them less professional.

2. It is interesting, though, that 72 percent of the moderates support such research. This may show that moderates are less sure of their views on various issues than are either conservatives or liberals and are more desirous, therefore, of independent support for the positions they do take.

3. For more information on the internal struggles of the John T. and Catherine D. MacArthur Foundation, see Nielsen (1985, pp. 100–115). Similar stories can be written about Joseph Pew and the Pew Charitable Trusts, and Ray Kroc (of McDonald's fame), his widow Joan, and the Joan Kroc Foundation.

4. The twelve questions pertaining to the philanthropic ethos were analyzed using the principal factors technique with a varimax rotation. The factor analysis retained three factors, which together accounted for 49 percent of the variance. Variables were retained on a factor if they had a loading of 0.33 or better. Factor scores were computed using the regression method, retaining all indicators. Three items did not load on the extracted factors.

5. Several questions are independent of (i.e., not statistically correlated with) these dimension of foundation culture. These include questions about funding of unbiased academic projects, matching donee orientation with the foundation's, and whether foundations do more harm than good.

6. For statistical purposes, these were scored as 1 (increase), 2 (stay the same), and 3 (decrease).

7. The twenty-five questions on spending preferences were analyzed using the principal factors technique with a varimax rotation. Three factors were extracted, which

together accounted for 45 percent of the variance. Variables were retained with a 0.38 loading or better. Factor scores were computed using the regression method, retaining all indicators.

8. A question is raised as to why we assign liberal responses higher scores and conservative responses lower scores. We do so primarily to make it consistent with our earlier work. However, insofar as political ideology is an interval and not a ratio variable, the conclusions of any statistical analysis are not affected by the direction in which the scale is scored. Thus we name each of our ideological factors after the "liberal" end of the dimension, and sometimes in the text we refer to political ideology as political liberalism.

9. To make the data analysis easier to follow, these correlations were computed with the signs of the progressivism and the foundation innovation factors reversed so that liberalism would be positively correlated with progressivism and foundation innovation.

10. There is also a statistically significant negative relationship between liberalism and support for medical research that is not shown here ($r = -.17$, $p \leq .05$).

11. Only a few respondents belong to foundations that rely on independent reviewers (thirty-eight). Of these thirty-eight, 45 percent think of them as influential, while only four respondents think of them as very influential.

12. See page 79 on how we created scores.

CHAPTER 8

FOUNDATIONS AND THEIR PUBLIC POLICY GRANTS

So far we have shown that a polarized foundation elite guide philanthropy in the United States. While most members of the foundation elite are either conservative or moderate, a large number appear to be advocates of major social change, for their own world of large-scale philanthropy as well as for U.S. society in general. How do such attitudes, conservative as well as liberal, translate into the reality of grant making?

One might assume that foundations support more conservative than liberal public policy projects. Since the political views of the foundation elite, conservative as well as liberal, extend to other arenas, it is not unreasonable to expect that political views extend to project funding. In reality, however, most projects are not conservative projects. They are either nonideological or liberal. This chapter demonstrates this point, starting with a brief discussion of our procedure of classifying grants.

DEFINITIONS AND PROCEDURES

The procedure we used to study public policy grants is similar (not identical) to the procedure we used to create the sampling frame for the survey. We began with the same 844 foundations that gave $1 million or more in total grants, as noted in the eleventh edition of the *Foundation Directory* (Foundation Center, 1987). We then used the Foundation Center publication *Grant$ for Public Policy and Political Science* (1988), which lists the public policy grants made by each foundation in previous years. With few exceptions, the grants on the Foundation Center's preliminary list of public policy grants were made in 1986 or early 1987.

We excluded grants such as those for buildings, the arts, and hunger or other emergency relief unless the foundation described the grant in terms of its social, political, or economic ramifications.[1] For example, we would not classify a general grant to the local symphony as a public policy grant because it was not worded in terms of its larger implications. We would include that grant in our public policy study if the same foundation earmarked the grant for inner-city residents to equalize access to the arts. The goal would be increasing mass participation, which we think embodies the sociopolitical goal of increasing egalitarianism.

Public policy grants, however, are not merely those that are in subject areas also funded by government. This would lead us to include every grant, including those for schools, the arts and humanities, and the sciences, projects normally not thought to be particularly relevant to public policy. It is more indicative of the increasing nonprofit dependence on government funding than it is of the politicization of public policy issues. Such an approach would also require access to the tax returns of all the 844 foundations. The foundations are required to report *all* their grants. To complete such a study would take us beyond our limited resources and time.

We found that approximately 27 percent of those 844 foundations (225) made at least one public policy grant. This group funded 4,738 grants totaling $386,470,000.

We then categorized the grants according to substantive sphere (international relations, agricultural policy, health, etc.). We also classified them according to whether they were for research, workshops, conferences, or were "action grants." Last we scored them by ideology, using the issues and dimensions of ideology developed in chapter five.

If a grant lacked any explicitly ideological orientation, we scored the grant as ideologically neutral. In a few cases, the grant or recipient had a distinct value orientation but did not fall readily into either the conservative or the liberal camp. These included grants dealing with freedom of religion, support for Israel, and freedom of the press. We classified such grants as "ideological but neither conservative nor liberal."

If, however, a grant had an identifiable ideological slant, we scored it as conservative or liberal, based on matching the description of the grant with our list of conservative and liberal positions along the dimensions described above. Instead of placing the grants on a multipoint ideological scale, we used a simple dichotomy of conservative-versus-liberal. We believed attempting finer distinctions like right, conservative, center-right, center, center-left, liberal, or left would in all probability lack consistency and reliability. The larger the number of categories and distinctions required, the more unreliable the classification scheme would be.

We must also clarify the term *moderate*. We do not believe there is a "moderately" ideological position on any of the issues defined above, except in the following sense. A foundation dispensing no ideological grants of any kind is nonideological, not moderate. A foundation supporting an equal number of liberal and conservative grants would have an ideological score placing it squarely in the center. To the extent we are scoring specific positions, we intend the dichotomous categories "conservative" and "liberal" to be analogous to the standard public opinion categories "agree" and "disagree" and the category of "neutral" akin to the public opinion category of "no opinion" and the unique residual category of "neither."[2]

To determine the ideology of a foundation, as opposed to a grant, we use the average (mean) ideological score of its grants. In other words, we measure the ideological slant of a foundation based on the collective score of the public policy projects that foundation chooses to support.

Before undertaking our data analysis, we must define one more concept—that of a politicized grant. We define politicized grants as those which can be categorized as either liberal or conservative. We do not use the term pejoratively. Aside from the few we were unable to classify as liberal or conservative, we defined two types of grants as nonpoliticized. The first type is politically neutral. For example, a neutral grant would be one granted to Harvard University's Kennedy School of Government, with no explicit purpose stated. Almost all grants to university-based programs or researchers were coded as neutral because we usually found it difficult to determine the projects' ideology. Given that most academics in the humanities and social sciences are politically liberal (see, for example, Ladd and Lipset, 1976), our analysis likely understates the number of liberal grants. The second type of nonpoliticized grant exhibits a value orientation, but not one that is liberal or conservative. A value-oriented nonpoliticized grant would be one made in support of a free press, a goal shared by liberals and conservatives alike.

The information we report about foundation grants is of two types: the number of grants made and the average dollar amount per grant. We report both findings because the average dollar amount per grant bears no relationship to the number of politicized grants made by a foundation ($r = 0.01$).[3] In total, we found 187 politicized foundations.

THE IDEOLOGICAL ORIENTATION OF FOUNDATIONS

Most public policy grants and most public policy foundations are liberal. When foundations award grants with an ideological slant, they make many more liberal grants. Of the 4,738 public policy grants in our study, 57 percent (2,705) are politicized; 44 percent (2,094) of all public policy grants are liberal, and 13 percent (611) are conservative. This gives us a liberal-to-conservative grant ratio of more than 3 to 1 (see Figure 8.1).

The remaining 43 percent of the grants (2,033) are split among three categories: 37 percent (1,771) are neutral; less than 1 percent (47) are ideological but neither liberal nor conservative; and 5 percent (215) go to organizations we were unable to identify.

We find similar patterns if we look at total dollars awarded for public policy

Figure 8.1
The Ideological Slant and Size of Public Policy Grants

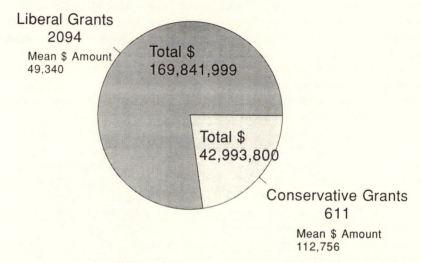

Liberal Grants
2094
Mean $ Amount
49,340

Total $
169,841,999

Total $
42,993,800

Conservative Grants
611
Mean $ Amount
112,756

Public Policy Grants

grants. Of the $386,470,000 distributed in public policy grants, $212,839,800 (roughly 55 percent) go to politicized groups. Liberal groups receive $169,841,999, or 44 percent of the total funding for public policy. This amounts to roughly four times as much as that awarded to conservative recipients ($42,993,800). Neutral groups receive $162,590,000; and $3,856,911 (1 percent) go to groups that are neither liberal nor conservative. The remainder ($7,188,504) goes to groups that we are unable to classify.

The data, however, also show that when foundations become involved in public policy, most end up with at least 1 ideological grant. Of the 225 foundations that made public policy grants in the mid–1980s, only 48 awarded only nonpoliticized grants.

When foundations get involved in ideological projects, they overwhelmingly favor liberal causes. Of the 187 foundations that fund at least one politicized project, the typical one makes an average of 11 liberal and 3 conservative grants.

In the next section, we devise an "ideology score" for each public policy foundation. We measure a foundation's ideological slant by calculating the ratio of liberal grants to all politicized grants for each foundation. The lowest possible score on this scale is 0, indicating that the foundation in question makes only conservative grants. The highest possible score is 1.00, which means that the foundation makes only liberal grants. A foundation's ideological score of 0.50 means that the foundation makes an equal number of conservative and liberal grants. In our scoring system, we exclude the 48 foundations that distribute no politicized grants.

The mean ideological score for all foundations is 0.77. This indicates that the typical foundation directed 77 percent of all ideological grants to liberal causes or programs. The mean ideological score, however, understates the liberal bias among public policy foundations. Another way to measure a foundation's ideological slant is to use the median score. The median score is that score at which half the politicized foundations have scores less than the median, while the remaining foundations have scores above it. The median ideological foundation score is 0.98. This means that half the public policy foundations receive a score of 0.98 or better. In other words, half the public policy foundations award almost all their politicized grants (98 percent of them) to liberal groups.

A third way to demonstrate the overwhelmingly liberal orientation of public policy giving is to look at the distribution of foundations around the score of 0.50, which is the midpoint of the scale, which indicates that the foundation makes half its politicized grants to liberal recipients and half to conservative. Approximately 65 percent of foundations (147) make more than half their grants to liberal groups, while only 18 percent (40 foundations) award a majority of grants to conservative groups or individuals.

At the extreme end of the scale, 40 percent of all public policy foundations (91 foundations) support only liberal causes while a mere 7 percent (15) favor solely conservative groups. Only 3 percent (6 foundations) balance their grant making ideologically by dividing their politicized grants evenly between liberal and conservative recipients.

Is the liberal preponderance among grants perhaps a function of the Ford Foundation? Because Ford, by all measures, is the largest foundation in the world, the 4-to-1 ratio of liberal to conservative public policy grants may be due to this foundation. For example, in our sample year (1987), Ford supported 520 public policy grants (about 11 percent of the total in our sample). It awarded about 18 percent of the total dollar value of all grants. Ford made 12.5 percent of all liberal grants in our sample and spent $45,865,000. Ford supported only 17 of the 611 conservative projects, spending only $1,610,124. This is less than 3 percent of all conservative grants.

Deleting Ford from the analysis above still gives us a sample slanted toward the left. It does not materially affect our conclusions. Roughly 2,000 grants are liberal grants awarded by other foundations, and roughly 600 are conservative grants awarded by foundations other than Ford. This gives us a 3-to-1 ratio of liberal to conservative grants.

In short, regardless of what measure we use, public policy foundations generally favor liberal over conservative recipients. Furthermore, it is no surprise that the Ford Foundation bestows the largest number of liberal grants. According to Figure 8.2, Ford makes more than twice as many liberal grants as does the next most liberal foundation, which is the John D. and Catherine T. MacArthur Foundation, of the celebrated MacArthur "genius" awards. The foundation that ranks third is the J. Roderick MacArthur Foundation, founded by John D. MacArthur's son. The most liberal of corporate philanthropies,

Figure 8.2
The Ten Most Ideological Foundations Based on Number of Liberal Grants Given

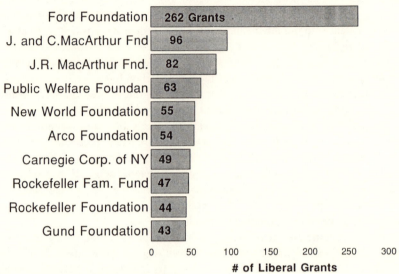

The Ten Most Liberal Foundations

the Arco Foundation, comes in sixth. Other large foundations—Carnegie Corporation, the Rockefeller Family Fund, and the Rockefeller Foundation—also make the top ten.

At the conservative end of the continuum, the John M. Olin and Smith Richardson foundations support the largest numbers of conservative projects (see Figure 8.3). Four of the top ten are corporate foundations—the Amoco Foundation (which comes in third), the Alcoa and Rockwell foundations (seventh and eighth), and the Ford Motor Company Foundation (tenth). Ironically the Ford Motor Company Fund, the corporate foundation that is part of the Ford Motor Company, is the tenth most conservative foundation, while its general-purpose, near-namesake the Ford Foundation ranks first in terms of liberal grants.

Comparing foundations that give the most to liberal causes with those that give the most to conservative causes illustrates most concretely the predominance of liberal grant giving. No foundation supports as many conservative projects as the number of liberal projects supported by the Ford Foundation and the two MacArthur Foundations. Only the Smith Richardson and John M. Olin foundations even approach the numbers of the largest liberal givers.

It is surprising, however, to find that liberal projects receive considerably less per grant. On average, the typical foundation gives $49,340 per liberal grant and $112,756 per conservative grant. This discrepancy is mildly puzzling given the greater total wealth of liberal foundations, but it may reflect the fact that there are fewer conservative recipients competing for available funds.

Figure 8.3
The Ten Most Ideological Foundations Based on Number of Conservative Grants Given

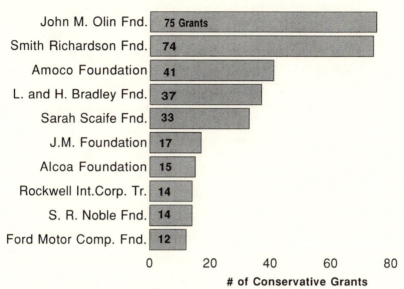

The Ten Most Conservative Foundations

Besides supporting many liberal projects, the John D. and Catherine T. MacArthur Foundation is the most generous to each recipient (see Table 8.1). The foundation awards on average almost a half-million dollars per liberal project. The Robert Wood Johnson Foundation is the second most generous to each liberal recipient, awarding $381,932 per liberal project. The foundation, established in the late 1960s by the son of the founder of the Johnson & Johnson company, focuses on the U.S. health care system but supports fewer liberal projects (fifteen) than many smaller foundations, such as the Public Welfare Foundation and the New World Foundation.

Five of the other foundations most generous to individual liberal projects support fewer than ten liberal projects. Furthermore, the Pew Memorial Trust and the Henry J. Kaiser Family Fund make mostly nonideological grants.

The Ford Foundation does not make this particular top ten of liberal foundations. While supporting the largest number of liberal recipients, it is relatively less generous per recipient. It bestows on average only $175,057 for each liberal project.

Table 8.1 also shows the most generous conservative donors, as measured by average dollar amounts. They include the Tandy, Hilton, and McCune Foundations, the J. Howard Pew Freedom Trust, and the John A. Hartford Foundation. We must note, however, that these top five made fewer than five conservative grants each. Given the small number of conservative public policy grants, these foundations can hardly

Table 8.1
The Most Ideological Foundations, Based on Mean Dollar Amount Per Grant

The Ten Most Liberal Foundations

Foundation	Mean Amount Given per Liberal Grant	Number of Liberal Grants
1. John and Catherine MacArthur Foundation	437,159.24	96
2. Robert Wood Johnson Foundation	381,931.93	15
3. Richard King Mellon Foundation	366,666.67	3
4. Andrew W. Mellon Foundation	362,857.14	14
5. Joan B. Kroc Foundation	303,333.33	3
6. Jessie Ball DuPont Religious Charitable and Educational Fund	255,000.00	1
7. W. K. Kellogg Foundation	211,867.45	20
8. Pew Memorial Trust	191,750.00	4
9. William and Flora Hewlett Foundation	183,700.00	20
10. Henry J. Kaiser Family Foundation	176,016.33	6

The Ten Most Conservative Foundations

Foundation	Mean Amount per Conservative Grant	Number of Conservative Grants
1. Anne Burnett and Charles D. Tandy Foundation	2,000,000	1
2. Conrad N. Hilton Foundation	1,594,878	1
3. McCune Foundation	750,000	1
4. J. Howard Pew Freedom Trust	280,000	4
5. John A. Hartford Foundation	260,476	2
6. Sarah Scaife Foundation	136,667	33
7. Lynde and Harry Bradley Foundation	109,519	37
8. Smith Richardson Foundation	76,156	74
9. M. J. Murdock Foundation	70,640	5
10. John M. Olin Foundation	55,600	75

match the sustained effort of liberal foundations like the John D. and Catherine T. MacArthur Foundation.

Others among the top ten foundations most generous to conservative recipients also disburse many more grants. They include the Scaife Foundation, which awards an average of $136,667 for 33 grants, the Bradley Foundation (an average of $109,519 for 37 grants), Smith Richardson (an average of $76,156 for 74 grants), and the John M. Olin Foundation (an average of $55,600 for 75 grants).

There is clearly a discrepancy between those foundations that support large numbers of liberal and conservative projects and those that choose to focus concerns more narrowly by awarding extremely large amounts but to fewer projects. Some founda-tions, moreover, award relatively few politicized grants but prefer to support nonpol-icy projects.

In the next section we rank foundations in terms of the proportion of resources de-voted to politicized grants. A politicized foundation is one in which politicized grants dominate that foundation's funding. We divide the number of each foundation's pol-iticized grants by the total number of grants (public policy plus nonpolicy, the latter including funds for new buildings, charity, and so on) for each foundation. We then divide how much money a foundation spends on politicized grants by the total amount of all grant money given.

As Table 8.2 shows, the most politicized foundations, with a few exceptions, are liberal. The most politicized of the conservative foundations is the Smith Richardson Foundation, which ranks third. If we base the ranking on the percent of dollars given to politicized projects versus total dollars awarded for all projects, the conservative Sarah Scaife Foundation comes in fifth.

While the Ford Foundation is the largest foundation in the United States, the lead-ing politicized foundation, as well as one of the leading U.S. liberal ones, is the J. Roderick MacArthur Foundation. The foundation tops both lists by a considerable margin. A total of 79 percent of all its grants are politicized, almost all of them liberal; 84 percent of its funds go to politicized grants. Unfortunately, we remove from one set of calculations the liberal, much larger, and better-known John D. and Catherine T. MacArthur Foundation only because the foundation did not report the total number of grants they make. However, they rank ninth in terms of the percentage of politi-cized to total dollars disbursed, with 45 percent of all its awards going to politicized projects.

In general, four highly conservative foundations spend a considerable proportion of all funds on politicized projects, but, in toto, many more liberal foundations do the same. The liberal J. Roderick MacArthur Foundation, the New World Foundation, and the Rockefeller Family Fund are more politicized than any conservative founda-tion. These also provide further support for our general contention that liberal foun-dations had greater influence on the public policy agenda than conservative ones, even in the 1980s.

An Excursus on Corporate Foundations

Public policy funding by corporate foundations is a recent development—noteworthy, yet poorly explored. As late as 1985, such scholars as Waldemar Nielsen overlooked corporate foundations when writing about big foundations in the United States. In his survey of corporate philanthropy, sociologist Michael Useem (1987, p. 345) reports that about half of nearly 800 firms maintain a corporate foundation. The activities of the corporate foundation are separate from a company's direct giving policies.

On the face of it, we would expect corporate foundations to reflect the interests of the corporate world and to fund conservative causes, especially projects that

Table 8.2
The Most Politicized Foundations

Foundation	Politicized as % of Total #	Slant	Liberal as % of Politicized
J. Roderick MacArthur	79	liberal	99
Rockefeller Family Fund	59	liberal	100
Smith Richardson	47	conservative	5
New World	43	liberal	89
John M. Olin	42	conservative	5
Sarah Scaife	40	conservative	3
General Service	35	liberal	100
Robert Sterling Clark	32	liberal	100
C.S. Fund	24	liberal	100
Sherman	24	liberal	100
New York	23	liberal	100
Mary Reynolds Babcock	22	liberal	100
Woods Charitable	21	liberal	97
Ford	16	liberal	94
Carnegie Corp.	15	liberal	98
George Gund	15	liberal	96
Bradley	14	conservative	3
Eli Lilly	14	liberal	55
Joyce Mertz-Gilmore	13	liberal	91
W. Alton Jones	13	liberal	100

Foundation	Politicized $ as % of All Grant $	Slant	Liberal as % of Politicized
J. Roderick MacArthur	84	liberal	99
New World	63	liberal	89
Eli Lilly	61	liberal	55
Rockefeller Family Fund	58	liberal	100
Sarah Scaife	56	conservative	3
General Service	54	liberal	100
Smith Richardson	54	conservative	4
Robert Sterling Clark	49	liberal	100
John D. & Catherine T. MacArthur	45	liberal	98
Rockwell International	42	conservative	42
Woods Charitable	40	liberal	97
Pew Memorial	32	liberal	80
Mary Reynolds Babcock	32	liberal	100
C.S. Fund	32	liberal	100
Columbia	31	liberal	100
John M. Olin	30	conservative	5
New York	29	liberal	100
Needmor	28	liberal	100
Charles K. Blandin	23	liberal	71
Z. Smith Reynolds	23	liberal	100

reduce government regulation and generally promote free enterprise. Useem himself suggests that corporations have an interest in "the preservation of the social system within which the corporation operates" (1986, p. 354). At most, we would expect them to provide "bricks and mortar" grants, of which Nielsen (1985) is so derisive. The conservative nature of corporate foundations also follows from the ruling class model of philanthropy discussed in chapter three.

This view of conservative corporate philanthropy is mistaken. Corporate foundations constitute 24 percent of the total number of foundations that support one or more politicized projects. More strikingly, corporate foundations follow the lead of their independent brethren. A total of 80 percent of independent foundations are liberal, with 50 percent or more of their politicized grants funding liberal projects; 77 percent of corporate foundations are liberal.[4]

An extensive discussion of the liberalism of corporate foundations is beyond the scope of this chapter. Several possible reasons why they are liberal, however, come to mind. The most important reason is probably a sophisticated version of "follow the leader." Corporate foundations are relatively new institutions. The corporate executives who head these foundations, in their search for models to follow, may be inclined to imitate established philanthropies, as Irving Kristol (1978) suggests. As these are predominantly liberal, it follows that corporate foundations follow predominantly liberal grant-making policies. A second possibility is that corporate foundations believe that funding liberal projects is in their interest, as good-will gestures to liberal groups with which they contend. Another possibility is that corporate philanthropy for liberal projects results from litigation, possibly in the area of either employment discrimination or environmental impact. This line of argument is supported historically. Contrast the hue and cry raised over congressional allegations of conservative "tainted money" of the original Rockefeller philanthropy (discussed in chapter two) with the relative silence of liberal groups concerning today's corporate philanthropy. The public interest groups are generally quick to detect and condemn corporate malfeasance, both real and alleged. The lack of complaint among them is especially noteworthy. Because the corporate foundation is as liberal as its independent counterparts, we will not discuss them separately for the remainder of the chapter.

The liberalism in the grant making versus the equal proportion of *conservatives and liberals* in our survey poses an apparent and unanticipated paradox. How can the overwhelming liberalism of public policy giving be squared with the factor that there are more conservatives than liberals among the foundation elite? Due to the confidentiality requirements of our survey, we cannot match individual survey respondents with foundations. We therefore cannot be entirely sure of the answer. However, the most likely explanation for the discrepancy between the survey results and the grant coding has to do with their differing universes. The public policy foundation universe ($n = 225$) comprises only 27 percent of the foundations in the survey universe ($n = 844$). This disjunction is important because we believe that leaders of public policy foundations are probably more liberal than those in foundations that do not get involved in policy affairs.

The relationship between staff influence and respondent liberalism among those surveyed is also an indicator that the foundation elite involved in policy projects are more liberal than other foundation leaders. Those respondents who rely on staff are more liberal than those respondents who report little or no staff influence (see chapter seven).

In our public policy grants data, we find that the number of foundation staff correlates highly with the total number of public policy grants ($r = .91$) and with the number of liberal grants awarded (r = .76). In other words, large foundations tend to support liberal projects and are likely to have a larger staff than smaller foundations. We assume, therefore, that the leaders of the larger foundations are more liberal and have more influential staff.

FUNDING RESEARCH VERSUS FUNDING SOCIAL ACTION

We note in chapter two how the big foundations shifted priorities during the 1960s, moving away from pure research to emphasizing funding for social action. While foundations still look to social science knowledge to provide the basis for policy action, the impetus for many is now "to do something." The more conservative foundation elite are more sympathetic to research today. Liberals are more supportive of social action. This section compares funding research versus social action projects.

We classified all public policy grants as for research, "action," conferences and workshops, or miscellaneous purposes. A total of 35 percent of public policy projects are for research (n = 1,634), 58 percent of the grants are for action, (n = 2,723), 5 percent are for conferences and workshops (n = 257), and the remaining 2 percent (n = 124) are for other purposes or unknown.

Proportionately, conservative grants are more likely to be given for research than are liberal grants. Liberal grants are more likely to be made for action purposes. For example, 55 percent of conservative grants are for research projects, 42 percent are oriented toward "doing something," and 3 percent are for conferences or workshops. In contrast, and in line with our earlier expectations, foundations disburse only one-fourth of all liberal grants for research purposes, 4 percent of liberal projects are for conferences and workshops, and three of four liberal grants go toward "action" projects.[5]

In short, a larger proportion of conservative grants than liberal grants go for research. Liberal proposals tend to be action-oriented projects. However, since there are so many more liberal grants overall, more research grants are awarded to liberal recipients.

Of the foundations in this study, 68 percent make at least one research grant, while the typical foundation makes an average of eleven. Whether they prefer action over research differs by whether they are generally nonpoliticized, liberal, or conservative. Of the thirty-eight nonpoliticized foundations, only eight foundations support some form of public policy research, making between one and three research grants worth an average of $103,125 each.

Of those foundations that give more than half of their percentage of their politicized grants to liberals, 78 percent of them support at least one public policy research project. Each liberal foundation averages ten research grants.

As expected, Ford awards the largest number of research grants among liberal philanthropies, followed by the John D. and Catherine T. MacArthur and Rockefeller foundations; the Carnegie Corporation; the Shell Companies, Andrew W. Mellon, Alfred P. Sloan, Exxon Education, and AT&T foundations; and Amer-

Figure 8.4
Foundation Support of Public Policy Research: Liberal Foundations

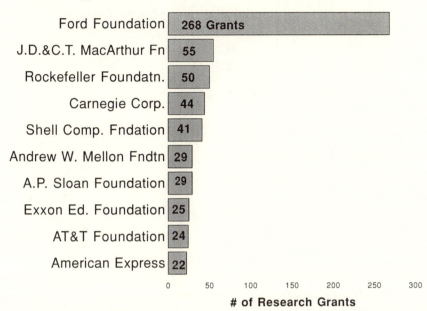

# of Research Grants

ican Express. Four of the ten (Shell, Exxon, AT&T, and American Express) are corporate foundations (see Figure 8.4).

Three out of four conservative foundations also support research projects (see Figure 8.5). These thirty foundations make more research grants than either liberal or nonpoliticized foundations. They average fifteen research grants per foundation. Since conservative foundations make fewer grants in all areas, this is consistent with our earlier expectation that conservative foundations focus a much larger proportion of their funding on the generation of new ideas than do liberal and nonpolitical philanthropies.

Among conservative foundations, the John M. Olin Foundation makes the largest number of research grants, followed by Smith Richardson, Amoco, Scaife, Bradley, Ford Motor Company Fund, Alcoa, Pew Freedom Trust, Texaco, and the J. M. Foundation. As we found with our ten liberal grant makers, four—Amoco, Ford Motor, Alcoa, and Texaco—are corporate foundations.

In terms of the average dollar amount, the typical conservative foundation gives more per research grant than do liberal and nonpoliticized foundations. Liberal foundations average $71,744 per research grant; those on the conservative side average $197,280.

While many foundations support research, how many foundations support research proposals with opposing views? How much ideologically diverse research do public policy foundations support? In chapter seven, we demonstrate that conservative foundation leaders are more likely than liberals to insist that

Figure 8.5
Foundation Support of Public Policy Research: Conservative Foundations

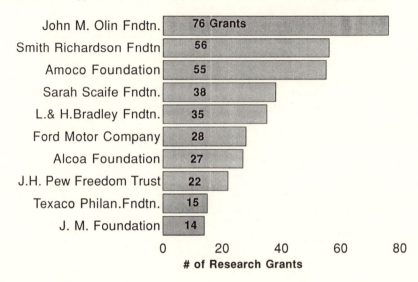

recipients share the ideological predispositions of the foundation that supports them. Do liberal foundations in fact "tolerate" more ideological diversity among recipients interested in the pursuit of knowledge?

Table 8.3 shows that liberal foundations are no more hospitable to research with an opposing ideological slant than are conservative philanthropies. Conservative foundations give more than half their research awards to conservative research projects, roughly one in three to ideologically neutral recipients, and one in ten to liberal research.

Liberal foundations prefer to give research grants to neutral institutions (52 percent), followed by liberal (41 percent) and conservative (7 percent) projects, although the liberal predisposition to favor neutral recipients probably understates the liberal slant of their research projects. These research recipients include a large number of university-based projects, which are coded as neutral since the ideological slant of the research being proposed is not discernible. Because academics as a group are liberal, the degree of liberal slant in research is probably understated.

Conservative philanthropies, once pictured by critics as a haven for crude and unsophisticated operators, clearly are now more involved than their liberal counterparts in supporting public policy research. We believe they have come to support research because, as the challenging group, conservatives have had to come up with new ideas and a new policy paradigm to compete with liberal policy makers (e.g., Nash, 1976; Kristol, 1978). We take up this issue in somewhat more detail when we discuss the role of journals and think tanks in promoting the conservative cause.

Table 8.3

Consistency in Foundation Funding of Public Policy Research

```
How Liberal Foundations Distribute Grants, By Type of Grant
and Ideology of Recipients (%).
```

Grant Type	Ideology of Recipients			
	Conservative	Liberal	Neutral/Neither	
Research	7	41	52	(1153)
Action	4	64	32	(2213)
Conference	3	43	55	(221)

N=3587

```
How Conservative Foundations Distribute Grants, By Type of Grant
and Ideology of Recipients (%).
```

Grant Type	Ideology of Recipients			
	Conservative	Liberal	Neutral/Neither	
Research	51	10	32	(441)
Action	43	15	41	(375)
Conference	45	0	55	(29)

N=845

Spheres of Activity

What areas of public policy do foundations support? Many classifications are possible because public policy foundations support an enormous range of activities and vast numbers of different groups. Since many grants have multiple purposes, we coded each grant for its two most prominent spheres of activity.[6] To keep the coding relatively simple, we limited the list to twenty-one spheres of activity, including one for grants to general-purpose think tanks.

According to Figures 8.6 and 8.7, almost two-thirds of all foundations support civic affairs. This includes such activities as voter registration drives and local government internships. Community-urban affairs projects and those dealing with international relations are also popular. Roughly 40 percent of all foundations fund projects in law, economics, education, health, and the environment. One-third support general-purpose think tanks. These are of special interest because of their role in creating and disseminating both domestic and foreign policy research. Also, 30 percent support media projects, and 30 percent fund activities relating to minority affairs.

Conservative and liberal foundations have few substantive fields in common, except for civic affairs, where 70 percent of conservative foundations and 69 percent of liberal philanthropies support projects in this field. In most other areas, they have strikingly different priorities. Two of three liberal foundations make grants in community-urban affairs and international relations. Roughly half make grants in law, education, the environment, economics, and health and minority programs. One in three liberal foundations fund media studies and general-

Figure 8.6
Foundation Spheres of Interest, Total

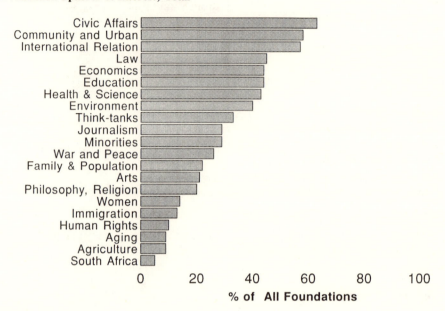

% of All Foundations

Figure 8.7
Foundation Spheres of Interest, Liberal and Conservative

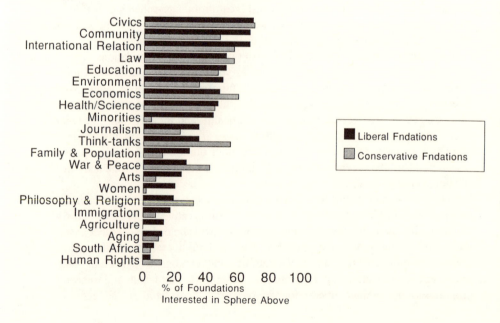

% of Foundations
Interested in Sphere Above

purpose think tanks. On the other hand, 60 percent of conservative foundations prefer to target funds in economics, followed closely by international relations, law, and public policy think tanks. Roughly half support community-urban affairs projects, education, and grants in health and medicine. A total of 44 percent fund proposals in the field of war and peace; and roughly one in three supports proposals dealing with the environment.

In terms of mean amount of dollars spent per grant proposal, foundations in general spend mostly on health issues, which average $106,985 per grant (see Table 8.4). The next largest mean dollar amounts go to proposals dealing with the environment.

Liberal and conservative foundations have somewhat different spending priorities. Based on the average amount spent, the largest policy area by far for liberals is the environment, with an average of $105,021 per grant from seventy-four foundations. Liberal foundations also generously fund health, the arts, South African affairs, media studies, and population issues. Minority affairs and war and peace rank seventh and eighth, while community affairs and international relations are ninth and tenth.

In terms of mean dollar amounts for conservatives, aging and health issues rank first and second respectively, followed by think tanks, economics, and South Africa. Sixth are war and peace issues, followed by human rights, community affairs, philosophy-religion, and media studies.

IDEOLOGICAL CONSENSUS WITHIN SUBJECT AREAS

How ideologically diverse is funding in particular areas? Which spheres are dominated by conservative projects, and which are dominated by liberal ones? Are there certain spheres in which recipients are more ideologically balanced or neutral?

Liberal foundations channel more than half of their grants to liberal recipients in ten of twenty-one spheres (see Table 8.5). They are the most ideologically consistent on projects dealing with women and minority issues. Almost all their funding in these areas is for liberal projects. Liberal foundations overwhelmingly favor liberal projects on war and peace (86 percent), the environment (82 percent), human rights (72 percent), and law (71 percent). To a lesser degree, they also fund mostly liberal proposals in family issues (69 percent), journalism (68 percent), immigration (61 percent), and community and urban affairs (58 percent). There are only seven spheres (economics, civic affairs, international relations, health, agriculture, education, and philosophy-religion) in which liberal foundations support a larger proportion of neutral proposals than liberal ones. Liberal foundations give conservatives even fewer grants in all spheres as compared to neutral projects, with the exception of the South Africa issue. In this sphere, which consists of only a few grants, liberal foundations fund more conservative than neutral proposals.[7]

Conservative foundations make most grants to conservative recipients in eight

Table 8.4
Mean Dollars in Various Spheres of Interest

All Large Public Policy Foundations

Sphere	Mean $ Given	Number of Foundations
health/sce	106,985	96
environment	97,805	90
S. Africa	93,715	12
arts	82,084	47
fam/pop	79,485	49
journalism	76,287	65
aging	75,947	21
think tank	72,698	75
economics	62,348	98
minorities	60,478	66
war	59,671	59
phil/rel	56,059	46
community/urban	53,435	130
education	51,760	100
int. rel.	53,220	129
human rights	48,466	23
agriculture	45,081	21
civics	44,173	141
law	40,315	101
women	37,868	32
immigration	32,104	30

Liberal Foundations			Conservative Foundations		
Sphere	Mean $	Number	Sphere	mean $	Number
environment	105,021	74	aging	164,385	4
health/sci	98,725	69	health/sci	163,796	18
arts	98,082	36	think tank	126,496	22
S. Africa	97,458	10	economics	110,105	24
journalism	87,184	51	S. Africa	75,000	2
family/pop.	85,387	42	war	59,007	17
minorities	61,853	64	hum. rights	56,086	5
war	60,280	40	community	50,788	19
community	57,078	98	phil/rel	44,115	13
int. rel.	56,242	98	journalism	43,642	9
education	56,076	76	education	33,709	19
phil/rel	55,888	28	environment	27,157	14
aging	55,138	17	family/pop	26,700	5
think tank	51,053	52	int. rel.	25,886	23
civics	48,914	101	law	25,205	23
economics	47,096	70	civics	24,235	28
human rights	46,349	8	minorities	16,500	2
agriculture	44,563	19	arts	11,400	5
law	43,436	77	immigration	8,200	5
women	39,143	30	women	7,500	1
immigration	36,885	25	agriculture	0	0

spheres: human rights (82 percent), journalism (82 percent), philosophy-religion (81 percent), think tanks (70 percent), law (68 percent), family and population (67 percent), war and peace (56 percent), and economics (54 percent). In education, they fund a plurality of conservative recipients (45 percent). For eight other spheres (civic issues, health and science, immigration, community affairs,

Table 8.5
The Ideological Slant of Grants by Different Spheres of Activity (percentage)

Liberal Foundations

	Ideological Slant of Grant				# of
Sphere	Liberal	Conserv.	Neutral	Neither	Grants
Women	99	0	1	0	78
Minorities	93	2	5	0	211
War	86	2	12	0	298
Env	82	1	17	0	248
Humrghts	72	7	4	16	94
Law	71	13	14	1	227
Fam	69	4	26	1	140
Jour	68	3	24	5	154
Immig	61	8	26	5	62
Commun	58	2	40	0	349
Think Tank	48	30	23	0	115
S. Africa	47	42	11	0	19
Aging	46	4	42	8	26
Econ	42	10	48	0	351
Civics	42	4	54	0	412
IR	39	3	58	0	654
Hlthsci	38	1	60	2	256
Agri	37	3	57	3	40
Educ	30	5	65	0	243
Arts	26	0	74	0	76
Phil/rel	19	8	67	6	52

Conservative Foundations

	Ideological Slant of Grant				# of
Sphere	Conser.	Liberal	Neutral	Neither	Grants
Humrghts	82	9	6	3	34
Jour	82	5	11	3	38
Phil/Rel	81	3	11	5	62
Think Tank	70	10	19	0	118
Law	68	12	16	3	73
Fam	67	17	17	0	6
Civics	35	11	54	0	100
Econ	54	9	37	0	138
S. Africa	50	50	0	0	2
War	56	8	36	0	77
Educ	45	14	41	0	29
Hlthsci	28	8	64	0	36
Immig	25	25	50	0	4
Commun	22	21	57	0	58
IR	21	18	61	0	130
Env	10	40	50	0	20
Aging	0	0	100	0	4
Agri	0	0	0	0	0
Arts	0	0	100	0	9
Minorities	0	100	0	0	2
Women	0	100	0	0	1

international relations, environment, aging, and arts), conservative foundations most frequently fund recipients with no explicit ideological orientation. Conservative foundations, however, support proportionately more liberals in five areas: women, minorities, the environment, immigration, and South Africa. It should be noted that these also are areas in which conservative foundations award few grants of any kind.

FOUNDATION PLURALISM AND IDEOLOGICAL POLARIZATION

The view that foundations are pluralistic is part of the conventional wisdom of the foundation world. This claim, however, is ambiguous. At the very least, we need to distinguish between a pluralism of sphere or subject matter of the grant and a pluralism of ideological slant. The data on public policy projects allow an assessment of pluralism in even greater detail, particularly as it relates to individual spheres.

We compare the results of conservative and liberal public policy grants with the survey findings regarding the kinds of projects conservative and liberal members of the foundation elite prefer. Many categories in the survey and the grant study are not the same (some of which are due to the passage of time and others to limitations of survey space necessary for the survey questionnaire), but many sufficiently overlap to make the comparison fruitful in helping us understand the basis on which grants are made.

We examine the two kinds of foundation pluralism—a pluralism of ideological slant and pluralism of approach (subject area)—and categorize them according to four types of overall ideological bias. First, we have ideologically neutral spheres. These are subjects where the majority of grants made by both liberal and conservative foundations are ideologically neutral. The second type of overall "bias" consists of spheres that are highly polarized. In polarized subject areas, liberal foundations primarily reward liberal recipients and conservative foundations predominantly support conservative projects. Third, there are those subject areas that are highly skewed toward the right, where conservative foundations largely support conservative recipients while liberal foundations primarily award grants that are neutral or conservative. Last, there are spheres that are highly skewed toward the left, where liberal foundations principally fund liberal recipients while conservative philanthropies support either neutral or liberal undertakings.

Ideologically Neutral Spheres

Health policy, agricultural policy, the arts, international relations, and civic affairs tend to be overall ideologically neutral. When conservative and liberal foundations support such programs, they fund nonideological recipients. This finding parallels the finding stated in chapter seven that spending preferences that make up the dimension of "health and welfare spending" do not correlate with political liberalism.[8] In our survey, a majority of conservative and liberal foundation leaders favor increased spending for health and welfare issues, such as those on health care cost containment, but also for disability, AIDS research, and the problems of the homeless.

Polarized Spheres

Table 8.6 lists the polarized and ideologically slanted subject areas in public policy funding. Five spheres—human rights, war and peace, journalism, law, and family and population—exhibit a good deal of polarization. Conservative and liberal foundations disburse a majority of their funds in these spheres to conservative and liberal recipients, respectively.

War and Peace and Human Rights. We present human rights and war and peace issues together because they reflect the strong underlying polarization among the foundation elite regarding foreign policy in the Reagan era. Our opinion survey finds that foreign policy issues make up one distinct ideological dimension. These translate into the spending preferences discussed in chapter seven. Conservatives and liberals differ sharply on spending preferences regarding peace initiatives, arms control, and human rights. Liberal foundation leaders support an increase in funding for these programs; conservatives oppose it.

The grants data show that funding human rights programs is highly polarized. Conservative donors give roughly four of five human rights grants to conservative recipients. Liberal foundations award roughly three-fourths to liberal recipients.

Conservative involvement in actual funding for human rights programs at first seems inconsistent with our survey finding, but the inconsistency is really superficial. Liberal foundations are generally more involved in the problems of human rights and, as Table 8.6 shows, make many more grants in this area than do conservative philanthropies. When conservative foundations become involved in human rights projects, they are primarily concerned with human rights abuses under communism. In practice, the distinction means that liberal foundations largely fund programs dealing with the human rights problems of U.S. allies, while conservative foundations focus almost exclusively on human rights problems in Soviet-bloc nations.

For example, the John M. Olin Foundation supported such causes as a "communications project on Soviet human rights performance" and "activities of [the] Nicaraguan Human Rights Commission" (Foundation Center, 1988, pp. 104, 105). In contrast, the J. Roderick MacArthur Foundation supported a project to foster human rights in South Korea and funded a documentary film on the human rights situation in Guatemala (Foundation Center, 1988, p. 34).

This grant-making pattern is similar in the sphere of war and peace. Conservative foundations give roughly half their grants to conservative groups (although one in three go to more neutral organizations like the Council on Foreign Relations). Liberal foundations award roughly four in five of their war-and-peace grants to liberal groups. For example, the John D. and Catherine T. MacArthur Foundation supported the Center for Defense Information (which also received $500,000 from the Joan B. Kroc Foundation), the Center for National Security Studies, and Lawyers Alliance for Nuclear Arms Control, among many others (Foundation Center, 1988, pp. 36–39).[9]

Table 8.6
The Politicization of Public Policy Spheres

<u>Highly Polarized</u>

| | Ideological Slant of Grant | | | | |
	Conserv.	Liberal	Neutral	Neither	Ns
Human Rights					
Conservative Found.	82	9	6	3	34
Liberal Found.	7	72	4	16	94
Journalism					
Conservative Found.	82	5	11	3	38
Liberal Found.	3	68	24	5	154
Law					
Conservative Found.	68	12	16	3	73
Liberal Found.	13	71	14	1	227
Fam					
Conservative Found.	67	17	17	0	6
Liberal Found.	4	69	26	1	140
War					
Conservative Found.	56	8	36	0	77
Liberal Found.	2	86	12	0	298

<u>Skewed, Conservative</u>

	Conserv.	Liberal	Neutral	Neither	Ns
Philosophy/religion					
Conservative Found.	81	3	11	5	62
Liberal Found.	8	19	67	6	52
Think tank					
Conservative Found.	70	10	19	0	118
Liberal Found.	30	48	23	0	115
Econ					
Conservative Found.	54	9	37	0	138
Liberal Found.	10	42	48	0	351

Table 8.6 (continued)

Skewed, Liberal

Immig					
Conservative Found.	25	25	50	0	4
Liberal Found.	8	61	26	5	62
Commun/urban					
Conservative Found.	22	21	57	0	58
Liberal Found.	2	58	40	0	349
Env					
Conservative Found.	10	40	50	0	20
Liberal Found.	1	82	17	0	248
MInorities					
Conservative Found.	0	100	0	0	2
Liberal Found.	2	93	5	0	211
Women					
Conservative Found.	0	100	0	0	1
Liberal Found.	0	99	1	0	78

The Media. Media issues also exhibit considerable polarization. Conservative foundations give roughly eight of ten grants to conservative groups. Liberal foundations give almost 70 percent to liberal causes.

Conservative foundations often make these grants in support of conservative intellectual journals. In their view, these journals provide alternatives to what they see as the liberal-dominated media. These journals, and conservative public policy think tanks, are part of a larger strategy of institution building. The Sarah Scaife Foundation, for example, funded projects like the Media Institute, a conservative press watchdog, while the Bradley Foundation gave money to such conservative intellectual journals as *The National Interest* and *The American Spectator* (Foundation Center, 1988, pp. 143–44).

On the other end of the spectrum, the Scherman Foundation, a small New York–based donor, funded the Media Access Project, a liberal press watchdog and an important part of the public interest movement (McCann, 1986, pp. 18, 61). The Media Access Project also received support from other liberal foundations, such as the J. Roderick MacArthur Foundation and Rockefeller Family Fund (Foundation Center, 1988, pp. 35, 109).

Public Interest Law. Public law and constitutional rights are extremely important in promoting or preventing social change. While this surely would have surprised those who created U.S. foundations, public interest law emerged in the aftermath of the Tax Act of 1969. Congress prohibited involvement in electoral politics, but with a sympathetic Supreme Court, litigation (or the threat of litigation) emerged as a key instrument of change for liberals, especially for those in the public interest movement (McCann, 1986, pp. 228–29). Because the law has become one of the crucial means available for advancing foundation-sponsored social change, it plays an important role in other highly polarized spheres such as women's issues, minority affairs, and the environment (McCann, 1986).

According to one detailed and sympathetic study of the movement, most public interest law firms received more than half their funding from private foundations during the 1970s (McCann, 1986, p. 54). They depend especially, but not exclusively, on the Ford Foundation (see also Nielsen, 1985). They also receive support from the Carnegie and Rockefeller foundations and many other liberal foundations. Not surprisingly, the survey data presented in chapter seven show that liberal foundation leaders strongly support funds for increasing access to legal services. Conservatives strongly oppose it.

As expected, grants made under the rubric of the public law and constitutional rights are sharply divided between liberals and conservatives. Roughly two-thirds of grants made by conservative foundations go to conservative recipients. Liberal recipients receive 71 percent of liberal foundations' support for public interest law.

The Ford Foundation awarded $600,000 to the American Civil Liberties Union Foundation for "litigation, advocacy and technical assistance to groups challenging race-based discrimination in areas of voting rights, employment, and capital punishment" (Foundation Center, 1988, p. 75). They gave another $400,000 to the Puerto Rican Legal Defense and Education Fund for similar types of litigation (p. 84). The Mary Reynolds Babcock Foundation funded the Southern Environmental Law Center; and the Wallace Alexander Gerbode Foundation aided the Asian Law Caucus's tenant's rights projects.

Political tactics, if perceived as successful, are often imitated by the opponents of those who pioneered them. Thus, conservatives in the late 1970s developed their own public interest law movement. The Sarah Scaife Foundation supported groups like the Washington Legal Foundation, a conservative public interest law firm, and the Federalist Society, devoted to reviving federalism and serving as a forum for conservative legal scholars and law students.

A subarea of activity in the sphere of law is prisoners' rights and the issue of capital punishment. Among foundation leaders surveyed, there are large liberal-conservative differences on such questions as support for the death penalty and on whether the courts are too easy on criminals. While liberal foundations are not as active as they were in the 1970s (see, for example, the discussion in Magat, 1979, pp. 108–11, 154–56, for a brief summary), it is still the liberal foundations that fund projects in the field of prisoners' rights.

Family and Population. Family and population issues are also highly polarized, although conservative foundations make only six grants in this area. Both the actual grant making and the funding preferences of foundation leaders reflect a basic disjunction between conservatives and liberals on issues of expressive individualism, especially abortion and gay rights.

Liberal members of the foundation elite are strongly in favor of increasing support for birth control, while conservatives are content with the status quo. Moreover, the data on public policy grants show that most conservative foundations do not support prolife groups, which would be the natural counter to liberal support for family planning.

Liberal foundations are very active in this field, making 140 grants in the year reported. No single recipient, however, received a disproportionate number of grants in that year. Planned Parenthood received only 10 of the 140.

Other forms of support from liberal foundations included a grant from the Robert Sterling Clark Foundation to the Center for Population Options "to conduct policy analysis and public education on key teen pregnancy issues, and work with major youth serving organizations in fostering adolescent access to family planning services and information" (Foundation Center, 1988, p. 72), in addition to the *MS.* Foundation's Reproductive Rights Project and the National Abortion Rights Action League. Gay rights in the mid–1980s, however, had not yet become an issue of general foundation interest, although the one grant in support of gay rights was made by a liberal foundation.

Spheres of Liberal Predominance

Liberal foundations and liberal donees dominate five spheres. Whereas conservative foundations give less than half their grants to conservative recipients, liberal foundations award more than 50 percent of their funds to liberal projects. These five areas of liberal foundation–liberal recipient dominance are immigration, community and urban affairs, the environment, women, and minorities.

Immigration. Of the grants made by conservative foundations in the field of immigration, only one was to a conservative recipient. In sharp contrast, over half the sixty-two grants made by liberal foundations were to liberal groups. Some of these projects helped obtain public services for immigrants and refugees. Other recipients (the American Civil Liberties Union, for example) challenge U.S. immigration policy, sometimes in the form of providing asylum for political refugees from El Salvador and Guatemala.

Community and Urban Affairs. Conservative foundations disburse most of their community and urban affairs grants to neutral organizations. Liberal foundations support groups like the Urban Institute, which alone received a total of twenty-five grants in the year studied. Community Action Programs are prominent recipients. The Center for Community Change, created by the Ford Foundation "to enhance the voice of the poor in their own destiny" (Nielsen, 1985, p. 64), received two grants of $100,000 apiece from the Ford and Florence and John Schuman foundations (Foundation Center, 1988, pp. 65, 77).

The Environment. Liberal foundations have long dominated environmental issues. Foundation support has helped develop new organizations like the Environmental Defense Fund (EDF) and helped in radicalizing older ones like the Sierra Club (McCann, 1986, p. 47). Foundation support in developing the organizational infrastructure is critical to its existence. For example, two of the major environmental organizations that specialize in environmental litigation, the Environmental Defense Fund and the Natural Resources Defense Council

(NRDC), were established primarily with the assistance of Ford and other liberal foundations (Echard, 1990, pp. 133–38, 167–72).

Liberal foundations gave 82 percent of their 248 environmentally related grants to liberal recipients. In addition to the EDF and NRDC, receiving 5 and 15 grants respectively, they included the Environmental Policy Institute (with 9 grants), the Sierra Club Foundation, the Environmental Action Coalition, and the Environmental Action Foundation. (For a brief discussion of the Ford Foundation's role in the environmental movement, see Magat, 1979, p. 186.)

The relative quiescence of conservative foundations in this area provides a striking contrast to the picture of liberal activity. Conservative foundations awarded twenty grants focused on the environment. Only two went to conservatives. Ten of these grants were ideologically neutral, while the rest slanted toward the left.[10]

How do these findings fit with our data on funding preferences and ideology? Liberal and conservative survey respondents favor increasing support for the preservation of the environment. Liberals, however, support it much more strongly. Similarly, while a majority of conservative foundation leaders think that our environmental problems are serious, many more liberals hold that view.

We believe that many conservatives favor the goal of environmental protection but are also suspicious of litigation and regulation, which are characteristically favored by liberals to achieve that end. Lacking a distinctively conservative paradigm for dealing with environmental problems, and facing scarce foundation resources, conservative foundations may restrict funding, as reflected in the grants data.

Minorities and Women. The leftward tilt is most pronounced on issues dealing with minorities and women. We find in chapter five that conservatives are strongly opposed to and liberals strongly support affirmative action for blacks and women. Similarly, in chapter seven we find that liberals are far more likely to support increases in funding for programs for women, women's studies, African American studies, programs for blacks, and programs for gays than are conservatives, who generally favor reducing spending for these kinds of programs.

Both survey findings are consistent with the grants data. Conservative foundations awarded only 2 grants in the minorities sphere while awarding only 1 dealing with women's rights. These were all given to liberal recipients. Liberal foundations gave over 90 percent of their 211 grants for minority affairs to liberal groups and 99 percent of their 78 grants on women to liberal groups. The National Association for the Advancement of Colored People (NAACP) Legal Defense and Educational Fund, for example, received 4 grants, including 1 from the Ford Foundation. The Mexican American Legal Defense and Educational Fund received 6, including 1 from the liberal New World Foundation.

In the area of women's issues, the Ford Foundation made grants to the National Organization for Women (NOW) Legal Defense and Education Fund, the Women's Equity Action League, and the Women's Research and Education Institute, while the Rockefeller Foundation made a grant to the Women's Legal Defense Fund.

Liberal grant making, however, is less supportive of affirmative action for women than of family and abortion issues. The former receives considerably less funding from liberal grant makers (78 grants) than do organizations working in the fields of abortion and population control (140).

Spheres of Conservative Predominance

We next discuss conservative predominance in grant making. We define this sphere as that in which conservatives give most of their grants to conservative groups while liberals give most funds for either neutral or conservative projects. There are only three spheres like this: religious and philosophical issues, public policy think tanks, and economics.

Religious and Philosophical Issues. Conservative foundations actually make more grants related to religious and philosophical issues than do liberal foundations. This is one of only two spheres in which they predominate. Conservative foundations make roughly 80 percent of their religious and philosophy grants to conservative recipients such as the Ethics and Public Policy Center, the Rockford Institute, and the Institute on Religion and Democracy.

Liberals give a majority of their grants to neutral organizations, mostly universities. However, as noted earlier, since many university faculty are sympathetic to liberal goals, it is quite easy for liberal foundations to support philosophical views within the university.

Think Tanks. Conservative think tank predominance marks a major change in the political environment and played a role in the election of presidents Reagan and Bush (see Smith, 1991, pp. 167–213, 270–294, which provides a list of think tanks). Our data allows for some examination of who funds which think tanks. For simplicity, we define the general-purpose think tank as one that covers issues, in both foreign and domestic policy areas, such as the Brookings Institution and the American Enterprise Institute. When funding goes to one of these general think tanks, and when the foundation provides no detailed project description, we code it as a grant for the all-purpose policy think tank. For example, certain policy projects concentrating on domestic economic issues of the Urban Institute or the Manhattan Institute for Policy Research are not counted as general think tank projects because they confine the particular project to domestic affairs. These would be coded as projects in economics.[11] Moreover, since recipients are coded on a grant-by-grant basis, the grants to the Cato Institute are coded primarily as economics/research, even though we recognize that Cato deals with foreign policy as well as domestic issues.

We find that conservative foundations make slightly more grants to general think tanks than do liberals (118 grants and 115 grants, respectively). Think tank support comprises almost one-fifth of all conservative grants but only 5 percent of all liberal grants. Conservative foundations overwhelmingly fund conservative public policy think tanks, but liberal philanthropies spread their funds across the ideological spectrum. For example, 70 percent of conservative foundation funding goes to conservative policy think tanks, such as the Heritage Foundation and the American Enterprise Institute. Liberal foundations dispense almost 30 percent of their grants to conservative think tanks, roughly one in four to neutral public policy institutions, and 48 percent to such think tanks as the Brookings Institution and Aspen Institute for Humanistic Studies.

Economics. Conservative foundations disburse most of their economic grants to conservative donees, although 37 percent of grants go to neutral proposals. Liberal foundations distribute roughly 40 percent of their economics grants for liberal projects, but roughly half go to neutral recipients.

Conservative recipients, generally interested in deregulation, include institutions like the Cato Institute and the Heritage Foundation. Liberal recipients include organizations like the Center on Budget and Policy Priorities, which received ten grants from such donors as the New World Foundation, Primerica Foundation, John D. and Catherine T. MacArthur Foundation, Rockefeller Brothers Fund, Rockefeller Family Fund, Scherman Foundation, Mary Reynolds Babcock Foundation, and the Ford Foundation (which accounted for three of the ten).

CONCLUSION

Liberal and conservative foundations have developed striking differences in strategies for attaining or retaining power in the larger polity. Conservative foundations target their support to think tanks and to philosophical-religious projects, while conservative funding of economics proposals represents the hope that economic thinking can help shape greater public sympathy for free-enterprise institutions. The overall design represents commitment to developing an alternative paradigm to liberal-dominated policy research.

In the mid–1980s, liberals devoted much of their grantmaking activities to the environment, family and population problems, women, and minorities, partly as a rhetorical strategy for seizing the moral high ground in the political debate. Expressions of concern in these areas forced conservatives to compete on unfavorable rhetorical terrain, with liberals able to point to their allegedly greater concern. Liberalism claimed to do more "for" these groups or interests, while labeling conservative ideology as rendering "cold-hearted" support of the traditional white male status quo or, at best, being unsympathetic to the plight of the disenfranchised and disadvantaged.

The relative success of liberal efforts is shown by typical conservative responses, which often consist of simply ignoring family and population issues, concerns over the environment, problems of minorities, and women's issues. There is no obvious alternative conservative paradigm in these areas.

Support for abortion rights, minorities, women's issues, and the poor (in the form of urban projects and economic policies) reflects liberalism's belief that philanthropic support of public affairs encourages greater participation by those outside the circles of power. The empirical data on these foundations show that liberal foundations take seriously Jane H. Mavity and Paul Ylvisaker's (1977) claim that private philanthropy in public affairs should pursue the expansion of rights, participation, and resources of those who lack them.

Consensus does exist in the public policy world over the issues of civic affairs, health and science, and international relations, where both liberal and conservative foundations support mostly neutral grant recipients. Major ideological dissension exists in the other spheres where a conservative or liberal foundation will not fund proposals by an ideologically opposed recipient. At best, a conservative or liberal foundation might fund an ideologically neutral recipient but not seek ideological balance by funding an equal proportion of conservative and liberal proposals. Thus, despite the prominence of a few conservative foundations and a few conservative grant recipients limited to certain fields, foundation support in public affairs clearly slants to the left.

NOTES

1. A few foundations inadvertently included such grants on their lists.

2. We also believe that those who categorize themselves as "moderates" are generally less certain of their beliefs compared to those who characterize themselves as either "liberal" or "conservative." One bit of evidence from our survey supports this point. Self-styled moderates are more supportive of objective and unbiased research than either conservatives or liberals. We interpret this to mean that they are less certain of their beliefs—that is, more open-minded.

3. The total amount given by each foundation also correlates highly with the number of grants ($r = 0.79$).

4. Despite major differences in methodology, these results are generally consistent with those of the Capital Research Center as well (e.g., Olasky, 1991; Meiners and Laband, 1988; Bennett, 1989).

5. Interestingly enough, 7 percent of neutral grants and 23 percent of ideological but nonpoliticized grants support conferences and workshops.

6. We recoded the data several times to create these categories. Each trial coding was followed by modifications and additions to the total number of categories as new entries were discovered and added to the list of codes.

7. The coding here was based on the division current in the early years of the Reagan administration between the administration's policy of constructive engagement, which we defined as the conservative position, versus divestiture, condemning human rights abuses, and maintaining South Africa as a pariah state, which was the liberal position.

8. Arts and agriculture were not offered as potential spending preferences in the survey.

9. Of course, the public policy grants were made and the survey completed before the collapse of communism in Eastern Europe and the subsequent disintegration of the Soviet Union in the fall of 1991. However, we expect that the policy differences between liberals and conservatives will remain relevant in the event of new foreign threats to the

United States because they ultimately reflect sharp differences in underlying values and because the question of who deserves the credit for the collapse of communism also remains an issue.

10. For detailed descriptions of the histories and current activities of the liberal environmental groups that are recipients of foundation grants, see Jo Kwong Echard's work (1990).

11. The Urban Institute, however, received twenty-five grants, while the Manhattan Institute received eleven.

CHAPTER 9

POLARIZATION, PLURALISM, AND THE
PROBLEM OF SOCIAL ORDER

Throughout this book, we have shown the many ways in which the foundation elite is a sharply polarized strategic elite and not a mere extension of the upper class. The sociodemographic data demonstrate clearly that foundation leaders are far from being part of the WASP establishment that scholars often picture them to be. Only one in three of the foundation elite are white Anglo-Saxon Protestants. While wealthier than members of other elite groups, many have risen from less affluent origins and are substantially more mobile than members of the most liberal of elite groups, public interest leaders.

Moreover, the foundation elite is the most politically noncohesive and politically polarized of elite groups in the United States. While roughly 40 percent are conservative, almost one-third are liberal. In contrast, other elite groups are either predominantly conservative or predominantly liberal.

Furthermore, some issues are more polarizing than others. Philanthropy leaders are most polarized on questions of collectivist liberalism. The conservative foundation leaders are as ideologically conservative as the business leaders, while foundation liberals are as liberal as the public interest group leaders. Foundation leaders are also polarized on issues of affirmative action, crime, and foreign policy. The foundation elite, however, are not particularly polarized on expressive individualism. The gap between conservative and liberal foundation leaders is not as large concerning this as it is on other issues.

Despite political polarization, foundation leaders do hold to a philanthropic ethos, parts of which are not related to political ideology. There is strong support for an autonomous nonprofit sector to provide a safety net against unfettered *laissez-faire* capitalism. At the same time, foundation leaders think philanthropy should support projects ignored by the welfare state.

Foundation leaders, regardless of ideology, also partake in the American tradition of voluntarism and progressivism. Many think organized philanthropy should promote some larger societal good, regardless of political ideology. Political liberalism does inject itself in support for innovative, anti–status quo foundation practices and preference for social change spending.

In actual public policy grant making, however, our data show that the much vaunted philanthropic pluralism does not extend to the ideological sphere. Foundation pluralism is, in fact, much more limited. Most foundation spending for public policy projects tilts toward the left, despite all the talk among foundation professionals on the virtues of philanthropic pluralism.

Our public policy data show that foundations support a variety of approaches to the same problem, which James Douglas and Aaron Wildavsky (1978) note is one type of philanthropic pluralism. This "project pluralism" means that foundations on the whole do not concentrate their support on a few donees (with the exception of funding the relatively few general-purpose think tanks).

Foundations, in trying many different approaches to the same problem, spread their funds around to many recipients. In specific areas such as the public interest movement, we find that the American Civil Liberties Union (ACLU) receives much support from foundations. Other groups such as the National Association for the Advancement of Colored People (NAACP), the Puerto Rican Legal Defense Fund, and the Southern Poverty Law Center also receive considerable foundation support. In the field of family and population issues, Planned Parenthood, despite its prominence, received only 10 of the 140 grants distributed in the year our study was carried out.

General strategy among foundation leaders, thus, seems to be what Douglas and Wildavsky (1978) call foundation procedural pluralism. "By supporting a wide variety of projects, foundations could hope that some would work, even though each one had a low probability of success. . . . They could try some of this and some of that" (Douglas and Wildavsky, 1978, p. 35). This is reflected in foundations covering a wide variety of subject areas—economics, international relations, family and population issues, media studies, affirmative action programs, community organizations, civic affairs, health and medicine, and so on. A few like the Henry J. Kaiser and Robert Woods Johnson Foundations concentrate on health care and develop a corresponding board and staff with considerable specialization and expertise. Others like Rockefeller and Ford have some programs that depend on staff and board expertise. On the whole, many of the large public policy foundations retain their general-purpose character and support many projects in a wide variety of public policy arenas.

Nonetheless, there is a paradox. A majority of the foundation elite are either conservatives or moderates; roughly 40 percent are conservative. In terms of actual public policy funding, however, liberal grants outnumber conservative grants by roughly four to one.

Several factors produce the disjunction, but the most important reason why most public policy funding tilts toward the left is that conservatives on the whole favor traditional, nonideological types of funding. Conservatives are not in favor of increasing social change spending, but only a few conservative respondents actively favor cutting most social change programs. Most think these programs should remain at current levels of support. Only two types of projects—funding for gays and funding for African American studies programs—are targeted for cuts by a majority of conservatives.

The prominent, ideologically conservative foundations, a product of the late 1970s, are unique in this regard. Recall that three in four foundations support *no* public policy project of any kind, conservative or liberal. These foundations, which scholars like Waldemar Nielsen label "conservative," are those that stay out of public policy funding or, at best, support noncontroversial, nonideological projects. These "traditionalist" foundations offer a contrast to the ideologically conservative ones, which knowingly support projects tilted toward the right. These include free-market approaches toward environmental problems, and public interest law firms supporting right-to-work cases. However, while liberal grants outnumber conservative ones four to one, the average conservative grant is more than twice the amount of the liberal one.

We believe the disparity in average dollar amounts awarded conservative, liberal, and neutral recipients reflects the relatively few conservative researchers and activists among nonprofit donees. As many conservative commentators lament, the best and brightest conservatives go into business. This leaves other arenas—government and politics, culture and education, and health and human services—generally open to liberal dominance. This is why liberals receive more grants and have available a greater total of funds. Each conservative project accounts for a substantial share of conservative money, but far fewer conservatives work in the nonprofit sector.

Theorists that promote the view of foundations as extensions of upper-class rule are thus correct in one regard. The foundation world on the whole is very traditional, acting as they claim "to support the status quo." In the case of traditional foundation behavior, this means historically *not* supporting ideological projects, either on the right or on the left. In addition, most foundations today do not fund any public policy projects.

The upper-class theorists are wrong, however, to equate a lack of support for social change projects with an explicit conservative ideology as applied to philanthropy. Moreover, they are wrong to define liberalism as merely "sophisticated conservatism" (Fisher, 1983) that modifies the system via the welfare state in order to save it.

The real problem, and one that lies beneath our disagreement with many theorists on the left, has to do with the meaning of the term *conservative*. The next section discusses the confusion over the term *conservative* and how it has been misapplied to the study of foundations.

As we have shown, most foundations are *ideologically* neither liberal nor conservative. They are neutral and avoid public policy funding. We call them traditional. This is a conservatism of sentiment, not of belief.

LIBERALISM, CONSERVATISM, AND IDEOLOGICAL SOPHISTICATION

To be a conservative can mean being consciously ideological with regard to a host of political and social issues, as we have used the term throughout this book. It can also refer to a temperament that instinctively hates anything that changes. Conservatives by temperament are, in fact, what John Stuart Mill talks about when calling conservatives "stupid." In his treatise *Considerations on Representative Government* (1972) Mill states, "Conservatives, as being by the law of their existence the stupidest party, have much the greater sins of this description to answer for" (p. 261). Sociologist Karl Mannheim (1971) claims the same about the genesis of conservative thought. Conservatism, according to Mannheim, is not an ideology at all but is bound up with traditional modes of action, that is, "the taken-for-granted world."

In the American case, Irving Kristol (1978), prominent neoconservative intellectual, argues that conservatism is traditional Americanism and, like all traditional modes, instinctive and unreflective. American conservatism (i.e., of sentiment) sensitizes persons to particulars, not to abstract ideas. This affinity to the particulars makes them resistant to the lures of ideological thinking.

More than just resistant to ideological thinking, this type of American conservatism is inherently suspicious of change. It is bound up with such gems of wisdom as "if it ain't broke, don't fix it," and "if it is not necessary to change, it is necessary not to change." The result, Kristol speculates, is an aversion to innovation based upon mere theoretical speculation (1978, p. 121). Ironically, this aversion to speculative thought is responsible for American conservatism's relative lack of success.

In repeated studies of the general public, political scientists find that only a few Americans think clearly and without prompting about political issues, political parties, and candidates in ideological terms, conservative or liberal. Philip Converse, in his classic study of American voter ideology (1964), finds that only one in forty voters uses *any* kind of abstract concept (e.g., affirmative action, free enterprise, law and order, extremist, isolationism) to evaluate candidates. Others (Nie, Verba, and Petrocik, 1976; Neuman, 1986) find proportionately more ideologues—up to 17 percent of the general public by the mid-seventies. The overwhelming majority of the voting public, however, choose candidates based on narrow (and undefined) group interest (e.g., is he good for labor?), what Converse (1964) calls "the nature of the times" (e.g., has the economy gotten better or worse?), or purely personal characteristics.

Nonideological thinking that does not like change, either good or bad, is a form of traditionalism. This traditionalism is what the radical scholars of philanthropy consistently confuse with programmatic conservatism. Because traditionalism is instinctive and unreflective, it naturally leads individuals to support the status quo, whatever that status quo may be. This innate traditionalism instinctively finds repugnant an explicitly ideological (or programmatic) conservatism. This may explain why many traditional foundations steer away from funding an ideologically explicit, conservative agenda but choose to limit funds to traditional institutions.

The irony of such funding strategies is that some traditional institutions, such as universities and the mainline American churches, have also become prominent sites for radical scholarship and activism (on the religious elite, see Lerner, Rothman, and Lichter, 1989). The mainline Protestant leadership is decidedly to the left of most other leadership groups on most ideological dimensions. The Catholic elite is also liberal, with the exception of issues related to expressive individualism (e.g., abortion, homosexuality). The religious elite and U.S. intellectuals generally are also the most ideologically consistent and the most ideologically sophisticated of all elites (Lerner, Nagai, and Rothman, 1991). In the case of the university, this is especially true in the humanities and social sciences, with such programs as women's studies, critical legal studies (in the law schools), gay and lesbian studies, and other forms of "multicultural" curricula.

In contrast to traditionalists, liberals and radicals act from more coherent thought systems. Much of the explicitness, we believe, relates to their favoring change. Favoring change forces an intelligent person to think about and articulate the kind of change being favored. Rarely are U.S. elites in favor of change simply for its own sake.

Our survey data generally show this split in ideological sophistication among U.S. elites—between liberal elite groups, which are ideologically coherent, and traditionally conservative elite groups, which are considerably less so. The latter on the whole lack the same kind of political sophistication and coherence possessed "naturally" by liberal elites and those of the left (Lerner, Nagai, and Rothman, 1991).

Concerning philanthropy, then, most conservative and moderate foundation leaders are traditionalists when it comes to funding (i.e., conservatives of sentiment), even though many may have fairly consistent political attitudes. They are traditionalists because traditionalists do *not* want to fund public policy grants, and most foundations stay away from public policy funding.

The programmatically conservative foundations, however, are a different breed altogether. They are on the "cutting edge" of the right, forming a policy idea network along with such journals of opinion as *The National Review* and *The American Spectator* and with think tanks such as Heritage, Hoover, and the American Enterprise Institute. Because they are explicitly promoting an ideological agenda like their liberal counterparts, their work can be characterized as what sociologist Richard Colvard calls "risk capital philanthropy" (1964, p. 728). Philanthropoid Frank Emerson Andrews first articulates this idea of "foundation[s] as venture capital providers": "The new [foundation] doctrine asserted that the funds of foundations were largely the venture capital of philanthropy, best spent when invested in enterprises requiring risk and foresight, not likely to be supported either by government or the private individual'' (1956, p. 12).

If typical American conservatism is one of sentiment and habits, then the agenda of these progammatically conservative foundations is explicitly innovative and riskier. Funding ideas and theories—in short, the abstract rather than what Kristol (1978) calls the particulars—goes against the temperament of the traditionalist. Hence, risk capital philanthropy, whether on the right or on the left, is unpopular within the foundation world. It is inherently more uncertain and has a greater rate of failure.

When risk capital philanthropy succeeds, however, there is a major paradigm shift. It is no accident that William Galston, an advisor to Walter Mondale during his losing presidential bid, could credit the network of programmatically conservative groups—the foundations, think tanks, and activist nonprofits—with creating a new "ideas industry" (Nielsen, 1985, p. 56). He claims, "It's almost impossible to overrate the importance of ideas in politics. . . . Ronald Reagan won last time on the strength of ideas" (quoted in Nielsen, 1985, p. 56). It is an idea that occurs naturally to liberals but not to all conservatives.

THE IMPACT OF POLITICIZED FUNDING

Despite the rise of the programmatic conservative foundation, public policy funding is still slanted toward the left. What then are the consequences of a liberal tilt in public policy grant making? What, for that matter, are the consequences of programmatically conservative foundations and conservative recipients in a world that is predominantly liberal? What are the ramifications of politicization and ideological conflict?

One result, ironically, has been polarization of the pluralism of ideas in the foundation world and of the policy arena in general. Another result, mostly due to long-term liberal dominance, is a subtle moving toward the left among conservatives of sentiment. Liberal foundations have had their impact, especially upon traditionals who come to accept the tenets of modern liberalism as the common-sense view of the world.

Polarized Pluralism

Politicization and sharpened ideological conflict permit the existence of some diversity of thought in the foundation world today. Whatever the general tilt of that world, diverse ideas do get a hearing, and diverse projects are tried. The vision of the marketplace of ideas comes to at least some fruition here. Foundations, liberal and conservative alike, have made large investments in the creation and dissemination of ideas and experimental programs, which probably would not have emerged and been developed without their support.

The new policy network—in effect, an alternative power elite—includes these policy foundations and their public policy recipients, along with key players in government. The foundation becomes a part of the policy network when it encourages government to deal with victims of larger social forces "by identifying programs and policies . . . that convert isolated and discretionary acts of private charity into regularized public remedies that flow as a matter of legislated right" (Mavity and Ylvisaker, 1977, pp. 797–98).

In the "new politics," business and labor no longer dominate the policy arena. Logrolling and bargaining no longer work as mechanisms for resolving disputes. Key players now lack the same kind of interest group benefits that business and labor actively seek from government.

Social movements, think tanks, and intellectuals set the ideological tone. Foundations support them. As a result, the policy arena moves from mainstream to radical politics (Lowi, 1988, pp. viii-xxi). Theodore J. Lowi argues that liberals and conservatives in old-style "mainstream politics" conducted an incrementalist and centrist policy making, where politics was the art of compromise. In the new form, positions are polarized. Much of the radicalization, however, started in the 1960s with the rise of the New Left and the counter-culuture—a point we must stress. The "new politics" include issues such as affirmative action, school prayer, gun control, crime, and abortion. Leaders mobilize supporters around absolutist positions and reject compromise. Language defining policy problems changes from the more mainstream concepts of "error," "utility," "entitlement," and "accountability," to moral absolutes—"sin," "civic virtue," "rights," and "commitment."

It can be argued that policies and politics of polarization weaken the legitimacy of the U.S. political culture. For people to retain their political identification, they must adopt policy preferences increasingly moving to the left or right. Or they could change their political self-identification (e.g., flipping from liberal to conservative, as did a number of prominent neoconservatives). People, however, also could become sufficiently dismayed to reject the political culture entirely and search for a new charismatic leader. The prospect of a majority disillusioned with the U.S. political culture poses grave risks to foundations. High-risk endeavors combined with little openness and no short-run political accountability run the risk of populist backlash among mass segments already disillusioned with U.S. politics.

What then does this say about philanthropic pluralism? The philosophy of philanthropic pluralism is predicated on the belief that reasonable persons cannot and do not agree on what constitutes the common good and the best way to achieve it. Yet, one cannot truly have conflict among equals, when some ideas and projects rely on government for enforcement or implementation. Programs that act as pilot programs for government action or projects that lead to government intervention (i.e., funding for the ACLU) ultimately depend on the *power* of government. Pluralism is harder to achieve when the power of government lies behind some programs but not others.

Promoting certain views by university administrations parallels, we believe, government-connected foundation projects. Philosopher David Sidorsky (1987) compares academic versus philanthropic pluralism. He notes that when universities advocate some views but not others, they force dissenting opinions underground.

In the last analysis, programs that rely on government for more funding, large-scale implementation, widespread regulation, and systematic enforcement potentially undercut potential projects that are openly in conflict. Do the latter find alternative sources of funding, or, like academic opinions, are they ignored? Or are some thought "racist," "elitist," "un-American," or "immoral" (i.e., illegitimate)?

Current conditions present a potential for foundations to confront the problem of the new polarized politics, and how government-nonprofit relations relate to the ideal of philanthropic pluralism. They also present a potential for foundations to deal with the *concurrent* problems of market and government failure as, for example, in the inner city. Their role straddles the new and old power elite. In these more unstable times, public policy foundations can play a pivotal role in finding a new, common ground. Ironically, they could also fund irrelevant proposals, projects that turn out badly, or those that are very unpopular. Such, unfortunately, is the nature of venture-capital philanthropy.

The problems of polarized pluralism that stem from ideologically conservative challenges to liberal policy networks are only one aspect of politicized foundations and public policy funding. The other problem is the dominance of the adversary culture among strategic elites and its impact on nonideological leadership groups.

One consequence of liberal dominance has been the gradual adoption of liberalism as the conventional wisdom. Many of the ideas that form part of the liberal agenda today, especially collectivist liberalism, affirmative action, and expressive individualism issues, were in fact quite radical at first (see Rothman, Lichter, and Lichter, forthcoming). How does such liberal dominance occur among foundations?

Much of the ideological slide is a function of the structure of the typical foundation. By contrasting the world of foundations and nonprofit recipients to that of markets and governments, we can talk about the difficulties inherent in the relationship between the foundation and the recipient. Because a foundation leader, especially without the appropriate technical training, cannot easily evaluate projects, there are difficulties in choosing amongst grant requests submitted by professionals and experts in the nonprofit sector. How do foundation leaders know whom to trust? We begin our discussion with an analysis of how the nonprofit sector (foundations and nonprofit recipient organizations such as charities, universities, and hospitals) differs from the economy and government.

The Three Sectors

Many writers divide nonfamilial life in the United States into three basic spheres: the market, politics, and the nonprofit sector, which means the many nonprofit associations, both voluntary and commercial, characteristic of U.S. life but largely ignored in academic research until recently. (See, for example, Nielsen, 1979; Hansmann, 1987; and Douglas, 1987).

To highlight the differences among sectors, especially in terms of feedback mechanisms, we use this tripartite classification in discussing foundations and grant recipients. We recognize, however, that the boundaries are not as distinct as they might seem in theory. Many nonprofit organizations today receive most of their funding from and do much of their work with related federal and state agencies (see Salamon, 1987). We thus treat the distinction as one among ideal types.

The first sector, the economy, consists of markets composed of firms and customers. In highly simplistic terms, market equilibrium consists of providing what customers want. It is a simple exchange relationship, whereby each side—the firm and the customer—is free to pursue its respective interests. Individual self-interest results in a quid pro quo between firm and customer. The firm-customer relationship of mutual benefit is pursued over a wide range of goods and services and leads to rationality of the market's "invisible hand."

The electoral arena provides the political analogy to markets. Most rational-choice theories of electoral politics start with the assumption that the goal of political parties is to win elections (e.g., Coleman, 1972; Davis and Hinich, 1968; Downs, 1957; Hotelling, 1929; see Page, 1978 for review of literature). The political parties are like firms.

These theorists also assume that voters identify themselves along a left-to-right, liberal-to-conservative continuum. The idea behind rational theories of elections and government is that political parties will strategically place themselves along this liberal-conservative continuum to attract just enough voters to win. The idea is that a political party, in order to win an election in our two-party system, need appeal only to 50 percent plus one individual voter, although more votes would be better. Rather than trying to please all the voters, they aim to please the minimum majority. The other party, the one that does not give the majority what they want, loses the election.[1] Once in office, the party in power must retain its majority. Subsequent elections become a referendum on party performance, and the logic of governing is to provide a sufficient mix of policy positions to satisfy the minimum percentage of voters necessary to win. Voters (who are analogous to consumers in the marketplace) express their preferences through polls and elections. In the long run, politicians act to satisfy voters. They act as voters want them to act.

If we apply these analogies to foundation behavior in the third sector, we find that foundations are analogous to consumers and voters. Just as consumers have the money sought by firms, and voters have the votes sought by politicians, foundations have something (grant money) that nonprofit applicants—such as universities, social movements, and think tanks—want. Grant recipients provide the product, as do firms and politicians.

If we draw an analogy between the foundation–grant applicant relationship and the consumer-firm/voter-politician relationships, we see the problems foundations face in the process of dispensing funds. There are few foundations, especially in the public policy arena, but many potential recipients. For example, our public policy sample includes 225 foundations and over 4,000 funded projects. We have no idea how many requests for funds were turned down.

In contrast, the voter's choices are simpler. Each voter has to choose between one Democrat and one Republican candidate in most electoral contests.

The oligopsony is the market parallel to the foundation-applicant relationship. In an oligopsony, a few customers are wooed by many firms. In a labor market, a few employers are courted by many job seekers.

The political parallel to the foundation-recipient relationship is the relationship between government agencies and interest groups. The Department of Defense, for example, is the sole "consumer," pursued by many military suppliers. Jane H. Mavity and Paul Ylvisaker (1977, p. 795) allude to the asymmetrical balance of power between foundation and grant applicants when they compare the grant-making process to the legislative one and the foundation to a private legislature.

We pursue the analogy further because the differences highlight the uneasy relationship among foundations, public policy, and politics today. In the same way that the legislature limits contact with most interest groups and constituents, foundations screen out most communications received from the outside world. For foundations, an overwhelming number of communications are requests for money. The parallel for those of us not in the foundation world would be the pleas we receive daily through the mail, in magazines, and on television and radio for donations to fight hunger, homelessness, poverty, illiteracy, disease, and a host of other societal ills. Deciding who or what groups should receive government support is the same decision faced by foundations.

Compounding this problem of deciding among many applicants is that the foundation, unlike the consumer or voter, does not materially benefit directly from recipient output (see Hansmann, 1987). Consumers benefit directly from the products and services delivered by firms. Voters receive benefits and taxes, thanks to their elected officials. The foundation "purchases" services or a product in the form of awarding a grant, but the difference is that these outputs either go to a third party or contribute to "the public good." The concept of the "public good," however, is so vague and ill-defined that the foundation cannot easily determine its impact (Hansmann, 1987, p. 30).

One concrete example is foundation funding for individual scholarships in higher education, versus individual students "purchasing" (i.e., paying tuition) directly for higher education from a particular university program. The payer who directly receives the benefits (in this case, students who pay their own tuition) gets better feedback regarding whether the services expected were delivered at all, much less how well a particular program and university performed. The foundations are removed from directly receiving the benefits of providing the scholarship. The foundation that provides the scholarship is like the scholarship student's parents, only even more distant; the foundation has an even harder time evaluating the quality of the product since its relationship with the scholarship recipient is even more distant.

The foundation faces other problems when the contribution goes toward the "public good." As Henry Hansmann points out (1987), the foundation (or any donor) cannot know whether that particular contribution produces a corresponding increase in the quality or quantity of that good. An example would be a $5,000 grant to a peace group in the Middle East. There is really no way to know whether this grant produces $5,000 worth of improvements in the Middle East relations.

A foundation, regardless of its distinctive identity and history, is thus an organization lacking feedback. In markets and politics, feedback comes in the form of increasing profits and winning elections. There are "measuring rods" by which firms and politicians can evaluate their performance. Consumers and firms have money as their standard; voters and parties have opinion polls and elections. Firms that attend to consumer wants make profits; parties that do what voters want win elections. Consumers and voters are also aided by the reputation of the firm or political party and by relying on sources they trust (see Downs, 1957, pp. 220–237). Federal agencies, consumer-oriented magazines, and competitive advertising help consumers make choices among products. This process is most important when consumers lack the expertise to evaluate product quality—for example, when purchasing microcomputers.

All foundations face the problem of finding criteria by which to sort applicants into categories of deserving and undeserving. Foundations and applicants do not have money, opinion polls, or elections as appropriate standards for measuring behavior; all that is readily available to them is the language of good intentions (the grant proposal). The grant proposal, however, is a vague substitute for currency and votes. To deal with the lack of an easy performance measure, foundations resort to other, more elaborate mechanisms. As a result, many foundations rely on the professional reputation of their applicants or ideological labels if the foundation works within an explicit ideological framework.

Relying on ideological labels, however, is not limited to foundations. All nonspecialists, whether they act in the role of voters, consumers, or donors, sometimes rely on ideological labels along with information provided by the various media and public opinion polls as guides for taking appropriate action when faced with more technical policy concerns. Ideological labels, in fact, act as informational short cuts for the nonspecialists. One example is the field of health and medical care. If noted congressional liberals and trusted news sources support a certain health care reform policy, and if the voter is a liberal, the voter often will support the policy outright rather than conduct his or her own individual policy analysis. This is especially true if he or she does not have the technical background. Even if he or she has the background, however, the individual will more likely rely on labels. To personally construct a model based on the medical, social, political, and economic costs and benefits of proposed health care policy innovations takes time.

What happens when the governmental arena undergoes a policy shift either to the right or to the left? Let us assume, first of all, that to the highly interested, politically sophisticated person, retaining her or his political self-identification, even in the face of cognitive dissonance, means holding on to a core identity as liberal or conservative, Democrat or Republican. When politics and policies shift, many of these politically sophisticated persons nonetheless seek to retain their ideological self-labels.

In order to retain the liberal label over time, it is not uncommon for committed liberals to shift policy preferences to match the label. Thus, being a liberal in the early 1960s meant supporting the Voting Rights Act of 1965. A liberal today includes supporting affirmative action, environmentalism, and a woman's right to choose. Wildavsky (1991) captures much of the shift in the U.S. political culture in his chapter "Egalitarianism on the Rise?" (1991, pp. 63–98). He describes several indicators pointing to rising radical egalitarianism. We list three in chapter seven that characterize a core social-change-oriented group within the foundation elite. The characteristics include a critical number of believers, many of them holding these beliefs intensely, and many of them altering key institutions. Wildavsky argues that a further indicator of a rise in radical egalitarianism is a shift in public policy debate (1991, p. 65), which becomes increasingly dominated by egalitarian concerns. Because liberalism is progressively identified with egalitarianism, one adopts these positions in order to maintain one's self-identification as a liberal.

Liberal and traditional foundations are more beholden to such intellectual shifts. Those who see themselves as "conservative by sentiment," but shy away from supporting explicitly ideological programs, turn the power to identify social problems and solutions over to liberal foundations. Thus, while they overstate the case, foundation critics on the right, who view the foundation elite as part of the adversary culture, grasp an important part of the truth. A critical mass of foundation leaders and foundations partakes of this adversary viewpoint and continues to push for social change and to push foundation practices increasingly toward the left.

NOTE

1. Versions of this paradigm in political science go as far back as H. Hotelling in 1929 and remain important in political science today. For a summary of the literature, see Benjamin I. Page (1978, pp. 10–28).

APPENDIX 1

SURVEY METHODOLOGY

DEFINING FOUNDATIONS WITH IMPACT

The common mode of determining the universe of relevant foundations in other studies of foundations is to consider foundation assets (see, for example, Colwell, 1980; Nielsen, 1972, and 1985). The size of assets is a good indicator of organizational wealth, but we believe that foundation spending is a more direct measure of impact. Using spending as a measure enables us to include those foundations mandated to spend themselves out of existence. It also eliminates foundations with large assets that make few grants (see Nielsen, 1985, pp. 227–34, for a discussion of one glaring example). We limit our universe of foundations to those that distributed over $1 million in grants in the fiscal year reported in the 1987 *Foundation Directory* (Foundation Center, 1987).

Because our studies of U.S. elites are national in scope, we sought to find a similar group of foundation elites. To accomplish this, we limited the foundations in our universe to those with impact that went beyond the local arena. We defined these as foundations that did *not* limit their grants to a particular city (e.g., ''Giving limited to New Bedford, Massachusetts'') (Foundation Center, 1987). We are confident of the national scope of the list of foundations, developed from the data provided by the *Directory*. It is the standard reference for grant seekers across the country, from those working for the smallest nonprofit organizations to major research universities. More importantly, *The Foundation Directory* asks foundation officers to explicitly report any limitations on grant disbursement.[1] A total of 844 foundations met these criteria.

THE SAMPLE AND THE SURVEY

The initial sample of 289 persons was randomly chosen from the universe of trustees and officers of the 844 independent and corporate foundations previously discussed. More literally, we compiled a list of all officers and trustees and selected the sample from this list using a random number table. Each individual, whether an officer or trustee, had an equal probability of being selected for the sample. (Unfortunately, our confidentiality requirements made it impossible to distinguish between officers and other trustees.) It is thus possible that two or more individuals associated with the same foundation could be in the sample, and undoubtedly there were foundations where no officers or board members were selected.

The questionnaire consisted of twenty pages of questions on a wide variety of political and social issues and a considerable amount of demographic information similar to those we have used to study other U.S. leadership groups. In addition, we asked our respondents about issues facing foundations today. These included: (1) general questions about the nature of philanthropic foundations; (2) questions on who makes critical decisions in their foundation; and (3) questions about the kinds of proposals foundations should fund.

Prior to conducting the survey, the questionnaire was pretested on a sample of foundation executives and members of boards of trustees not in our universe. After some revisions, the survey itself was conducted from May 1989 to February 1990 in the form of a mail questionnaire. In order to achieve as high a response rate as possible, we sent out four consecutive mailings, each of which was followed up by phone calls to urge respondents to complete the questionnaire. After the fourth wave, we concluded that it might take 6 or more additional months and thousands of dollars to raise the response rate still further. The survey ended with 126 respondents, giving us a response rate of 43.6 percent. In reaching this figure, we did not delete from the original sample of 289 the 70 persons who were unreachable (e.g., those who were spending the year in Europe). If we delete these 70, we obtain a response rate of 58 percent.[2] (See Dillman, 1978, pp. 48–52, for an extensive discussion of the differences in the calculation of response rates for mail surveys and for telephone interviews.)

Because our response rate was somewhat lower than usual, we completed some additional analysis to try to locate possible response biases. One technique we employed was to correlate the order in which questionnaires were returned with other respondents' characteristics as a crude approximation to nonresponse. This procedure assumed, not unreasonably, that the more time a respondent took to return the questionnaire, the more similar he or she was to the typical nonrespondent. In order to examine this, the questionnaires were numbered sequentially in the order in which they were returned. We then correlated every variable used in our subsequent analyses (and some that were not) with the order in which the questionnaires were returned. Fortunately, only five of the eighty-six correlations thus generated were statistically significant, a finding which was most likely explained by chance alone. In particular, self-identified political ideology, a seven-point scale which was a crucial variable in our analysis, was negligibly correlated with the order in which questionnaires were returned ($r = .04$).[3]

In addition, we were able to compare respondents and nonrespondents on certain demographic and organizational characteristics. We found that there was no difference between respondents and nonrespondents in their gender and in the size of foundation assets. There was a difference between respondents and nonrespondents in the number of staff employed by their foundation. Respondents were more likely than nonrespondents to come from organizations with more staff. (However, if the Ford respondents are dropped from the calculation, there would be no statistically significant difference between the two groups.)

Compared to our studies of other elite groups, individual members of the foundation elite can be easily identified if one merely knows certain demographic characteristics of the individual, the foundation position, and the name of the foundation. To insure confidentiality, we did not ask our respondents what their exact job titles were or the names of the foundations for which they worked. We cannot identify which respondents are members of the donor family, are noteworthy elites from other institutions, or are the career professionals. This limits our ability to address the relationship between type of foundation elite (e.g., family member versus foundation professional) and other variables, but it upholds our commitment to insuring the confidentiality of respondents. This limitation, however, does not extend to answering the question of overall mobility within the foundation elite. We asked our respondents about their social background—race, sex, age, where they went to school, and, most important for our assessment of whether the foundation elite is better characterized as a strategic elite or an upper-class group, their parents' occupation and educational attainment.

NOTES

1. According to *The Foundation Directory* (Foundation Center, 1987, pp. 1i–1iii), there are four types of foundations: the independent foundation, the company foundation, the community foundation, and the operating foundation.

- The independent foundation is a private foundation whose primary activity is making grants. Although its assets are derived from a single donor or family, the independent foundation is separate from the individual donor. The Ford, John D. and Catherine T. MacArthur, and Rockefeller foundations, for example, are all independent foundations established by individual donors.
- The company foundation, the second most common type, derives its funds from the profit-making corporation but is legally independent from it. The primary activity of the corporate foundation is to make grants, not profits. A recipient thus could receive separate contributions from the company foundation and from the company itself (for example, the Coca Cola Foundation and the Coca Cola Company).
- The community foundation, a newer type, is classified by the Internal Revenue Service as a public charity that makes grants for charitable purposes in a specific community. Funds come from the public, in contrast to an individual donor family or single corporation, and are held in an endowment. Interest generated from the endowment is distributed as grants.
- The operating foundation is a private foundation whose primary purpose is to conduct its own programs. The J. Paul Getty Trust, for example, runs the J. Paul Getty Museum and six other programs in the arts and humanities. The Russell Sage Foundation runs its own programs that focus on basic research, conferences, and seminars in the social and behavioral sciences.

The Foundation Directory (1987) lists 4,100 independent foundations, compared to 781 company, 160 community, and 107 operating foundations.

2. On the difficulties of obtaining a higher response rate, Dr. James Wiley, assistant director of the University of California Survey Research Center, writes,

Respondents are extremely well insulated by secretaries, administrative assistants, and others who take messages, promise to "bring it to their attention if you'll send another copy" and produce myriad other diversionary tactics that are hard to combat. . . . Never have we encountered the kind of objections made to the questionnaire or even about the procedures (with one man objecting that we were presumptuous in sending something to him by mail)." (Personal correspondence with the authors, January 14, 1990)

The response rate of Teresa Jean Odendahl, Elizabeth Trocolli Boris, and Arlene Kaplan Daniels's study on career patterns (1985) is 33 percent, while the response rate of Allen H. Barton's survey of the very wealthy is 31 percent (1975). Since our response rate is lower than usual, we consider the findings suggestive rather than statistically definitive.

3. The five variables that were statistically significantly correlated with the order of return did not form any kind of coherent set.

None of the attitudes toward philanthropy, none of the structural variables, and none of the variables measuring political interest were significantly correlated. Two of twenty-four questions on spending priorities, two of forty-one attitudinal questions, and one of nine demographic measures were statistically significant. Only two of the correlation coefficients were as high as 0.20, and none were higher than 0.25. The five questions that were significantly correlated were: (1) family income while growing up ($r = .17$, $p < .05$); (2) increasing, maintaining, or decreasing funding for international student exchanges ($r = -.20, p < .03$); (3) increasing, maintaining, or decreasing funding for human rights ($r = .19, p < .04$); (4) whether or not the government should guarantee jobs ($r = .19, p < .04$); and (5) whether or not the United States needs a complete restructuring of its basic institutions ($r = .25, p < .006$). The latter two questions were in four-point Likert format.

SAMPLES OF AMERICAN ELITES

Bureaucrats. High-ranking bureaucrats make up the sample from the Office of Personnel Management's *List of Senior Executive Personnel*. Political appointees are excluded. Half the sample is drawn from "activist" agencies, which include: the Civil Rights Division of the Justice Department, the Environmental Protection Agency (EPA), the Department of Housing and Urban Development (HUD), the Federal Trade Commission (FTC), Action, Consumer Products Safety Commission, Equal Employment Opportunity Commission (EEOC), and the Department of Health and Human Services. The other half were from "traditional" agencies: Commerce, Agriculture, Treasury, Immigration and Naturalization Service (INS), and the Bureau of Prisons. Interviews were conducted in 1982, with a response rate of 85 percent. The final sample size is 200.

The Business Elite. Upper and middle management personnel were randomly drawn from the official company lists of four Fortune 500 companies and of one firm selected from *Fortune* lists of the 50 leading retail outlets, banks, and public utilities, respectively. As a requirement for cooperation, the names of the corporations cannot be publicly disclosed. Interviews were conducted in 1979. The response rate is 96 percent; the final sample size is 242.

Congressional Aides. The random sample of congressional aides was drawn from key committee and personal staff listed in the *Washington Monitor's 1982 Congressional Yellow Book* and cross-checked with the *Congressional Staff Directory*. The interviews were conducted in 1982, with a response rate of 71 percent. The final sample size is 134.

Federal Judges. The random sample of federal judges consisted of those on the bench as of February 1982. Ten at the appeal level and ten district judges were randomly selected from each chosen circuit. The first subsample from New York, Chicago, Los Angeles, and Washington, D.C., was interviewed in 1984; the second subsample from Dallas/Fort

Worth, Detroit, St. Louis, San Francisco, Minneapolis/St. Paul, and North Carolina was interviewed in 1985. The response rate for all samples is 54 percent; the final sample size is 114.

Labor Union Leaders. The random sample consists of presidents and secretary-treasurers from national unions and trade associations with 1,000 or more members, and presidents, vice presidents, research directors, and business managers of major locals, based on the U.S. Department of Labor's *Directory of National Unions and Employee Associations* and subsequently updated through phone calls. There are two subsamples, one from Washington, D.C., New York, Chicago, and Los Angeles done in 1984, the second from Detroit and Minneapolis/St. Paul in 1985. The response rate is 54 percent; the final sample size is 95.

Corporate Lawyers. The random sample of elite corporate lawyers consists of partners from New York and Washington, D.C., law firms with more than 50 partners, based on the *Martindale-Hubbell Law Directory*. Interviews were conducted in 1982. The response rate is 66 percent; the final sample size is 150.

The Media Elite. The media sample consists of a random sample of journalists and editors from the *New York Times*, *Washington Post*, *Wall Street Journal*, *Time*, *Newsweek*, *U.S. News and World Report*, and the news organizations at NBC, ABC, CBS, and PBS. The sampling frame was derived from internal phone directories and the names of individuals listed on mastheads in the case of news magazines. Staff members with responsibility for news coverage were chosen in consultation with knowledgeable people. A computer-generated random sample was chosen from this pool of names. Interviews were conducted in 1979. The response rate is 74 percent; the final sample size is 238.

The Military Elite. The military elite are a random sample of field grade officers from the Pentagon phone book and from the class roster of the National Defense University (NDU). The Pentagon sample consists of general and flag grade officers; the NDU sample consists of noncivilian students mostly at the rank of colonel, commander, and above. Interviews were conducted in 1982. The response rate is 77 percent; the final sample size is 152.

The Movie Elite. The random sample is drawn from a list of writers, producers, and directors of the fifty top-grossing films made between 1965 and 1982, based on *Variety*. Interviews were conducted in 1982. The final sample size is ninety-six; the response rate is 64 percent.

The Public Interest Elite. The random sample is drawn from lists of presidents and members of boards of directors of formal lobbying groups, based on *Public Interest Profiles*, *Washington Five*, and the *Encyclopedia of Associations* and lists of attorneys in public interest law firms drawn from *Public Interest Law: Five Years Later*, and *Balancing the Scales of Justice*. Knowledgeable individuals were also consulted. Equal numbers were drawn from lobby groups and public interest law firms and restricted to Washington, D.C., and New York City. Interviews were conducted in 1982. The response rate is 84 percent; the final sample size is 158.

Religious Elite. In order to find the most influential religious leaders, we contacted the leaders of those Christian denominations with 1 million or more members and the editors of leading religious periodicals such as *Christian Century* (we used their published list of the most influential religious leaders of 1982) and *Christianity and Crisis* and asked them to nominate the most influential religious figures in the United States. We asked them to include the leading figures from the major Christian denominations, leaders of religiously based social action groups, editors of religious journals, and theologians. These nominees provided the basis of our sample. Names that appear on multiple lists were included in our preliminary listing, which was sent out for further review by many of the above groups and individuals. Once again, only consensual choices were retained in our final sample. Among our respondents were the heads of Protestant churches and Catholic orders, university and seminary presidents, editors of major religious publications, prominent "televangelists," and individuals in leadership positions in such organizations as the National Council of Churches, the Moral Majority, the National Conference of Catholic Bishops, the Religious Roundtable, and the National Association of Evangelicals. The interviewing was conducted in 1984 and 1985. The final sample size is 178; the response rate is 77 percent.

The Television Elite. The television sample is based on a reputational sampling frame of an initial list of 350 writers, producers, and executives associated with the development of 2 or more successful prime-time television series. Interviews were conducted in 1982. The response rate is 60 percent; the final sample size is 104.

The interviewing firms were: Response Analysis Corporation, Princeton, New Jersey; Metro Research, Washington, D.C.; Depth Research, New York, New York; Carol Davis Research, Los Angeles, California; Joyner Hutcheson Researchers, Atlanta, Georgia; Arlene Fine Associates, Chicago, Illinois; Davideen Swanger, Dallas, Texas; High Scope Research, Detroit, Michigan; Quality Control Services, Minneapolis/St. Paul, Minnesota; Bartlett Research, San Francisco, California; and Field Service, Inc., St. Louis, Missouri. All interviewers were employees of the firms and received special training, orientation seminars, and preliminary practice interviews. Response Analysis supervised the pretesting of the original questionnaire.

*QUESTIONS AND THEIR FACTOR
LOADINGS ON EACH FACTOR
MEASURING POLITICAL IDEOLOGY
AMONG U.S. ELITES*

System Alienation	Loading
The American legal system mainly favors the wealthy	.49
The American private enterprise system is generally fair to working people	.44
The United States needs a complete restructuring of its basic institutions	.63
Big corporations should be taken out of private ownership and run in the public interest	.47
The structure of our society causes most people to feel alienated	.56
The main goal of U.S. foreign policy has been to protect U.S. business interests	.57

Expressive Individualism	Loading
It is a woman's right to decide whether or not to have an abortion	.52
Lesbians and homosexuals should not be allowed to teach in public schools	.59
It is wrong for a married person to have sexual relations with someone other than his or her spouse	.54
It is wrong for adults of the same sex to have sexual relations	.81

Collectivist Liberalism	Loading
Less government regulation of business would be good for the country	.46
It is not the proper role of government to insure that everyone has a job	.48
Our environmental problems are not as serious as people have been led to believe	.38
The government should work to substantially reduce the income gap between the rich and the poor	.58

Foreign Policy	Loading
We should be more forceful in our dealings with the Soviet Union even if it increases the risk of war	.61
It is important for America to have the strongest military force in the world, no matter what it costs	.60
It is sometimes necessary for the CIA to protect U.S. interests by undermining hostile governments	.50

Crime	Loading
There is too much concern in the courts for the rights of criminals	.57
America should retain the possibility of relying upon the death penalty for persons convicted of first degree murder	.56

Affirmative Action	Loading
Special preference in hiring should be given to blacks	.79
Special preference in hiring should be given to women	.68

Note: Factor loadings for the first three factors are taken from the twelve elite group factor analysis. The factor loadings for the death penalty question are taken from the factor analysis of philanthropy data. The remainder of the factor loadings are taken from the eight elite group factor analysis.

*COVER LETTER AND "SOCIAL
LEADERSHIP IN AMERICA: A SURVEY"*

UNIVERSITY OF CALIFORNIA, BERKELEY

BERKELEY · DAVIS · IRVINE · LOS ANGELES · RIVERSIDE · SAN DIEGO · SAN FRANCISCO SANTA BARBARA · SANTA CRUZ

SURVEY RESEARCH CENTER

BERKELEY, CALIFORNIA 94720

May 22, 1989

Dear

Philanthropic foundations play an increasingly important role in supporting many of America's most important social and cultural achievements. Yet there has not been a detailed study of what those involved in directing such foundations think about the philanthropic mission and its relation to the social and political issues facing society. To help us learn more about the role of philanthropy, we are sending questionnaires to a scientific sample of officers and trustees of foundations which make a significant contribution to American social and political life. While participation is voluntary, we hope we can count on your cooperation.

This investigation is part of a larger study of the political and social attitudes of leadership groups in the United States. In the past, we have conducted surveys of U.S. district and appellate judges, the makers of our most popular television shows and motion pictures, high-ranking military officers, America's religious elite, leaders of America's major public interest groups, high ranking members of the federal civil service, the CEO's of Fortune 500 companies, and other groups.

In order to insure that the opinions of a good cross-section of decision makers are represented, it is important that only YOU complete your copy of the questionnaire. In some foundations, two or more representatives happened to fall into our sample. Because almost all our questions ask for opinions rather than factual data, we need separate questionnaires completed by as many of the individuals in our sample as possible.

Please be assured of complete confidentiality. No one reading the final report will be able to determine who participated or who said what. We have pre-numbered all questionnaires to help us determine which questionnaires have been returned and who needs reminders. Once the data have been collected and checked for major omissions, serial numbers (and any other identifying information which you may have added) will be removed.

If you would like to receive a summary of our findings, please use the enclosed post card. The summary will be sent to interested participants as soon as data analysis is complete.

Please return your completed questionnaire to the Survey Research Center in the enclosed envelope at your earliest opportunity. If you have questions about the survey, please write or call me. My telephone number is (413) 585-3569.

Thank you in advance for your help.

Sincerely,

Robert Lerner, Ph.D., Principal Investigator
Center for the Study of Social
    and Political Change
Smith College

R1830
4/26/89

SOCIAL LEADERSHIP IN AMERICA:

A SURVEY

A WORD ABOUT FILLING OUT THIS QUESTIONNAIRE:

- Please try to answer all the questions.

- Please remember that most questions ask for <u>your personal opinion</u> --
  not necessarily the same as your foundation's official position.

- Most questions can be answered simply by circling a number or checking
  a box. Unless the instruction tells you to circle or check all that
  apply, please mark only one answer to a question.

- We recognize that surveys like this tend to oversimplify issues. If
  you wish to comment on a question or qualify your answer, feel free to
  use the space in the margins or on the last page of the questionnaire.
  (Your comments will be read and incorporated in our analysis).

- If you feel that some questions are too black and white, try to pick the
  answer that comes closest to your own -- just as you would if you were in
  the polling booth and had to choose between two candidates who were less
  than perfect.

- If any questions are confusing or if you need another kind of help,
  please feel free to call Dr. Robert Lerner at (413) 585-3569.

THANK YOU VERY MUCH FOR YOUR HELP.

Sponsored by the Center for the Study of Social and Political Change,
Smith College, Northampton, Massachusetts 01063 in collaboration with
the Survey Research Center, University of California at Berkeley.

CONFIDENTIAL   CONFIDENTIAL

#___ ___ ___

- 1 -

I.   LEADERS AND MOVEMENTS

Below is a list of 12 different individuals or groups active in political affairs.
For each one, please circle one number, indicating how strongly you approve of that
person or group.

	Disapprove Strongly	Disapprove Somewhat	Approve Somewhat	Approve Strongly	Have no opinion
A. Ronald Reagan.........	1	2	3	4	5
B. Margaret Thatcher.....	1	2	3	4	5
C. Fidel Castro..........	1	2	3	4	5
D. The Sandinistas.......	1	2	3	4	5
E. The Moral Majority....	1	2	3	4	5
F. Edward Kennedy........	1	2	3	4	5
G. Ralph Nader...........	1	2	3	4	5
H. Jeane Kirkpatrick.....	1	2	3	4	5
I. John Kenneth Galbraith	1	2	3	4	5
J. Milton Friedman.......	1	2	3	4	5
K. Andrew Young..........	1	2	3	4	5
L. Gloria Steinem........	1	2	3	4	5

- 2 -

II. NEWS SOURCES

For each of the following sources of news or opinion, please circle one of the seven
numbers, indicating how much faith you have in that source. For example, if you
consider a particular source as NOT AT ALL RELIABLE, circle the "1" on that line. If
you think the source is VERY RELIABLE, please circle the "7" for that item. If the
reliability of a source falls somewhere in between, please choose one of the
intermediate positions, noting that "4" is the MIDDLE POSITION.

	YOUR FAITH IN THIS NEWS SOURCE *(Please circle one number for each)*							Totally unfamiliar with it
	Not at all reliable ↓						Very reliable ↓	↓
A. Time Magazine..........	1	2	3	4	5	6	7	8
B. Newsweek...............	1	2	3	4	5	6	7	8
C. U.S. News and World Report.................	1	2	3	4	5	6	7	8
D. National Review........	1	2	3	4	5	6	7	8
E. New Republic...........	1	2	3	4	5	6	7	8
F. New York Review of Books.................	1	2	3	4	5	6	7	8
G. The Nation.............	1	2	3	4	5	6	7	8
H. Commentary.............	1	2	3	4	5	6	7	8
I. Public Interest........	1	2	3	4	5	6	7	8
J. New York Times.........	1	2	3	4	5	6	7	8
K. Public television...... (PBS)	1	2	3	4	5	6	7	8
L. TV network news........	1	2	3	4	5	6	7	8
M. Washington Post........	1	2	3	4	5	6	7	8

- 3 -

III.   SOCIAL, POLITICAL AND ECONOMIC ATTITUDES

The following list of statements presents a considerable range of views on various issues in contemporary society. For each statement, please circle one number, indicating how strongly you agree or disagree with that point-of-view.

		Agree Strongly	Agree Somewhat	Disagree Somewhat	Disagree Strongly
A.	Less government regulation of business would be good for the country	1	2	3	4
B.	The American legal system mainly favors the wealthy	1	2	3	4
C.	The American private enterprise system is generally fair to working people	1	2	3	4
D.	Everyone should obey society's accepted moral rules	1	2	3	4
E.	It's a woman's right to decide whether or not to have an abortion	1	2	3	4
F.	It is not the proper role of government to insure that everyone has a job	1	2	3	4
G.	Under a fair economic system, people with more ability should earn higher salaries	1	2	3	4
H.	People who are willing to work hard should be allowed to get ahead	1	2	3	4
I.	Lesbians and other homosexuals should not be allowed to teach in public schools	1	2	3	4
J.	We should be more forceful in our relations with the USSR even if it increases the risk of war	1	2	3	4
K.	Our environmental problems are not as serious as people have been led to believe	1	2	3	4
L.	Government regulation of technology hampers society's progress	1	2	3	4
M.	The Government should work to substantially reduce the income gap between the rich and the poor	1	2	3	4

- 4 -

PART III (continued)

		Agree Strongly	Agree Somewhat	Disagree Somewhat	Disagree Strongly
N.	The U.S. needs a complete restructuring of its basic institutions	1	2	3	4
O.	Many risks we face are hidden from us by those in power	1	2	3	4
P.	Big corporations should be taken out of private ownership and run in the public interest	1	2	3	4
Q.	The structure of our society causes most people to feel alienated	1	2	3	4
R.	It is wrong for a married person to have sexual relations with someone other than his or her spouse	1	2	3	4
S.	It is right to discriminate in favor of racial minorities ...	1	2	3	4
T.	It is wrong for adults of the same sex to have sexual relations	1	2	3	4
U.	The U.S. has a moral obligation to prevent the destruction of Israel	1	2	3	. 4
V.	It is sometimes necessary for the CIA to protect U.S. interests by undermining hostile governments	1	2	3	4
W.	People with more important jobs should be paid more money	1	2	3	4
X.	The main goal of U.S. foreign policy has been to protect U.S. business interests	1	2	3	4
Y.	The government should ensure that everyone has a good standard of living	1	2	3	4
Z.	Special preference in hiring should be given to blacks	1	2	3	4
AA.	Special preference in hiring should be given to women	1	2	3	4
BB.	America offers an opportunity for financial security to all those who work hard	1	2	3	4

PART III (continued)

		Agree Strongly	Agree Somewhat	Disagree Somewhat	Disagree Strongly
CC.	Careful government planning is the best way to make sure that we continue to benefit from advances in technology	1	2	3	4
DD.	It is important for America to have the strongest military force in the world, no matter what it costs	1	2	3	4
EE.	In general, people are poor because of circumstances beyond their control rather than lack of effort	1	2	3	4
FF.	Almost all gains made by blacks in recent years have come at the expense of whites	1	2	3	4
GG.	Government should reduce the large differences in wealth in this country	1	2	3	4
HH.	A woman with young children should not work outside the home unless it is financially necessary	1	2	3	4
II.	The U.S. would be better off if it moved toward socialism .	1	2	3	4
JJ.	There is too much concern in the courts for the rights of criminals	1	2	3	4
KK.	Excessive public concern over environmental risk slows industrial innovation	1	2	3	4
LL.	In general, blacks don't have the chance for the education it takes to rise out of poverty	1	2	3	4
MM.	In general, blacks don't have the motivation or willpower to pull themselves out of poverty	1	2	3	4
NN.	America should retain the possibility of relying upon the death penalty for persons convicted of first degree murder	1	2	3	4
OO.	Religious prayer should not be allowed in the public schools	1	2	3	4
PP.	The federal budget should be balanced even if it means raising taxes	1	2	3	4

IV. GOALS FOR THIS COUNTRY

There are many differences of opinion about what this country's main goals should be during the next ten years. Below is a list of six different goals some people have suggested as the most important:

1. Maintaining a high rate of economic growth

2. Making sure that America has strong defense forces

3. Seeing that people have more say in how things get decided at work and in their communities

4. Progressing toward a less impersonal, more humane society

5. Fighting crime

6. Progressing toward a society where ideas are more important than money

A. If you had to choose only one, which of the six would you say is the most important goal for this country? *PLEASE ENTER ITS NUMBER BELOW:*

———————

B. And which of these would you say is the second most important goal for this country? *PLEASE ENTER ITS NUMBER BELOW:*

———————

C. Which of the six would you say is the least important goal for this country? *PLEASE ENTER ITS NUMBER BELOW:*

———————

D. Are there any other goals, not listed above, that you consider more important for this country during the next 10 years? *IF SO, PLEASE DESCRIBE THE ONE YOU CONSIDER THE MOST IMPORTANT OF ALL:*

1
☐ Yes, in my opinion, the most important goal is_____

2
☐ No, no others are more important than the six listed above

————————————————
————————————————

- 7 -

V.   INFLUENCE IN AMERICA

   A. For each of the eleven groups listed below, please circle one answer showing how
      much influence or power you think that group <u>actually</u> exercises on American life
      today. If you feel that a group actually has VERY LITTLE INFLUENCE nowadays, circle
      the "1" on that line. If you think the group has a A GREAT DEAL OF INFLUENCE,
      please circle the "7." If you think that the amount of influence the group
      exercises on current American life falls between these extremes, please circle one
      of the intermediate numbers, noting that "4" is the MIDDLE AMOUNT OF INFLUENCE.

AMOUNT OF INFLUENCE CURRENTLY HELD BY THIS GROUP

(Please circle one number for each)

	Very little influence						Great deal of influence
(1) Business leaders	1	2	3	4	5	6	7
(2) News media	1	2	3	4	5	6	7
(3) Intellectuals	1	2	3	4	5	6	7
(4) Labor unions	1	2	3	4	5	6	7
(5) Consumer groups	1	2	3	4	5	6	7
(6) Feminist groups	1	2	3	4	5	6	7
(7) Black leaders	1	2	3	4	5	6	7
(8) Federal government agencies	1	2	3	4	5	6	7
(9) Military leaders	1	2	3	4	5	6	7
(10) Religious leaders	1	2	3	4	5	6	7
(11) Foundations	1	2	3	4	5	6	7

- 8 -

PART V (continued)

B. Now, please rate the amount of influence you believe each of these groups SHOULD
   have on American life today (regardless of the amount of influence it actually has).

	AMOUNT OF INFLUENCE THIS GROUP SHOULD HAVE						
	(Please circle one number for each)						
	Very little influence ↓						Great deal influence ↓
(1) Business leaders	1	2	3	4	5	6	7
(2) News media	1	2	3	4	5	6	7
(3) Intellectuals	1	2	3	4	5	6	7
(4) Labor unions	1	2	3	4	5	6	7
(5) Consumer groups	1	2	3	4	5	6	7
(6) Feminist groups	1	2	3	4	5	6	7
(7) Black leaders	1	2	3	4	5	6	7
(8) Federal government agencies	1	2	3	4	5	6	7
(9) Military leaders	1	2	3	4	5	6	7
(10) Religious leaders	1	2	3	4	5	6	7
(11) Foundations	1	2	3	4	5	6	7

VI. VOTING AND IDEOLOGY

   A. For whom did you vote in each of the six Presidential elections indicated? *PLEASE CIRCLE ONE ANSWER FOR EACH ELECTION. IF YOU DID NOT VOTE IN THAT ELECTION, CIRCLE ONE OF THE .2 NUMBERS ON THE RIGHT.*

     (1) For whom did you vote in the 1968 Presidential election?

        1 - Humphrey   5 - Was ineligible to vote

        2 - Nixon   6 - Did not vote for another reason

        3 - Wallace

        4 - Other candidate
            (SPECIFY:_____)

     (2) For whom did you vote in the 1972 Presidential election?

        1 - McGovern   5 - Was ineligible to vote

        2 - Nixon   6 - Did not vote for another reason

        3 - Other candidate
            (SPECIFY:_____)

     (3) In the 1976 Presidential election?

        1 - Ford   5 - Was ineligible to vote

        2 - Carter   6 - Did not vote for another reason

        3 - Other candidate
            (SPECIFY:_____)

     (4) For whom did you vote in the 1980 Presidential election?

        1 - Reagan   5 - Was ineligible to vote

        2 - Carter   6 - Did not vote for another reason

        3 - Anderson

        4 - Other candidate
            (SPECIFY:_____)

     (5) In the 1984 Presidential election?

        1 - Mondale   5 - Was ineligible to vote

        2 - Reagan   6 - Did not vote for another reason

        3 - Other candidate
            (SPECIFY:_____)

     (6) For whom did you vote in the 1988 Presidential election?

        1 - Dukakis   5 - Was ineligible to vote

        2 - Bush   6 - Did not vote for another reason

        3 - Other candidate
            (SPECIFY:_____)

- 10 -

PART VI (continued)

B. Regardless of how (or whether) you've voted in recent presidential elections, which political party do you generally support? *PLEASE CIRCLE ONE.*

    1 - Democrats   2 - Republicans   3 - Another party   4 - Independent OR
                                       (SPECIFY:_____   no one party
                                         _____ *)*

C. While you were growing up, which political party did <u>your father</u> generally support? *PLEASE CIRCLE ONE.*

    1 - Democrats   2 - Republicans   3 - Another party   4 - Independent OR
                                         (SPECIFY:_____   no one party
                                         _____ *)*

D. And while you were growing up, which political party did <u>your mother</u> generally support? *PLEASE CIRCLE ONE.*

    1 - Democrats   2 - Republicans   3 - Another party   4 - Independent OR
                                         (SPECIFY:_____   no one party
                                         _____ *)*

E. Using the seven-point scale below, how would you describe the political views of each of the following people or groups?

	THE POLITICAL VIEWS OF THIS PERSON OR GROUP			
	(Please circle one number for each)			
	Conservative	Middle	Liberal	Have no idea
(1) Your own political views.........	1 2 3	4 5	6 7	
(2) The political views of most of the people with whom you work closely these days................	1 2 3	4 5	6 7	8
(3) Your father's political views when you were growing up.........	1 2 3	4 5	6 7	8
(4) Your mother's political views when you were growing up........	1 2 3	4 5	6 7	8

F. How often do you discuss political questions with your friends?

    1 - Never   2 - Seldom   3 - Occasionally   4 - Frequently

G. How often do you discuss political questions with your work colleagues?

    1 - Never   2 - Seldom   3 - Occasionally   4 - Frequently

H. How often did your father discuss political questions when you were growing up?

    1 - Never   2 - Seldom   3 - Occasionally   4 - Frequently

I. And how often did your mother discuss political questions when you were growing up?

    1 - Never   2 - Seldom   3 - Occasionally   4 - Frequently

VII.   THE ROLE OF PHILANTHROPIC FOUNDATIONS

The 12 statements below represent the views of different people regarding philanthropic foundations. For each statement, please circle one number, indicating how strongly you agree or disagree with that viewpoint.

	Agree Strongly	Agree Somewhat	Disagree Somewhat	Disagree Strongly
A. Philanthropic foundations should make up for the shortcomings of the private sector................	1	2	3	4
B. Philanthropic foundations should make up for the shortcomings of government programs..............	1	2	3	4
C. There should be greater government regulation of philanthropic foundations.......................	1	2	3	4
D. Today, most philanthropic foundations support the status quo......	1	2	3	4
E. Philanthropic foundations should primarily fund projects that have the large potential for large societal impact............................	1	2	3	4
F. When funding academic projects, philanthropic foundations should support only those that are objective and unbiased..............	1	2	3	4
G. On the whole, most philanthropic foundations do more harm than good	1	2	3	4
H. Philanthropic foundations should primarily fund projects where the philosophical orientation of the grantee matches that of the foundation........................	1	2	3	4
I. In making grants, the intentions of the original donor should be strictly followed	1	2	3	4
J. There should be minimum standards of philanthropic giving for foundations........................	1	2	3	4
K. Foundation assets should be invested only in companies that are socially responsible, even if it results in smaller earnings..................	1	2	3	4
L. Foundation employees should be encouraged to do volunteer work on their own time....................	1	2	3	4

- 12 -

PART VII (continued)

M. In deciding which grant proposals should receive funds, how much influence do each of the following kinds of people in your foundation have? *PLEASE CIRCLE ONE NUMBER FOR EACH, DEPENDING ON THAT GROUP'S INFLUENCE.*

Amount of influence this group tends to carry in deciding which grant proposals your foundation should fund

(Please circle one number for each)

	No influence at all						Great deal of influence
(1) Your foundation's officers....	1	2	3	4	5	6	7
(2) Other members of your Board of Trustees or Board of Directors................	1	2	3	4	5	6	7
(3) Foundation staff members who are not on the board..	1	2	3	4	5	6	7
(4) Independent reviewers.....	1	2	3	4	5	6	7

☐ Does not apply. We do not use independent reviewers

N. How often does your foundation review its goals? *CIRCLE ONE.*

    0 - Never ⟶ *IF NEVER, PLEASE SKIP TO P*

    1 - Less than once a year

    2 - Annually (once a year)

    3 - Semi-annually (twice a year)

    4 - Quarterly

    5 - Monthly

    6 - Other *(PLEASE DESCRIBE: _____)*

O. Who reviews your foundation's goals? *CIRCLE ALL THAT APPLY.*

    1 - Foundation officers

    2 - Other members of the Board of Trustees or Board of Directors

    3 - Foundation staff members who are not on the Board

P. Who establishes your foundation's grantmaking guidelines? *CIRCLE ALL THAT APPLY. IF RECOMMENDATIONS ARE MADE BY ONE GROUP AND FINAL DECISIONS MADE BY ANOTHER, PLEASE CIRCLE BOTH.*

    1 - Foundation officers

    2 - Other members of the Board of Trustees or Board of Directors

    3 - Foundation staff members who are not on the Board

- 13 -

PART VII (continued)

Q. How much support would you personally like to see each of the following kinds of projects receive from philanthropic foundations? *CIRCLE ONE ANSWER FOR EACH.*

Kind of project:	More than it gets now	The same as it gets now	Less than it gets now
(1) Medical research............	1	2	3
(2) Access to health care.......	1	2	3
(3) Health care cost containment	1	2	3
(4) AIDS research...............	1	2	3
(5) Birth control research......	1	2	3
(6) Programs for women..........	1	2	3
(7) Programs for blacks.........	1	2	3
(8) Programs for gays...........	1	2	3
(9) Programs for the disabled...	1	2	3
(10) Programs for the aged.......	1	2	3
(11) Access to legal services....	1	2	3
(12) Problems of the homeless....	1	2	3
(13) International student exchange	1	2	3
(14) Peace initiatives...........	1	2	3
(15) Arms control...............	1	2	3
(16) Human rights...............	1	2	3
(17) Environmental problems......	1	2	3
(18) Mathematics.................	1	2	3
(19) Genetics research...........	1	2	3
(20) IQ research.................	1	2	3
(21) Nuclear energy..............	1	2	3
(22) Economics...................	1	2	3
(23) Women's studies.............	1	2	3
(24) Sociology...................	1	2	3
(25) Afro-American studies.......	1	2	3

- 14 -

VIII.   BACKGROUND DATA

We also need some background information about the people in our survey to facilitate comparisons of responses of different kinds of participants. Please answer the following, remembering that all responses are strictly confidential.

A. Where did you live most of the time while you were growing up?

Name of State:_____   OR   Foreign country:_____

B. Which of the following best describes the area in which you lived most of the time while you were growing up? *CIRCLE ONLY ONE.*

   1 - Rural area

      2 - Small town (less than 25,000 people)

         3 - Suburb of a large city

            4 - Small city (25,000 - 99,999 people)

               5 - Fairly large city (100,000 - 999,999 people)

                  6 - Very large city (at least a million people)

C. What was the highest year or grade of school each of your parents completed? *CIRCLE ONE ANSWER FOR EACH.*

	Father's Education	Mother's Education
8th grade or less	1	1
Some high school	2	2
High school graduate	3	3
Some college	4	4
Graduate of 4-year college/university	5	5
Some graduate work	6	6
Graduate degree	7	7
Have no idea	8	8

- 15 -

Part VIII (continued)

D. Which of the following best describes your parents' occupation(s) during most of the time when you were growing up? *PLEASE CIRCLE ONE ANSWER FOR EACH.*

		Father's Usual Occupation	Mother's Usual Occupation
	Homemaker or not employed for pay	0	0
W H I T E C O L L A R W O R K E R S	<u>Major and minor professions</u> including physician, lawyer, college professor, clergyman, dentist, architect, social and physical scientists, accountants, artists, writers, engineers, librarians, musicians, pharmacists, social and welfare workers, nurses, etc..............................	1	1
	<u>Managers and owners</u>	2	2
	<u>Semiprofessions</u> including aviators, decorators, commercial artists, dancers, draftsmen, laboratory assistants, photographers, athletes, radio operators, showmen, surveyors, undertakers, etc...	3	3
	<u>Sales occupations</u> including realtors, automobile salesmen, insurance salesmen, manufacturer's representatives, retail clerks, route salesmen, door to door salesmen, demonstrators, etc..	4	4
	<u>Clerical workers</u> including bookkeepers, secretaries, stenographers, file clerks, etc............................	5	5
	Other white-collar workers *(PLEASE DESCRIBE:_____)*	6	
	(PLEASE DESCRIBE:_____)		6
B L U E C O L L A R W O R K E R S	<u>Farm or ranch owner</u>......................................	7	7
	<u>Farm, forest and fishing workers</u> excluding farm owners.....	8	8
	<u>Foremen</u>...	9	9
	<u>Protective occupations</u> including police, firemen, enlisted men in the armed services, guards, watchmen, etc..........	10	10
	<u>Skilled workers</u> including carpenters, plumbers, electricians, etc...	11	11
	<u>Semiskilled workers</u> including routemen, carpenter's helper, machinist, etc..	12	12
	<u>Unskilled workers</u> including laborers, street cleaners, janitors, etc..	13	13
	Other blue collar workers *(PLEASE DESCRIBE:_____)*	14	
	(PLEASE DESCRIBE:_____)		14

- 16 -

PART VIII (continued)

E. Thinking about the time when you were growing up, how would you say your family's income compared with most American families' income?

    1 - Well below average

      2 - Somewhat below average

        3 - Average

          4 - Somewhat above average

            5 - Well above average

              6 - Have no idea

F. To which of the following ethnic or nationality groups would you say you belong? *PLEASE CIRCLE ONLY ONE NUMBER FOR THE GROUP FROM WHICH YOU ARE MAINLY DESCENDED. USE "19" ONLY IF ETHNIC HERITAGE IS EQUALLY DIVIDED AMONG YOUR PARENTS AND/OR GRANDPARENTS.*

      1 - Afro-American

      2 - Chinese

      3 - English, Scottish or Welsh

      4 - French

      5 - German

      6 - Irish

      7 - Italian

      8 - Japanese

      9 - Eastern European Jewish

     10 - German or Austrian Jewish

     11 - Polish

     12 - Russian

     13 - Scandinavian

     14 - Central or South American

     15 - Mexican-American

     16 - Puerto Rican

     17 - Other Spanish

     18 - Other *(SPECIFY:_____)*

     19 - Evenly split between or among the following groups
         (PLEASE ENTER IDENTIFYING NUMBERS: _____)

PART VIII (continued)

G. In what religion were you raised? And what is your present religious preference, if any? *CIRCLE ONE ANSWER IN EACH COLUMN.*

	Religion when I was growing up	Present religious preference
Protestant *(PLEASE SPECIFY DENOMINATION)*	1 _____ (denomination)	1 _____ (denomination)
Roman Catholic..................	2	2
Jewish *(PLEASE SPECIFY ORTHODOX, CONSERVATIVE OR REFORM)*	3 _____ (denomination)	3 _____ (denomination)
Other religion *(PLEASE SPECIFY)*.	4 _____ (religion)	4 _____ (religion)
None, no religion..............	5	5

H. How often, if ever, did you attend religious services when you were growing up? How often do you attend now? *CIRCLE ONE ANSWER IN EACH COLUMN.*

	When I was growing up	At the present time
Every week (or almost weekly)	1	1
Once or twice a month...................	2	2
A few times a year.....................	3	3
Once or twice a year...................	4	4
Never.................................	5	5

I. What was the highest grade or year of school you completed?

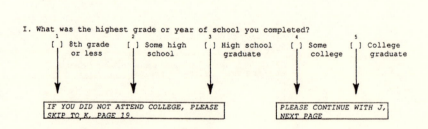

[ ] 8th grade or less   [ ] Some high school   [ ] High school graduate   [ ] Some college   [ ] College graduate

IF YOU DID NOT ATTEND COLLEGE, PLEASE SKIP TO K, PAGE 19.

PLEASE CONTINUE WITH J, NEXT PAGE

- 18 -

PART VIII (continued)

J. *IF YOU ATTENDED COLLEGE, PLEASE ANSWER THE FOLLOWING:*

(1) Please list below the name of each college/university you attended as an undergraduate student:

(2) What was your undergraduate college major?

My college major when I was an undergraduate   [ ] I left college without
was:_____   declaring a major

(3) What was the highest degree, if any, you received in college? *CHECK ONLY ONE.*

[ ] Attended college, no degree   [ ] Some graduate work, no graduate degree

[ ] A.A. degree (junior college)   [ ] Master's degree (M.A., M.S., etc.)

[ ] Bachelor's degree   [ ] Ph.D
(A.B., B.S., etc.)

[ ] M.D.

[ ] Other advanced degree
(PLEASE SPECIFY:____
_____)

| *IF NO GRADUATE DEGREE, PLEASE* | *IF ANY GRADUATE WORK, PLEASE* |
| *SKIP TO K, NEXT PAGE.* | *ANSWER (4) AND (5) BELOW* |

(4) Please list below the name of each college or university you attended as a graduate student:

(5) What was your major field as a graduate student?

PART VIII (continued)

K. In the first column below, please check the income group that includes your total
   personal income in 1988 <u>before taxes</u>; in the second column, please check your
   total family income during the same year. Both figures should <u>include income from
   all sources</u> -- including wages, salaries, interest, dividends and any other income.

	My own individual income	Total family income
Under $20,000	1	1
$20,000 - $29,999	2	2
$30,000 - $49,999	3	3
$50,000 - $74,999	4	4
$75,000 - $99,999	5	5
$100,000 - $199,999	6	6
$200,000 - $499,999	7	7
$500,000 or higher	8	8

L. How old were you on your last birthday?   _____ years old

M. Your sex? *CIRCLE ONE.*

                          1 - Male

                          2 - Female

N. What is your current marital status? *CIRCLE ONE.*

                          1 - Married

                          2 - Widowed

                          3 - Divorced

                          4 - Separated

                          5 - Never married

O. Which of the following best describes your race? *CIRCLE ONE.*

                          1 - Black

                          2 - White or Caucasian

                          3 - Other *(PLEASE SPECIFY:*_____

                              _____*)*

- 20 -

PART VIII (continued)

P. Please use the space below to tell us anything else you think we should know about the questionnaire or any of the questions.

Q. Please use the following space (or, if you prefer, write us a separate letter) to tell us about anything else that you think might help us understand your answers or might help us in future research efforts.

> YOUR CONTRIBUTION TO THIS PROJECT IS
> GREATLY APPRECIATED. THANKS AGAIN.

REFERENCES

Almond, Gabriel, and Sidney Verba. 1965. *The Civic Culture*. Boston: Little, Brown.

American Foundations and Their Fields. 1948. New York: American Foundations Information Service.

Andrews, Frank Emerson. 1956. *Philanthropic Foundations*. New York: Russell Sage Foundation.

Arnove, Robert. 1980. "Introduction." In Robert F. Arnove (ed.), *Philanthropy and Cultural Imperialism*, pp. 1–23. Boston: G. K. Hall.

Baltzell, E. Digby. 1964. *The Protestant Establishment: Aristocracy and Caste in America*. New York: Random House.

———. 1979. *Puritan Boston and Quaker Philadelphia*. Boston: Beacon Press.

Banfield, Edward C. 1974. *The Unheavenly City Revisited*. Boston: Little, Brown.

Barton, Allen H. 1975. "Consensus and Conflict Among American Leaders." *Public Opinion Quarterly* 38 (Winter): 507–30.

Bell, Daniel. 1973. *The Coming of Post Industrial Society*. New York: Basic Books.

———. 1976. *Cultural Contradictions of Capitalism*. New York: Basic Books.

———. 1980. "The New Class: A Muddled Concept." In Daniel Bell (ed.), *The Winding Passage: Essays and Sociological Journeys, 1960–1980*, pp. 144–64. Cambridge, MA: Abt Books.

———. 1992. "The Cultural Wars: American Intellectual Life, 1965–1992." *The Wilson Quarterly* 16 (Summer):74–107.

Bellah, Robert N. 1970. "Civil Religion in America." In Robert N. Bellah (ed.), *Beyond Belief: Essays on Religion in a Post-Traditional World*, pp. 168–89. New York: Harper and Row.

Bellah, Robert N., Richard Madsen, William M. Sullivan, Ann Swidler, and Steven M. Tipton. 1985. *Habits of the Heart*. Berkeley, CA: University of California Press.

Bennett, James T. 1989. *Patterns of Corporate Philanthropy: Ideas, Advocacy, and the Corporation*. Washington, DC: Capital Research Center.

Berger, Peter L. 1986. *The Capitalist Revolution: Fifty Propositions About Prosperity, Equality, and Liberty*. New York: Basic Books.

Berger, Peter, and Richard J. Neuhaus. 1977. *To Empower People: The Role of Mediating Structures in Public Policy*. Washington: American Enterprise Institute.

Berry, Jeffrey M. 1977. *Lobbying for the People: The Political Behavior of Public Interest Groups*. Princeton, NJ: Princeton University Press.

Bledstein, Burton J. 1976. *The Culture of Professionalism*. New York: W. W. Norton.

Boorstin, Daniel J. 1983. "From Charity to Philanthropy." In Brian O'Connell (ed.), *America's Voluntary Spirit: A Book of Readings*, pp. 129–41. New York: The Foundation Center.

Bremner, Robert H. 1977. "Private Philanthropy and Public Needs." In Commission on Private Philanthropy and Public Needs, *Research Papers*, volume II, part I, pp. 89–114. Washington, DC: Department of the Treasury.

———. 1988. *American Philanthropy*. Chicago: University of Chicago Press.

Brint, Steven. 1984. " 'New Class' and Cumulative Trend Explanations of Liberal Political Attitudes of Professionals." *American Journal of Sociology* 90 (July):31–71.

Brody, Deborah. 1988. "What's a Typical Foundation?" *Foundation News* 29 (November-December):52–54.

Bulmer, Martin. 1984. "Philanthropic Foundations and the Development of the Social Sciences in the Early Twentieth Century: A Reply to Donald Fisher." *Sociology* 18 (November):572–79.

Bulmer, Martin, and Joan Bulmer. 1981. "Philanthropy and Social Science in the 1920s: Beardsley Ruml and the Laura Spelman Rockefeller Memorial, 1922–29." *Minerva* 19 (Autumn):347–407.

Capital Research Center. 1986. "Victory—Finally—in Buck Trust Case." *Organization Trends* (September):1–3.

Carnegie, Andrew. 1983. "The Gospel of Wealth." In Brian O'Connell (ed.), *America's Voluntary Spirit: A Book of Readings*, pp. 97–108. New York: The Foundation Center.

Cochran, Thomas. 1985. *Challenges to American Values: Society, Business and Religion*. New York: Oxford University Press.

Cohen, Steven M. 1983. *American Modernity and Jewish Identity*. New York: Tavistock Publications.

Coleman, J. S. 1972. "Internal Processes Governing Party Positions in Elections." *Public Choice* 11:35–60.

Colvard, Richard. 1964. "Risk Capital Philanthropy: The Ideological Defense of Innovation." In George K. Zollschan and Walter Hirsch (eds.), *Explorations in Social Change*, pp. 728–48. Boston: Houghton Mifflin.

Colwell, Mary Anna. 1980. *Philanthropic Foundations and Public Policy: The Political Role of Foundations* Ph.D. dissertation. Berkeley: University of California.

Converse, Philip E. 1964. "The Nature of Belief Systems in Mass Publics." In David E. Apter (ed.), *Ideology and Discontent*, pp. 206–61. New York: Free Press.

Cornuelle, Richard C. 1965. *Reclaiming the American Dream*. New York: Random House.

Coser, Lewis A. 1970. *Men of Ideas: A Sociologist's View*. New York: Free Press.

Coser, Lewis A., Charles Kadushin, and Walter W. Powell. 1982. *Books: The Culture and Commerce of Publishing*. New York: Basic Books.

Davis, O. A., and M. Hinich. 1968. "A Mathematical Model of Policy Information in a Democratic Society." In J. L. Bernd (ed.), *Mathematical Applications in Po-*

litical Science, volume 2, pp. 175–205. Dallas, TX: Southern Methodist University Press.

Dewey, John. 1935. *Liberalism and Social Action*. New York: G. P. Putnam's Sons.

Dillman, Don A. 1978. *Mail and Telephone Surveys: The Total Design Method*. New York: John Wiley and Sons.

Domhoff, G. William. 1971. *The Higher Circles*. New York: Viking.

———. 1983. *Who Rules America Now? A View for the '80s*. Englewood Cliffs, NJ: Prentice-Hall.

Douglas, James. 1987. "Political Theories of Nonprofit Organization." In Walter W. Powell (ed.), *The Nonprofit Sector: A Research Handbook*, pp. 43–54. New Haven: Yale University Press.

Douglas, James, and Aaron Wildavsky. 1978. "The Knowledgeable Foundations." In *The Future of Foundations*, pp. 12–43. New Rochelle, NY: Change Magazine Press.

Downs, Anthony. 1957. *An Economic Theory of Democracy*. New York: Harper and Row.

Dunn, Marvin G. 1980. "The Family Office: Coordinating Mechanism of the Ruling Class." In G. William Domhoff (ed.), *Power Structure Research*, pp. 17–45. Beverly Hills, CA: Sage Publications.

Durkheim, Emile. 1947. *The Division of Labor in Society*. Trans. George Simpson. Glencoe, IL: The Free Press.

Dye, Thomas. 1986. *Who's Running America?* New York: Praeger.

Echard, Jo Kwong. 1990. *Protecting the Environment: Old Rhetoric, New Imperatives*. Washington, DC: Capital Research Center.

Ehrenreich, Barbara, and John Ehrenreich. 1977. "The Professional/Managerial Class." *Radical America* 11 (March-April):7–31.

Encyclopedia Americana: International Edition. 1993. Vol. 15, p. 633. Danbury, CT: Grolier, Inc.

Feldman, Stanley. 1983. "Economic Individualism and American Public Opinion." *American Politics Quarterly* 11 (January):3–29.

Fisher, Donald. 1980. "American Philanthropy and the Social Sciences: The Reproduction of a Conservative Ideology." In Robert F. Arnove (ed.), *Philanthropy and Cultural Imperialism*, pp. 233–68. Boston: G. K. Hall.

———. 1983. "The Role of Philanthropic Foundations in the Reproduction and Production of Hegemony: Rockefeller Foundation and the Social Sciences." *Sociology* 17:206–33.

Foundation Center. 1987. *The Foundation Directory*, 11th ed. New York: The Foundation Center.

———. 1988. *Grant$ for Public Policy and Political Science*. New York: The Foundation Center.

Frankena, William K. 1987. "Beneficence/Benevolence." In Ellen Frankel Paul, Fred D. Miller, Jr., Jeffrey Paul, and John Ahrens (eds.), *Beneficence, Philanthropy, and the Public Good*, pp. 1–20. Oxford and New York: Basil Blackwell.

Friedman, Milton. 1970. "The Social Responsibility of Business Is to Increase Its Profits." *New York Times Magazine* (September 13).

Geertz, Clifford. 1973. *The Interpretation of Cultures*. New York: Basic Books.

Glazer, Nathan. 1986. "Welfare and 'Welfare' in America." In Richard Rose and Rei

Shiratori (eds.), *The Welfare State East and West*, pp. 40–63. New York: Oxford University Press.

Gouldner, Alvin W. 1979. *The Future of Intellectuals and the Rise of the New Class*. New York: Continuum.

Gramsci, Antonio. 1975 trans. *Letters from Prison*, Lynne Lawner (trans. and ed.). London: Jonathan Cape.

Hall, Peter Dobkin. 1987. "A Historical Overview of the Private Nonprofit Sector." In Walter W. Powell (ed.), *The Nonprofit Sector: A Research Handbook*, pp. 3–21. New Haven: Yale University Press.

Hansmann, Henry. 1987. "Economic Theories of Nonprofit Organization." In Walter W. Powell (ed.), *The Nonprofit Sector: A Research Handbook*, pp. 27–42. New Haven: Yale University Press.

Hart, Jeffrey. 1973. "Foundations and Social Activism: A Critical View. In Fritz F. Heinmann (ed.), *The Future of Foundations*, pp. 7–42. Englewood Cliffs, NJ: Prentice-Hall.

Hartz, Louis. 1955. *The Liberal Tradition in America*. New York: Harcourt Brace.

Heale, M. J. 1968. "Humanitarianism in the Early Republic: The Moral Reformers of New York." *Journal of American Studies* (October):164–66.

Helfgot, Joseph. 1981. *Professional Reforming*. Lexington, MA: D. C. Heath.

Hofstadter, Richard. 1948. *The American Political Tradition*. New York: Vintage Books.

Hollander, Paul. 1981. *Political Pilgrims: Travels of Western Intellectuals to the Soviet Union, China, and Cuba, 1928–1978*. New York: Oxford University Press.

———. 1988. *The Survival of the Adversary Culture*. New Brunswick, NJ: Transaction Books.

Horowitz, Irving Louis, and Ruth Leonora Horowitz. 1970. "Tax-Exempt Foundations: Their Effects on National Policy." *Science* 168 (April):220–28.

Hotelling, H. 1929. "Stability in Competition." *Economic Journal* 39:41–57.

Inglehart, Ronald. 1977. *The Silent Revolution: Changing Values and Political Styles Among Western Publics*. Princeton, NJ: Princeton University Press.

Irwin, T. H. 1987. "Generosity and Property in Aristotle's *Politics*." In Ellen Frankel Paul, Fred D. Miller, Jr., Jeffrey Paul, and John Ahrens (eds.), *Beneficence, Philanthropy, and the Public Good*, pp. 37–54. Oxford and New York: Basil Blackwell.

Janowitz, Morris. 1978. *The Last Half Century: Societal Change and Politics in America*. Chicago: University of Chicago Press.

Jencks, Christopher. 1987. "Who Gives to What?" In Walter W. Powell (ed.), *The Nonprofit Sector: A Research Handbook*, pp. 321–39. New Haven: Yale University Press.

Jenkins, J. Craig. 1987. "Nonprofit Organizations and Policy Advocacy." In Walter W. Powell (ed.), *The Nonprofit Sector: A Research Handbook*, pp. 296–318. New Haven: Yale University Press.

———. 1989. "Social Movement Philanthropy and American Democracy." In Richard Magat (ed.), *Philanthropic Giving: Studies in Varieties and Goals*, pp. 292–314. New York: Oxford University Press.

Joseph, James A. 1988. "Private Philanthropy and South Africa." *Foundation News* (November/December):49.

Kadushin, Charles. 1974. *The American Intellectual Elite*. Boston: Little, Brown.

Kahl, Joseph A. 1957. *The American Class Structure*. New York: Holt, Rinehart and Winston.

Karl, Barry D., and Stanley N. Katz. 1981. "American Private Philanthropic Foundations and the Public Sphere, 1890–1930." *Minerva* 19 (Summer):236–70.

———. 1987. "Foundations and Ruling Class Elites." *Daedalus* 116 (Winter):1–40.

Kekes, John. 1987. "Benevolence: A Minor Virtue." In Ellen Frankel Paul, Fred D. Miller, Jr., Jeffrey Paul, and John Ahrens (eds.), *Beneficence, Philanthropy, and the Public Good*, pp. 21–36. Oxford and New York: Basil Blackwell.

Keller, Suzanne. 1963. *Beyond the Ruling Class*. New York: Random House.

Keppel, Frederick P. 1930. *The Foundation: Its Place in American Life*. New York: The Macmillan Company.

Kohn, Melvin L. 1973. *Class and Conformity: A Study in Values*. Homewood, IL: Dorsey Press.

Kramer, Ralph M. 1981. *Voluntary Agencies in the Welfare State*. Berkeley: University of California Press.

Kristol, Irving. 1978. *Two Cheers for Capitalism*. New York: Basic Books.

Ladd, Everett Carll, and Seymour Martin Lipset. 1976. *The Divided Academy: Professors and Politics*. New York: W. W. Norton.

Lasch, Christopher. 1977. *Haven in a Heartless World*. New York: Basic Books.

Laslett, John H. M., and Seymour Martin Lipset (eds.). 1974. *Failure of a Dream: Essays in the History of American Socialism*. Garden City, NY: Anchor Press.

Laslett, Peter. 1971. *The World We Have Lost: England Before the Industrial Age*, 2nd ed. New York: Charles Scribner's Sons.

Lawson, Alan. 1985. "The Cultural Legacy of the New Deal." In Harvard Sitkoff (ed.), *Fifty Years Later: The New Deal Evaluated*, pp. 155–86. Philadelphia: Temple University Press.

Leiby, James. 1978. *A History of Social Welfare and Social Work in the United States*. New York: Columbia University Press.

Lemann, Nicholas. 1991. *The Promised Land: The Great Black Migration and How It Changed America*. New York: Vintage Books.

Lerner, Robert, and Stanley Rothman. 1989. "The Media, the Polity, and Public Opinion." In Samuel Long (ed.), *Political Behavior Annual*, volume 2, pp. 39–76. Boulder, CO: Westview Press.

———. 1990. "The Adversarial Media." In Joseph B. Gittler (ed.), *The Annual Review of Conflict Knowledge and Conflict Resolution*, volume 2, pp. 159–93. New York: Garland Publishing.

Lerner, Robert, Althea K. Nagai, and Stanley Rothman. 1989. "Marginality and Liberalism among Jewish Elites." *Public Opinion Quarterly* 53 (Fall):330–52.

———. 1990. "Elite Dissensus and Its Origins." *Journal of Political and Military Sociology* 18 (Summer):25–39.

———. 1991. "Elite vs. Mass Opinion: Another Look at a Classic Relationship." *International Journal of Public Opinion Research* 3:1–31.

———. 1992. "Ideology and Philanthropy: A Survey of Foundation Elites." Unpublished manuscript.

Lerner, Robert, Stanley Rothman, and S. Robert Lichter. 1989. "Christian Religious Elites." *Public Opinion* 11 (March/April):54–58.

Levine, Robert A. 1970. *The Poor Ye Need Not Have With You: Lessons from the War on Poverty*. Cambridge, MA: MIT Press.

Lichter, S. Robert, Stanley Rothman, and Linda S. Lichter. 1986. *The Media Elite*. Bethesda, MD: Adler and Adler.

Lindeman, Eduard C. 1936. *Wealth and Culture*. New York: Harcourt, Brace.

Lipset, Seymour Martin. 1963. *The First New Nation*. New York: Basic Books.

Lowi, Theodore J. 1988. "Foreword: New Dimensions in Policy and Politics." In Raymond Tatalovich and Byron W. Daynes (eds.), *Social Regulatory Policy: Moral Controversies in American Politics*, pp. x-xxi. Boulder, CO: Westview Press.

Lubove, Roy. 1965. *The Professional Altruist: The Emergence of Social Work as a Career*. Cambridge: MA: Harvard University Press.

Luker, Kristen. 1984. *Abortion and the Politics of Motherhood*. Berkeley: University of California Press.

Macdonald, Dwight. 1989. *The Ford Foundation: The Men and the Millions*. New Brunswick, NJ: Transaction Publishers.

Macy, Michael W. 1988. "New Class Dissent Among Social-Cultural Specialists." *Sociological Forum* 3, 3 (Summer):325–56.

Magat, Richard. 1979. *The Ford Foundation at Work: Philanthropic Choices, Methods, and Styles*. New York: Plenum Press.

Manchester, William. 1988. *The Last Lion, Winston Spencer Churchill: Alone, 1932–1940*. New York: Dell Publishing.

Mannheim, Karl. 1971 trans. *From Karl Mannheim*, Kurt H. Wolff (trans. and ed.). New York: Oxford University Press.

Marris, Peter, and Martin Rein. 1972. *Dilemmas of Social Reform: Poverty and Community Action in the United States*, 2nd ed. London: Routledge and Kegan Paul.

Marx, Karl. 1978. "The German Ideology: Part I." In Robert Tucker (ed.), *The Marx-Engels Reader*, pp. 146–200. New York: W. W. Norton.

Matusow, Allen J. 1984. *The Unraveling of America: A History of Liberalism in the 1960s*. New York: Harper and Row.

Mavity, Jane H., and Paul Ylvisaker. 1977. "Private Philanthropy and Public Affairs." In Commission on Private Philanthropy and Public Needs, *Research Papers*, volume II, part I, pp. 795–836. Washington, DC: Department of the Treasury.

Mayhew, Leon. 1970. "Ascription in Modern Societies." In Edward O. Laumann, Paul M. Siegel, and Robert W. Hodge (eds.), *The Logic of Social Hierarchies*, pp. 308–23. Chicago: Markham Publishing Co.

McAdams, John. 1987. "Testing the Theory of the New Class." *The Sociological Quarterly* 28, 1 (Winter):23–49.

McCann, Michael W. 1986. *Taking Reforms Seriously: Perspectives on Public Interest Liberalism*. Ithaca, NY: Cornell University Press.

McCarthy, Kathleen D. 1982. *Noblesse Oblige: Charity and Cultural Philanthropy in Chicago, 1849–1929*. Chicago: University of Chicago Press.

McClosky, Herbert, and John Zaller. 1984. *The American Ethos*. Cambridge, MA: Harvard University Press.

McCraw, Thomas K. 1985. "The New Deal and the Mixed Economy." In Harvard Sitkoff (ed.), *Fifty Years Later: The New Deal Evaluated*, pp. 37–67. Philadelphia: Temple University Press.

Meiners, Roger E., and David N. Laband. 1988. *Patterns of Corporate Philanthropy: Public Affairs Giving and the Forbes 250*. Washington, DC: Capital Research Center.

Merton, Robert K. 1968. *Social Theory and Social Structure*. 1968 enlarged ed. New York: Free Press.

Mill, John Stuart. 1972 ed. *Considerations on Representative Government*, H. B. Acton (ed.). London: J. M. Dent.

———. 1975 ed. *On Liberty*, David Spitz (ed.). New York: W. W. Norton.

Mills, C. Wright. 1956. *The Power Elite*. New York: Oxford University Press.

Minogue, Kenneth R. 1963. *The Liberal Mind*. New York: Vintage Books.

Moynihan, Daniel P. 1970. *Maximum Feasible Misunderstanding*. New York: Free Press.

Muravchik, Joshua. 1992. "MacArthur's Millions." *The American Spectator* (January):34–41.

Murray, Charles. 1984. *Losing Ground: American Social Policy, 1950–1980*. New York: Basic Books.

Myrdal, Gunnar. 1944. *An American Dilemma*, 2 volumes. New York: Harper and Brothers.

Nagai, Althea K., Robert Lerner, and Stanley Rothman. 1989. "Philanthropy and Social Change." *Alternatives in Philanthropy* (May).

———. 1991. *The Culture of Philanthropy: Foundations and Public Policy*. Washington, DC: Capital Research Center.

Nash, George H. 1976. *The Conservative Intellectual Movement in America Since 1945*. New York: Basic Books.

National Opinion Research Center. 1990. *General Social Surveys, 1972–1990: Cumulative Codebook*. Chicago: National Opinion Research Center.

Neuman, W. Russell. 1986. *The Paradox of Mass Politics: Knowledge and Opinion in the American Electorate*. Cambridge, MA: Harvard University Press.

New York Times. February 16, 1968, p. 49.

———. May 15, 1968, p. 1.

———. May 19, 1968, p. 27.

———. May 30, 1968, p. 23.

———. June 13, 1968, p. 52.

———. March 2, 1969, p. 46.

———. January 28, 1970, p. 22.

———. February 9, 1970, p. 79.

———. November 19, 1970, p. 95.

———. June 24, 1979. "Giving Is Getting Reformed to Aid Those Most in Need," p. E27.

———. January 30, 1990, p. A18.

———. July 12, 1991, p. A29.

Nie, Norman H., Sidney Verba, and John R. Petrocik. 1976. *The Changing American Voter*. Cambridge, MA: Harvard University Press.

Nielsen, Waldemar A. 1972. *The Big Foundations*. New York: Columbia University Press.

———. 1979. *The Endangered Sector*. New York: Columbia University Press.

———. 1985. *The Golden Donors*. New York: E. P. Dutton.

Novak, Michael. 1988. "An Essay on 'Public' and 'Private.' " In *Philanthropy: Four Views*, pp. 11–25. New Brunswick, NJ: Transaction Publishers.

O'Connell, Brian (ed.). 1983. *America's Voluntary Spirit: A Book of Readings*. New York: The Foundation Center.

———. 1988. "Private Philanthropy and the Preservation of a Free and Democratic

Society.'' In *Philanthropy: Four Views*, pp. 27–38. New Brunswick, NJ: Transaction Publishers.

Odendahl, Teresa. 1990. *Charity Begins at Home: Generosity and Self-Interest Among the Philanthropic Elite*. New York: Basic Books.

Odendahl, Teresa Jean, Elizabeth Trocolli Boris, and Arlene Kaplan Daniels. 1985. *Working in Foundations: Career Patterns of Women and Men*. New York: The Foundation Center.

Olasky, Marvin N. 1985. *The Council on Foundations*. Washington, DC: Capital Research Center.

———. 1988. "Standards or Standardization?" *Alternatives in Philanthropy* (July).

———. 1990. "The Lessons of History: Robert Bremner's American Philanthropy." *Alternatives in Philanthropy* (July).

———. 1991. *Patterns of Corporate Philanthropy: Funding False Compassion*. Washington, DC: Capital Research Center.

———. 1992. *The Tragedy of American Compassion*. Washington, DC: Regnery Gateway.

Organization Trends. 1986. "Victory—Finally—in Buck Trust Case." (September):1.

Ostrander, Susan A. 1984. *Women of the Upper Class*. Philadelphia: Temple University Press.

Page, Benjamin I. 1978. *Choices and Echoes: Rational Man and Electoral Democracy*. Chicago: University of Chicago Press.

Payton, Robert. 1988. "Philanthropy in Action." In *Philanthropy: Four Views*, pp. 1–10. New Brunswick, NJ: Transaction Publishers.

Piven, Frances Fox, and Richard A. Cloward. 1971. *Regulating the Poor: The Functions of Public Welfare*. New York: Vintage Books.

———. 1979. *Poor People's Movements: Why They Succeed, How They Fail*. New York: Vintage Books.

Powell, Walter W. (ed.). 1987. *The Nonprofit Sector: A Research Handbook*. New Haven: Yale University Press.

Robert Wood Johnson Foundation. 1988. *Annual Report*. Princeton, NJ: Robert Wood Johnson Foundation.

Rogin, Michael Paul. 1969. *The Intellectuals and McCarthy: The Radical Specter*. Cambridge MA: MIT Press.

Roth, Guenther. 1968. "Personal Rulership, Patrimonialism, and Empire-Building in the New States." *World Politics* 20 (January):194–206.

Rothman, Stanley. 1979. "The Mass Media in Post-Industrial Society." In S. M. Lipset (ed.), *The Third Century: America as a Post-Industrial Society*, pp. 345–88. Stanford, CA: Hoover Institution Press.

———. 1986. "Academics on the Left." *Society Transaction* 23 (March/April):4–8.

Rothman, Stanley, and S. Robert Lichter. 1984. "Personality, Ideology and World View: A Comparison of Media and Business Elites." *British Journal of Political Science* 15, 1 (1984):29–49.

Rothman, Stanley, S. Robert Lichter, and Linda S. Lichter. Forthcoming. "Elites in Conflict." Unpublished manuscript.

Rotunda, Ronald. 1986. *The Politics of Language: Liberalism as Word and Symbol*. Iowa City: University of Iowa Press.

Rudolph, Lloyd I., and Susanne H. Rudolph. 1979. "Authority and Power in Bureaucratic and Patrimonial Administration." *World Politics* 31 (January):195–227.

Salamon, Lester M. 1987. "Partners in Public Service: The Scope and Theory of Government-Nonprofit Relations." In Walter W. Powell (ed.), *The Nonprofit Sector: A Research Handbook*, pp. 99–117. New Haven: Yale University Press.

Schumpeter, Joseph A. 1950. *Capitalism, Socialism, and Democracy*. New York: Harper and Row.

Shapiro, Robert Y., and John T. Young. 1989. "Public Opinion and the Welfare State: The United States in Comparative Perspective." *Political Science Quarterly* 1:59–89.

Shils, Edward. 1980. "Learning and Liberalism." In Edward Shils (ed.), *The Calling of Sociology and Other Essays on the Pursuit of Learning*, pp. 289–355. Chicago: University of Chicago Press.

Sidorsky, David. 1987. "Moral Pluralism and Philanthropy." In Ellen Frankel Paul, Fred D. Miller, Jr., Jeffrey Paul, and John Ahrens (eds.), *Beneficence, Philanthropy, and the Public Good*, pp. 93–112. Oxford and New York: Basil Blackwell.

Simon, John G. 1987. "The Treatment of Nonprofit Organizations: A Review of Federal and State Policies." In Walter W. Powell (ed.), *The Nonprofit Sector: A Research Handbook*, pp. 67–98. New Haven, CT: Yale University Press.

Sitkoff, Harvard. 1985. "The New Deal and Race Relations." In Harvard Sitkoff (ed.), *Fifty Years Later: The New Deal Evaluated*, pp. 93–112. Philadelphia: Temple University Press.

Smith, James Allen. 1991. *The Idea Brokers: Think Tanks and the Rise of the New Policy Elite*. New York: Free Press.

Smith, T. V. 1949. "The New Deal as a Cultural Phenomenon." In F.S.C. Northrop (ed.), *Ideological Differences and World Order*, pp. 208–28. New Haven: Yale University Press.

Stanmeyer, William A. 1978. "National Committee for Responsive Philanthropy." *Institution Analysis* 8 (August):1–17.

Sundquist, James L. 1968. *Politics and Policy: The Eisenhower, Kennedy, and Johnson Years*. Washington, DC: The Brookings Institution.

Sutton, Francis X. 1989. "Introduction." In Dwight Macdonald, *The Ford Foundation: The Men and the Millions*, pp. vii–xxi. New Brunswick, NJ: Transaction Publishers.

Theobald, Robin. 1982. "Patrimonialism." *World Politics* 34 (December):548–59.

Tocqueville, Alexis de. 1969. *Democracy in America*, ed. J. P. Mayer, trans. George Lawrence. Garden City, NY: Doubleday.

Trattner, Walter I. 1979. *From Poor Law to Welfare State*, 2nd ed. New York: Free Press.

Trilling, Lionel. 1965. *Beyond Culture*. New York: Viking Press.

Trolander, Judith Ann. 1987. *Professionalism and Social Change: From the Settlement House Movement to Neighborhood Centers, 1896 to the Present*. New York: Columbia University Press.

Useem, Michael. 1987. "Corporate Philanthropy." In Walter W. Powell (ed.), *The Nonprofit Sector: A Research Handbook*, pp. 340–59. New Haven: Yale University Press.

Verba, Sidney, and Gary R. Orren. 1985. *Equality in America: The View from the Top*. Cambridge, MA: Harvard University Press.

Walton, Ann D. and F. Emerson Andrews (eds.). 1960. *The Foundation Directory, Edition 1*. New York: Russell Sage.

Watson, Frank Dekker. 1922. *The Charity Organization Movement in the United States*. New York: The Macmillan Company.

Weaver, Warren. 1967. *U.S. Philanthropic Foundations: Their History, Structure, Management, and Record*. New York: Harper and Row.

Weber, Max. 1930 trans. *The Protestant Ethic and the Spirit of Capitalism*, Talcott Parsons (trans.). New York: Scribner's.

———. 1947 trans. "The Protestant Sects and the Spirit of Capitalism." In Hans Gerth and C. Wright Mills (eds.), *From Max Weber: Essays in Sociology*, pp. 302–22. London: Kegan Paul, Trench, Trubner and Co.

———. 1978 trans. *Economy and Society*. Roth, Guenter, and Klaus Wittich (eds.). New York: Bedminster Press.

Weisbord, Robert G., and Arthur Stein. 1970. *Bittersweet Encounter: The Afro-American and the American Jew*. New York: Schocken Books.

Whitaker, Ben. 1974. *The Philanthropoids: Foundations and Society*. New York: William Morrow.

Whyte, William F. 1955. *Street Corner Society: The Social Structure of an Italian Slum*. Chicago: University of Chicago Press.

Wildavsky, Aaron. 1982. "The Three Cultures: Explaining Anomalies in the American Welfare State." *The Public Interest* 69 (Fall):45–58.

———. 1991. *The Rise of Radical Egalitarianism*. Washington, DC: American University Press.

Wilensky, Harold L. 1975. *The Welfare State and Equality: Structural and Ideological Roots of Public Expenditures*. Berkeley and Los Angeles: University of California Press.

Wilensky, Harold L., and Charles N. Lebeaux. 1965. *Industrial Society and Social Welfare*. New York: Free Press.

Wilson, James Q. 1973. *Political Organizations*. New York: Basic Books.

Wooster, Martin Morse. 1990. "Using Their Own Judgment." *Alternatives in Philanthropy* (May):1–4.

Wright, Robert. 1990. "The Foundation Game." *The New Republic* 203, 19 (November 5):21–25.

Wuthnow, Robert, and Wesley Shrum. 1983. "Knowledge Workers and the 'New Class.' " *Work and Occupations* 10, 4 (November):471–87.

Ylvisaker, Paul N. 1987. "Foundations and Nonprofit Organizations." In Walter W. Powell (ed.), *The Nonprofit Sector: A Research Handbook*, pp. 360–79. New Haven: Yale University Press.

Zophy, Angela Howard (ed.). 1990. *Handbook of American Women's History*, pp. 537–38. New York: Garland Publishers.

Zurcher, Arnold J. 1972. *The Management of American Foundations: Administration, Politics, and Social Role*. New York: New York University Press.

INDEX

About the Authors

ALTHEA K. NAGAI is Senior Research Associate at the Center for the Study of Social and Political Change at Smith College.

ROBERT LERNER is Assistant Director at the Center for the Study of Social and Political Change at Smith College.

STANLEY ROTHMAN is Director of the Center for the Study of Social and Political Change at Smith College.